1990

# REBUILDING EUROPE'S BOMBED CITIES

*Also by Jeffry M. Diefendorf*

BUSINESSMEN AND POLITICS IN THE RHINELAND,
1789–1834

# Rebuilding Europe's Bombed Cities

*Edited by*

## JEFFRY M. DIEFENDORF
*Associate Professor of History*
*University of New Hampshire, Durham, USA*

MACMILLAN

First published 1990

Published by
THE MACMILLAN PRESS LTD
Houndmills, Basingstoke, Hampshire RG21 2XS
and London
Companies and representatives
throughout the world

Printed in Hong Kong


British Library Cataloguing in Publication Data
Rebuilding Europe's bombed cities.
1. Europe. Cities. Redevelopment, 1940–1970
I. Diefendorf Jeffry M, *1945–*
711'.4'094
ISBN 0–333–47443–0

# Contents

| | |
|---|---|
| List of Plates | vii |
| List of Figures | x |
| Acknowledgements | xi |
| Notes on the Contributors | xii |

1 Introduction: New Perspectives on a Rebuilt Europe    1
   **Jeffry M. Diefendorf**

2 Reconstructors' Tales: an Example of the Use of Oral
   Sources in the History of Reconstruction after the Second
   World War    16
   **Danièle Voldman**

3 Between Regionalism and Functionalism: French
   Reconstruction from 1940 to 1945    31
   **Rémi Baudoui**

4 Continuities in Belgian Wartime Reconstruction Planning    48
   **Pieter Uyttenhove**

5 Planning the Impossible: History as the Fundament
   of the Future – the Reconstruction of Middelburg, 1940–4    64
   **J. E. Bosma**

6 Warsaw: Destruction, Secret Town Planning, 1939–44,
   and Postwar Reconstruction    77
   **Stanislaw Jankowski**

7 People, Politics and Planning: the Reconstruction of
   Coventry's City Centre, 1940–53    94
   **Tony Mason and Nick Tiratsoo**

8 Hamburg: the 'Catastrophe' of July 1943    114
   **Niels Gutschow**

9 German Reconstruction as an International Activity 131
Friedhelm Fischer

10 The Lijnbaan (Rotterdam): a Prototype of a Postwar
Urban Shopping Centre 145
E. R. M. Taverne

11 The Reconstruction of the Buda Castle Hill after 1945 155
Erzsébet C. Harrach

12 Reconstruction of the City Centre of Dresden:
Planning and Building during the 1950s 170
Jürgen Paul

13 Reconstruction in the German Democratic Republic 190
Klaus von Beyme

14 Reconstruction: its Place in Planning History 209
Gordon E. Cherry

*Figures* 221

*Index* 229

# List of Plates

1   Middelburg: reconstruction plan, 10 December 1940

2   Middelburg: reconstruction plan for the town centre

3   Warsaw: the East–West Thoroughfare, 1949

4   Warsaw: the Old Town Square, rebuilt 1953

5   Warsaw: the Old Town Square, Piwna Street, 1944

6   Warsaw: the Old Town Square, Piwna Street, rebuilt 1953

7   Hamburg: the medieval core and the Cremon Island after the air raids in August 1943

8   Hamburg: resettlement of air-raid victims in emergency housing in a model neighbourhood; urban design by the town planning office, landscape design by Heinz Paulus, Autumn 1943

9   Hamburg: design for so-called war-homes with two flats which were to be converted after the war into a single home; design by Hans-Dieter Gropp and Karl Friedrich Fischer for civil servants of the Sanitation Board, November 1943

10  Rotterdam: the Lijnbaan plan

11  Rotterdam: the Lijnbaan under construction, with high-rise apartments and low shopping area

12  Budapest: Uri Street in 1945

13  Budapest: the White Dove restaurant on the corner of Uri Street

14  Budapest: Uri Street – façades from the Bástya Promenade, a block of buildings with new layout, and view of Uri Street's rebuilt façades

15  Dresden: river front, *c*. 1930

16  Dresden: design for buildings on north side of new Altmarkt and the magistrale, competition entry by Schneider architects' collective (1952)

17  Dresden: Altmarkt – new buildings on the east side beside Kreuzkirche, begun 1953

18  Dresden: Altmarkt – façades of new buildings on the west side, begun 1953

19  Dresden: outlines of new Altmarkt and magistrale (Ernst-Thälmann-Strasse) drawn over the street plan before destruction

20  Dresden: plan of city centre with completed buildings and projects (1959); architect: Hans Hunger of the municipal building department

21  Dresden: project of Zentraler Platz (Altmarkt) with tower house (1953); architect: Herbert Schneider

22  Dresden: design for House of Socialist Culture; architect: Rudolf Lasch (1959/60)

23  Dresden: air-view of Frauenkirche and Neumarkt before destruction

24  Dresden: city centre in 1947 with ruins of Royal Palace and Catholic Court Church

25  Dresden: House of the Socialist Culture

**Sources**

Plates 1 and 2 courtesy of J. E. Bosma; Plates 3–6 courtesy of Centralna Agencja Fotograficzna, Warsaw; Plates 7–9 courtesy of Niels Gutschow Collection; Plate 10 courtesy of Foto Geljon; Plate 11 courtesy of Foto KLM AERO CARTO; Plates 12 and 13 courtesy of Erzsébet C. Harrach Collection; Plate 14 courtesy of Budapest Föváros Levéltára; Plate 15 courtesy of Deutsche Fotothek, Dresden; Plates 16 and 21 from *Deutsche Architektur*, 2 (1953) 17, 181; Plate 17 from G. Krenz, *Architektur zwischen gestern und morgen: Ein Vierteljahrhundert Architekturentwicklung in der Deutschen Demokratischen Republik* (Stuttgart, 1974) Fig. 11; Plate 18 from U. Kuhirt (ed.), *Kunst der DDR 1945–1959* (Leipzig, 1982) Fig. 199; Plate 19 from *Deutsche Architektur*, 3 (1954) 242; Plate 20 from *Deutsche Architektur*, 8 (1959) 596; Plate 22 from *Deutsche Architektur*, 9 (1960) 670; Plate 23 from G. Eckardt, *Schicksale deutscher Baudenkmale*, vol. II (Berlin, 1978) p. 375; Plate 24 from F. Löffler, *Das alte Dresden* (Leipzig, 1982) p. 426; Plate 25 courtesy of PGH Film und Bild, Berlin.

# List of Figures

1  Plan of Middelburg centre, 1939                                221

2  Warsaw, 1939                                                   222

3  The Pabst Plan for Warsaw as a German city,
   1939–40                                                        222

4  Warsaw: destruction map, 1939–45                               223

5  Warsaw: clandestine town-planning – project for
   the redevelopment of the high bank in the city
   centre, 1943                                                   224

6  Warsaw: the First Reconstruction Plan, 1945                    225

7  Warsaw: the East–West thoroughfare                             226

8  Warsaw: the Muránów residential district, built on
   top of the Ghetto ruins                                        226

9  Hamburg: plan for the urban landscape after
   rebuilding, 1944                                               227

10  Budapest: ground plan of the Buda Castle Hill                 228

**Sources**

Figure 1 courtesy of J. F. Berghoef, 'Wederobvouw van Middelburg', *Forum*, (1946) p. 10; Figures 2–8 courtesy of the Stanislaw Jankowski Collection; Figure 9 courtesy of the Niels Gutschow Collection; Figure 10 courtesy of the Erzsébet C. Harrach Collection.

# Acknowledgements

For his help in organising the conference at which these papers were originally presented, I would like to thank Anthony Sutcliffe most sincerely. The Rockefeller Foundation made its wonderful conference centre in Bellagio, Italy, available to us for a week in June 1987, and the Cellis and their staff showed that their reputation as wonderful hosts is well deserved. The Volkswagen Foundation of Hanover, West Germany, provided a grant to pay most of the travel costs of the conference participants. To both foundations let me express our collective appreciation. My own travel expenses and administrative overheads were met by grants from the American Council of Learned Societies and the University of New Hampshire. My thanks, too, to Jeanne Mitchell of the History Department there for her help in administering the grants. Gordon Cherry of the University of Birmingham very kindly assumed responsibility for photocopying the conference papers.

The manuscript for this book was prepared while I held a visiting appointment at Stanford University. I greatly appreciate the advice of Jeff Fear and Claire Gresset during the editing of the papers. Dominique Fredregill typed several of them on to computer disks. Instruction and Research Information Services, Stanford's computing consulting office, translated some files into a format that I could edit, and that office was also able to digitise some of the transcripts.

Finally, I would like to thank Barbara Diefendorf for her advice and encouragement at all stages in this effort and all the contributors to this volume for having submitted their revised essays to me by the date requested. Such promptness is all too rare these days.

# Notes on the Contributors

**Rémi Baudoui** is an historian and urban planner engaged in research at the architecture school at Paris-Villemin and in teaching at the Institut d'Urbanisme de Paris. He recently worked on the 1987 Le Corbusier centennial exhibition at the Centre Georges Pompidou.

**Klaus von Beyme** is Professor of Political Science at the University of Heidelberg. He has written extensively on West German politics and has recently published a book on urban reconstruction in the two German states.

**J. E. Bosma** is an art historian working at the Institute for the History of Art at the University of Groningen and preparing a doctoral dissertation, 'The Reconstruction of the Netherlands 1940–54'.

**Gordon E. Cherry** is Professor of Urban and Regional Planning and Head of Department of Geography at the University of Birmingham, England. Well known for his historical research on the development of town planning in the United Kingdom, he is past President of the Royal Town Planning Institute and is the present chairman of the international Planning History Group.

**Jeffry M. Diefendorf** is Associate Professor of History at the University of New Hampshire, USA. He has written about early nineteenth-century Rhenish urban history and more recently has published a number of articles on German urban reconstruction after 1945.

**Friedhelm Fischer** did his doctoral dissertation on the planning of Canberra, Australia. He currently holds a research position in the urban planning section at the Technical University of Hamburg–Harburg, West Germany, where he is working on the international context of German postwar urban planning.

**Niels Gutschow** is a research fellow in the Department of Oriental Studies at the University of Kiel, West Germany. He has published numerous works on the architectural and urban history of Nepal as well as on urban reconstruction, architecture and historic preservation in West Germany. From 1978 to 1980 he was the officer for historic preservation in Münster.

**Erzsébet C. Harrach** studied architecture at the Technical University of Budapest. From 1957 to 1962 she worked as an architect for the Budapest city government; from 1962 to 1977 she was employed at the State Institute for the Protection of Architectural Monuments; and since 1977 she has been the head of the department of Architectural Plans and Maps at the Budapest City Archives. She has published numerous works on the preservation of historic monuments in Hungary.

**Stanislaw Jankowski** studied in Warsaw and Liverpool. Having participated in the Warsaw Uprising of 1944, he contributed to the rebuilding of the city as a member of the Town Planning Office from 1946 to 1976. He also worked as a planner in Iraq, Yugoslavia, Peru, Vietnam and Cyprus, and has been awarded major international as well as Polish prizes.

**Tony Mason** teaches in the Centre for the Study of Social History at the University of Warwick, England. He has written on the British general strike, the British soldier, and the social history of sport.

**Jürgen Paul**, Professor of Art History at the University of Tübingen in West Germany, has published numerous works on modern architecture and historic preservation in West Germany.

**Nick Tiratsoo** holds degrees from Thames Polytechnic and the London School of Economics and is currently Senior Research Fellow at the Centre for the Study of Social History, University of Warwick, England. He has worked on official histories of the British coal industry and British railways.

**E. R. M. Taverne** is Professor of the History of Architecture and Planning at the University of Groningen, Holland, having earlier studied and taught at the University of Nijmegen. He has been a member of the State Commission on Historic Monuments and has written on early modern as well as modern Dutch architectural history.

**Pieter Uyttenhove** studied architectural engineering at the University of Leuven, Belgium, and town planning at the Institut d'Urbanisme de Paris. He is currently doing research on planning history and preparing a doctoral dissertation on the history of leisure planning in France in the nineteenth and twentieth centuries.

**Danièle Voldman**, ingénieur de recherche at the Centre National de la Recherche Scientifique and the Institut d'Histoire du Temps Présent in Paris, is currently working on research comparing the experiences of reconstruction in France and Great Britain. She is the author and editor of several recent works on French planning history.

# 1 Introduction: New Perspectives on a Rebuilt Europe

## JEFFRY M. DIEFENDORF

In 1945, a great many of the cities of Europe lay in ruins. Some were the victims of long bombing campaigns conducted by both sides; some were damaged in the course of fighting between ground forces. The destruction was most widespread in Germany, where Allied bombers had rained high explosives and incendiary bombs on urban centres for more than three years, but large-scale destruction had also occurred in most of the other countries that had participated in the war. Cultural monuments that had stood for centuries had been reduced to rubble, and, in practical terms, the loss of masses of housing, schools, hospitals, transportation facilities and the like posed an immediate threat to the very survival of these urban centres. Observers in the summer of 1945, horrified at what they saw as 'biblical annihilation', expected that it would take generations to rebuild.

Clearly urban reconstruction was one of the greatest tasks ever faced by town planners, town authorities, and regional and national politicians, as well as by private citizens in their capacities as renters, property owners, architects and workers. It was, moreover, a task of enormous complexity, fraught with potential for conflict. We need only list some of the basic issues involved to appreciate the formidable job that policy-makers had to tackle.

How would the rubble and debris be cleared, and who would pay for it? How would building material and labour be allocated, and who would finance reconstruction? Even before the war, many historic cities had been candidates for extensive urban renewal because of unregulated growth during the decades of industrialisation and urban expansion; was it now possible to engage in urban renewal during reconstruction? Were new streets needed? New social amenities? Should and could the cities be so reorganised as to keep housing, industry, commerce and culture separated? What population density was desirable, and how could that density be obtained and maintained? How could the demand for immediate housing for a suffering population be reconciled with the time needed to design

1

and construct modern housing? Should historic cities be rebuilt in a way that retained or recaptured their traditional character? If so, did that mean that all, or only some, historic buildings should be rebuilt as they had been? Were the building and property laws adequate to guide decision-makers? Who would make the decisions – private individuals, town authorities, or regional and national authorities? How were urban needs to be weighed against other priorities?

This is already a long list of questions, and it could still be lengthened considerably. If the questions seemed overwhelming to policy-makers, so do the variety of answers that were offered pose a daunting challenge to scholarly analysis.

In 1956 Leo Grebler published a survey of the reconstruction of the bombed cities of Western Europe. He described what he had seen and recounted what people had told him.[1] The shape that reconstruction was taking was in most cases already clear in 1956, even if reconstruction was not yet complete, and many of Grebler's insights were keen. In the same year that Grebler's study appeared, a conference was held in Erfurt in the German Democratic Republic; the subject was the history of urban planning and reconstruction in historic cities, mostly in Eastern Europe.[2] The papers presented at this conference likewise contained many useful insights, in some cases because the participants had themselves been active in the reconstruction process.

But the Erfurt conference, like Grebler's survey, only touched the surface. New housing, streets and shopping centres were discussed, as well as the rebuilding of certain historic monuments. However, one does not find in the proceedings of the conference the deep conflicts, bitter struggles between individuals and heated debates over values that lay behind town planning and new construction. Viewing reconstruction as a postwar phenomenon, the scholars of the 1950s overlooked the extent to which wartime developments continued into the postwar period. Deeper insights into the process of rebuilding could only come with systematic archival research into newly available materials and systematic interviews with those who had been involved. Furthermore, only the passage of time could make it possible to consider the era of reconstruction in the broader context of the history of European cities in this century and to deal more objectively with the political legacies of the 1930s and 1940s.

In 1975 Western Europe celebrated a year devoted to the furtherance of historic preservation. One result was a new wave of scholarly interest in what historic cities had experienced during the war and postwar reconstruction. By the mid-1980s, scholarly work on reconstruction was being done all over Europe. Most of this work consists of detailed studies of developments in single cities or countries, but some consists of comparisons of the developments in different cities or countries. Research projects are underway comparing reconstruction in the Ruhr with that in Coventry, comparing French wartime plans for reconstruction with German reconstruction plans for occupied Lorraine and Alsace, and comparing English postwar reconstruction planning with reconstruction planning in Northern France.[3] These projects involve different teams of scholars and have been funded by different agencies and institutions. Among the nationally based studies, Dutch scholars in Gröningen have been working on reconstruction in that country, while Belgian urban historians have worked on reconstruction in Belgium after the First World War and have staged a major exhibition of their findings.[4]

A great deal of work is being done on reconstruction in Germany, the country that suffered the worst destruction. Niels Gutschow and Renate Stiemer have published important volumes with documents and commentary on Münster.[5] Gutschow and Werner Durth have prepared an enormous volume of documents on planning from 1940 to 1950; Durth has also published an extremely important multi-generational study of German architects and planners that deals with continuities from the early part of this century into the postwar world.[6] Provocative volumes on fascist architecture, edited by Hartmut Frank, and on housing policy under the Nazis, edited by Gerhard Fehl and Tilman Harlander, have raised questions about postwar developments in these areas.[7] Teams of scholars at the Technical Universities of Berlin, Munich and Hamburg have been engaged in intensive studies of those cities, and the bulletin published by the Deutsches Institut für Urbanistik in Berlin regularly contains notices of research on reconstruction underway at universities all over Germany.[8] There have been recent exhibitions with sections on architecture and planning in the 1950s, and, finally, the political scientist Klaus von Beyme has just published a volume comparing reconstruction in the two German states.[9]

With all of this detailed research going on, there has yet been no attempt to replace Grebler's early synthesis. Indeed, such an attempt would probably still be premature. Nevertheless, contacts between scholars in different countries and in different fields are helping turn reconstruction research into a community effort. In June 1987 a conference was held in Bellagio, Italy, for the purpose of sharing new insights gained with the advantage of added years since Grebler's work and the Erfurt conference. The eighteen participants who met for a week at the Rockefeller Conference Centre came to discuss their research on postwar reconstruction and, in two cases, their own direct participation in that process. Several scholarly disciplines were represented: social and urban history, geography, architectural and planning history, political science, architecture and town planning. Some of the papers presented dealt with reconstruction in individual cities, while others dealt with planning and building issues in a broader geographical framework. The conference, which represented the first attempt to bring together scholars from Eastern and Western Europe, yielded perspectives that were quite different from those in the studies of the 1950s.

The majority of the conference papers are to be found in the chapters that follow.[10] It was not easy to find an entirely coherent organisational scheme for this book. The arrangement chosen is thematic, chronological and geographical. The first paper (Chapter 2) appropriately addresses basic methodological questions, in this case in the context of French reconstruction. Chapters 2–8 in one way or another examine reconstruction in terms of continuities stretching back into the war years or prewar period, thereby providing a broad chronological framework for this subject. Moreover, Chapters 2–6 all deal with the experiences of countries occupied by the Germans and with wartime reconstruction planning. Chapters 7 and 8 deal with reconstruction concepts in cities in two of the main protagonists in the war, England and Germany. Chapters 9–13 focus more on postwar developments, the first two in Western Europe, the next three in Eastern Europe. The final chapter in the book, written after the conference, seeks to place the subject of urban reconstruction in a larger historiographical context.

Considered together, the papers and discussions at the conference pointed to a number of fascinating themes that help to illuminate what we already know about the reconstruction process but also suggest new areas for research. One of the most important themes common to much of this work is that one must not see the end of the war in 1945 as the starting point for reconstruction. This is true in several senses. Clearly, people began to think, and in some cases act, on reconstruction almost as soon as the destruction happened; they did not wait until the end of the war. Some of this activity was official. The damage often required immediate action, such as clearing streets of rubble, sealing off or dynamiting buildings that might cave in, repairing utility and water lines, repairing lightly damaged housing, and the like. A lot of practical experience was gained here that was put to use after 1945. In addition to these practical measures, planners, architects, but also private citizens without architectural training, composed essays, made sketches and thought about what the reconstructed cities should be like – while the war continued and the cities sustained further damage. To date, most of these unofficial suggestions remain unexamined, though many German proposals will appear shortly in the collection of documents edited by Durth and Gutschow. Most of the research has instead been devoted to official measures and to the debates over their implementation.

Almost everywhere, town planners viewed the bombing as an unprecedented opportunity to introduce radically modernising changes in the urban fabric on a scale that had been almost impossible in existing, built-up cities. Rebuilders of bombed cities could go beyond what Haussmann had done for nineteenth-century Paris. Generally speaking, planners wanted to use reconstruction to heal the 'unhealthy' metropolis left by the age of industrialisation, housing speculation and rapid, unplanned growth. At the same time, reconstruction planning often looked back to earlier conceptions of ideal urban forms; it was shaped by pre-existing institutions and laws and was guided by individuals with prewar or wartime experiences in reconstruction planning.

Sometimes, as Rémi Baudoui, Tony Mason and Nick Tiratsoo point out in their essays on Northern France and Coventry, this idea of healing the ills of the metropolis was expressed primarily in technical terms. That is, planners wanted to modernise the technical infrastructure of the cities to provide better streets, sanitation systems and modern housing with air, light and modern equipment. Because the mixture of industry and housing was viewed as inflicting bad air on urban residents (and we are not very distant from the old miasmic theory of disease), planners wanted to give rebuilt cities functionally distinct zones. Housing, industry, culture, government, recreation: each was to have its own separate location. This sort of thinking was found all over Europe during the war, in fascist and democratic countries, and it is certainly a part of the modern town planning movement. But one also found in Germany and in countries occupied by the Germans the use of the term 'unhealthy' in a social and political sense. That is, planners believed that crowded, contaminated housing produced, on the one hand, a politically radicalised working class, and on the other, a biologically weakened working class that could not make its proper contribution to the fatherland.

The most extreme views along these lines were to be found in Germany, though there were some hints also in Le Corbusier's Vichy era proposals for new cities. As Niels Gutschow shows in his paper, some German planners almost welcomed the destruction of the metropolis, arguing that the great industrial city was really already a 'dead' social form of human organisation. Instead of rebuilding the cities as they had been, even with technical improvements, these men suggested building either a number of smaller new cities, or greatly spreading out the old city in such a way that the city was dominated by the natural landscape, the soil, rather than the other way around. (This kind of thinking had its grim counterpart in Nazi plans to demolish Warsaw and replace it with a much smaller German city, purged of its original Polish, and Jewish, features.) The rubble produced by the bombing should perhaps be bulldozed and planted over, with the people relocated elsewhere. (It is interesting that a similar idea for the German cities was put forward by Martin Wagner after the war. Wagner had been Berlin's chief planner until his dismissal in 1933, after which he had ended up in America with Walter Gropius at Harvard University. After the war, from his Cambridge base, he railed at postwar German planners for trying to rebuild their bombed cities and urged them to abandon the ruins and start again with smaller new cities, quite unaware that he sounded like some of the most extreme proposals put forwarded under Nazi Germany.)

In Belgium, France and Germany, planners also looked back to the experiences during and after the First World War. They sought to build on those experiences or to improve upon what had been done, or not done, at that time. Pieter Uyttenhove observes that damage to Belgian cities had been more extensive in the First World War than in the Second, and it was felt that the absence of strong, centralised planning had resulted in a failure to modernise during rebuilding in the 1920s. Several of the same individuals who had been involved in rebuilding after 1919 and in trying to draft strong planning legislation in the 1920s seized the opportunity presented by the German occupation of 1940 to put their earlier concepts into action. The result was centralised town and regional planning and, for the first time in Belgium, the widespread application of modern planning concepts. The wartime approach to planning remained in place until the early 1960s and this shaped postwar reconstruction.

In Vichy France too, as Baudoui shows, reconstruction was centrally directed. A reconstruction ministry and several subordinate agencies, staffed by like-minded and similarly educated technocrats, sought to rebuild the towns of the Loire Valley in particular by applying modern planning techniques, though they also wanted to retain some form of typically regional architecture to help strengthen local loyalties and to attract future tourists. At the same time, and this again is something found in many places, they sought to provide a strong legal framework for postwar town planning. In his paper, J. E. Bosma indicates that similar developments can be found in reconstruction plans for Middelburg in the Netherlands, where authorities, directed from the Hague, sought to combine a modern urban structure with a traditionalist architectural style. In Nazi-occupied Norway, centralised reconstruction planning began in June 1940 under Norwegian leadership but with German supervision.[11]

German wartime reconstruction activity was especially interesting. On one level it drew upon experiences from rebuilding damaged towns in East Prussia during the First World War. Here planners and architects had been dispatched in 1914 to modernise damaged towns while using local building styles. When no truly interesting local style could be identified, one was made up and it became the basis not only for small-town reconstruction during the First World War but also during the Second World War. Before bombs fell on Germany, German teams were sent to rebuild re-annexed Alsace-Lorraine. They included not simply pro-Nazi architects but modernists like Rudolf Schwarz, who later became Cologne's first postwar planner.[12]

In her own big cities, German reconstruction planning started seriously (but relatively secretly) in the autumn of 1943 in Speer's ministry under the leadership of Rudolf Wolters and Konstanty Gutschow. Here reconstruction planning aimed at urban modernisation not unlike the prewar ideas of Fritz Schumacher, the progressive town planner of Hamburg and Cologne in the 1920s, though provision was still made for specifically National Socialist characteristics: parade streets, party buildings and the like. In fact, as Friedhelm Fischer notes in his paper, planners in Gutschow's Hamburg office were receiving, via Lisbon, news about British wartime planning legislation, which they admired for its modernity.

Mason and Tiratsoo show that in England reconstruction planners also drew upon earlier experience. Already before the war, in 1937, Coventry's new Labour-dominated City Council had chosen a new city architect (Donald Gibson) to draft a plan for a new city centre and for other reforms it felt were needed in this overgrown and poorly laid out city. Gibson was a strong believer in modern planning and architecture. When German bombing destroyed most of the city core, and when the wartime emergency atmosphere led to the creation of central planning and reconstruction agencies, the way appeared to be cleared for a modern Coventry. The move toward modern urban planning in London had also started before the war with the 1937 Barlow Report, which had called for urban decentralisation and decongestion. With regional and town planning institutionalised in the 1944 Ministry of Town and Country Planning, and with planning for the rebuilding of London in the hands of Patrick Abercrombie and William Holford, the technical modernisation of London was largely planned by the end of the war.[13]

Note that in all of these cases architecture took a subordinate place. These wartime reconstruction planners were first of all technocrats and bureaucrats interested in technically modern cities. They generally felt that their work – obviously necessary given the destruction – stood outside politics and was part of the European-wide trend toward urban planning. When architecture played a role, it usually followed a conservative aesthetic and resulted in the endorsement of regional styles. Even here, these styles were sometimes artificially concocted historicist façades, behind which stood relatively modern buildings made up of standardised elements.

It is safe to say that in most of Western and Northern Europe, these wartime approaches to the problem of rebuilding continued after the war, and they help explain both the rapidity of reconstruction (no one was really starting from scratch) and some of the mediocre architecture that appeared. Interesting new architecture was indeed relatively rare during reconstruction. Perhaps the crushing experiences of the war made it especially difficult to produce creative new building forms. It was not impossible, however: witness the Lijbaan shopping centre of Rotterdam, discussed by E. R. M. Taverne, which was a radical departure from the form of the prewar Dutch metropolis.

In Western Europe, of course, the German cities had suffered the most destruction, and more often than not, postwar German planners attempted to follow the path of technical modernisation, with less attention given both to development of new, modern building styles and to the preservation or recreation of historic buildings destroyed in the war. This was also true for Austria. Once again independent of Germany, the Viennese sought to re-establish continuity with the modern planning traditions of the 1920s but without any explicit endorsement of modern architecture in either the Bauhaus sense or the Succession style of the early twentieth century.[14]

The situation in what became the Soviet bloc in East-Central Europe was somewhat different. Here architectural style played a very important role in reconstruction because of its symbolic role in state building, though here too there was a commitment to technical modernisation of the large cities. On the whole, prewar or wartime planning ideas were less important here. The case of Warsaw is unusual in this respect.

The Nazis had made it their policy to try to obliterate the physical manifestations of Polish culture, and so, quite naturally, the Poles were set on rebuilding those cultural artefacts. During the German occupation, several groups of planners and architects worked secretly on reconstruction planning for Warsaw, and students prepared detailed drawings of important buildings. When the war ended these people came forward to lead reconstruction, and Stanislaw Jankowski recounts in his essay his own participation in this process. The historic core of the city was to be rebuilt as a replica of what had existed before, though in fact some modifications were made, such as a tunnel under the central city, which required demolition of some still-standing buildings. The firm commitment to historic recreation established a leading place for Polish craftsmen in such work. The rebuilding of historic areas in Polish cities like Danzig was followed by Polish artisans working on historic re-creations elsewhere, including the cities of the German Democratic Republic.

On the other hand, rebuilding Warsaw enjoyed such a high priority that reconstruction in other Polish cities – most of which suffered extensive damage – lagged behind.[15] During the first five years after the war there was an attempt at historic restoration, but in many towns the great demand for housing meant serious encroachments on the historic structure of Polish towns, encroachments that could not later be reversed. In common with other socialist states, moreover, the early 1950s saw the search for forms of supposedly socialist architecture – an effort that produced little in the way of good building.

The requirement to utilise a socialist style of architecture caused problems also for reconstruction in Budapest and in the

GDR. Erzsébet Harrach argues that in the Hungarian capital there was an early decision to rebuild in their historic form as many as possible of the buildings on the Castle Hill above the city because the buildings there represented a kind of architectural diary of Hungarian history. This was a slow process, even though it was facilitated by the expropriation of private property in the area. New uses had to be found for the buildings on the hill, which had formerly been an area containing many government buildings, foreign embassies, as well as private residences. New uses required compromises between new needs and historic forms. Reconstruction in this area is in fact still going on, more than forty years after the war. Ironically, the most famous building on the Hill is a piece of new architecture for a Western, capitalist enterprise – the Hilton Hotel, which incorporates major elements of historic buildings.

But while this effort at symbolic, historic recreation was going on, Budapest also faced the need to rebuild other damaged areas and to construct huge quantities of new housing. Unlike many of the other large cities of Central Europe, Budapest still continued to grow rapidly. In the Hungarian case, the demand for socialist realism in architecture meant that architects were ordered to imitate a kind of classicism that had no roots in Budapest. In this murky situation, very little new building was done at all until the 1960s, when newer architectural forms were again allowed.

Rebuilding in the German Democratic Republic was likewise influenced by this architectural mandate, as Klaus von Beyme and Jürgen Paul argue in their papers. On the one hand, the East Germans wanted to modernise their cities, to break completely from the German past and become a new modern, socialist state, with a modern Berlin as its capital. On the other hand, official policy required first the creation of new socialist parade squares and the imitation of Stalinist architecture. The most famous is Berlin's Stalinallee and its apartment buildings, but a Stalinist skyscraper was planned for Berlin's Alexanderplatz as well as for Dresden's main square. After Stalin's death, official style was supposed to imitate German classicism, and in the meantime truly historic but damaged structures, like the Hohenzollern palace in Berlin and the ruined Frauenkirche in Dresden, were either demolished or allowed to decay further. As in Poland and Hungary, considerable confusion about urban and architectural forms prevailed, which in turn both slowed the rebuilding process and gave it an unattractive face. Only in the later 1960s was there a turn toward more modern architectural forms. Instead of the skyscraper, a television tower became the dominant monument on Alexanderplatz, and towers of apartment houses rose near the old city centre.

In the 1970s there was also a turn in the GDR toward renewed interest in historic preservation and the recreation of historic buildings. Major restoration projects have taken place in East Berlin, including the creation of a brand new 'historic' Nikolai quarter with buildings brought and assembled there that had not been there before. In Dresden there are plans now for rebuilding the Frauenkirche, long after the building stones of the original were deliberately broken up and dispersed. Why this turnabout? In part it derives from a political strategy to lay claim to being the true heirs of what is best in the German tradition (whatever that is); in part it is a response to the realities of the tourist trade. Tourists, whether from East or West, want to visit attractively maintained or restored old cities, not bland new ones.

Whether in Western Europe or in the Soviet bloc, however, it is clear that rebuilding took place under a variety of severe constraints, such that neither property owners nor planners could in fact do what they wanted. Some of these constraints were practical: existing streets and utilities represented an enormous investment, and impoverished postwar Europe could not afford to abandon that investment and redesign cities according to planners' wishes. This was true in East and West, though in the West the commitment to private property ownership meant additional constraints on what planners could do. Everywhere there was a shortage of capital, skilled labour and building materials. Everywhere the highest priority had to be housing, which most often meant publically owned or subsidised housing according to relatively standardised models – models that have frequently turned out to be boring at best and, at worst, inadequate. And in many European states, political uncertainties caused changes in policy (a general trend away from planning in the West, fluctuating conceptions of planned cities in the East) and, at least in the early postwar years, discouraged long-term investment in buildings.

Given these very real constraints, it is remarkable how much was in fact accomplished in the ten to fifteen years after the war. How many people today – including the residents of those cities – realise that a Florence or Vienna or Hamburg suffered as much wartime damage as they did? The historical record is needed to show the youngest postwar generations just how much their urban environments have been changed by the accidents of war and the deliberate actions of their fellow residents. Moreover, we must recognise that there was a positive side to the constraints within which the rebuilders worked. Modernisation could not proceed at a pace that would have allowed it to erase entirely centuries of urban life. In Germany, for example, most people's favourite city is Munich, where in fact reconstruction authorities tried but failed to make many changes in the city's structure.

Was European reconstruction a success or failure? The answer depends on one's point of view, so no definitive answer may be possible. A pragmatist might argue that given the magnitude of the task, especially in the area of housing, and the scarcity of resources, the quantitative achievement certainly calls for applause, even if the results were often neither imaginative or attractive. An observer sensitive to aesthetic issues, however, might deplore the instances where damaged buildings were demolished to make way for wider streets or parking lots or modern skyscrapers.

Although the papers presented in Bellagio covered many aspects of postwar reconstruction, there are still important issues to be researched. In his essay, Fischer shows that German planners followed planning activities in other countries, even during the war and early postwar years when they were supposedly isolated. Clearly more research is needed on the flow of planning ideas across all of Europe's borders before a satisfactory general account of the reconstruction process can be ventured. In addition, there are countries that suffered urban destruction during the Second World War but were not covered in papers presented at the Bellagio conference. Cities from Austria to Greece had to be rebuilt. Spanish cities were damaged in a civil war that some might argue was the opening phase of the Second World War.[16] It would be extremely interesting to know how the Soviet Union dealt with the task of reconstruction. And, of course, there was the vast urban destruction of Asian cities, whose reconstruction might instructively be compared with that process in Europe.

There are also important questions of methodology and sources that need to be considered. Representatives of different disciplines are apt to claim a certain primacy for materials central to their own fields. Scholars thus differ on the relative importance of written documents as opposed to sources that require visual analysis: plans, drawings and photographs. In her paper on French reconstruction, Danièle Voldman discusses some of the problems raised by oral history. For example, she found that former reconstruction officials were nostalgic about their days of public service and incapable of real self-criticism. Thus even though they had been officials, they nevertheless blamed government bureaucracy, or the political parties, or the shortages of building materials and labour, or financial difficulties – but never themselves – for the failure to realise their aim of transforming French town planning. The technocrats held themselves blameless. They were also reluctant to reflect on their behaviour as citizens who stayed at their posts during the German occupation and thus worked with or for their conquerors. The analysis of such selective or distorted recollections of the past, Voldman indicates, requires great care on the part of the historian.

In spite of the fact that oral histories are not always trustworthy, they remain an important resource. Unfortunately, the actors of that period are rapidly dying off and it is essential to collect their personal histories. Moreover, many of these retired planners and architects still possess invaluable collections of documents, plans and drawings, many of which are not duplicated in public archives. Unfortunately, many city and even regional and national archives are not well equipped to solicit and care for these materials, especially when they are overwhelmed by the volume of documents already being turned over by public agencies. Urban historians of all sorts need to encourage the collection and conservation of these irreplaceable sources for the history of Europe's cities.

Finally, the papers presented at Bellagio should go far to provide an interpretative framework for further research. The importance of continuities between prewar ideas on urban planning, wartime planning and postwar reconstruction is very clear, as is the significance of cross-national influences. In spite of hostilities in war and deep political divisions in peacetime, the individuals responsible for rebuilding the bombed cities were not isolated from events and ideas in other countries. Moreover, just as scholars are now able to demonstrate continuities with earlier periods, so they will increasingly have to place the era of reconstruction within the greater context of the history of Europe's cities in the whole twentieth century. Gordon E. Cherry's concluding essay in this volume is a step in that direction. After all, concepts of the ideal city and tastes in architecture have changed several times in this period. An evaluation of the successes and failures in rebuilding must take into account not only what was wanted, what was possible, and what was done during the years after the war, but also how well the achievement of reconstruction has stood the test of time.

## Notes

1. Leo Grebler, *Europe's Reborn Cities*, Urban Land Institute Technical Bulletin 28 (Washington, D.C., 1956).
2. *Städtebau. Geschichte und Gegenwart*, Deutsche Bauakademie, Schriften des Instituts für Theorie und Geschichte der Baukunst, 2 vols (Erfurt, 1956).
3. Tony Mason and Dietmar Petzina head the Ruhr/Coventry project; Rémi Baudoui and Hartmut Frank are comparing wartime reconstruction in France and Germany; and Anthony Sutcliffe and a group of French scholars at the Institut d'histoire du temps présent in Paris have worked in French–English comparisons. Here one should note the recent publication of *Images, discours et enjeux de la réconstruction des villes français après 1945*, ed. Danièle Voldman, Cahiers de l'institut d'histoire du temps présent nr 5 (Paris, 1987).
4. Some of the work of E. R. M. Taverne and J. E. Bosma is discussed in their papers in this volume. An exhibition on Middelburg and a conference on German influences on Dutch reconstruction planning is scheduled for November 1988. See also E. R. M. Taverne, 'Ouds ontwerp voor het hofplein', *Plan*, 12 (1981) pp. 30–4. For Belgium, see especially Marcel Smets (ed.), *La réconstruction en Belgique après 1914* (Brussels, 1985). A recent publication dealing with English reconstruction is Gordon E. Cherry and Leith Penny, *Holford: A Study in Architecture, Planning and Civic Design* (London and New York, 1986).
5. Niels Gutschow and Renate Stiemer, *Dokumentation Wiederaufbau der Stadt Münster* (Münster, 1982) and *Dokumentation Wiederaufbau: Materialsammlung*, Beiträge zur Stadtforschung, Stadtentwicklung, Stadtplanung, vol. 6 (Münster, 1980).
6. Werner Durth and Niels Gutschow, *Träume in Trümmern: Planung des Wiederaufbaus im Westen Deutschlands, 1940–1950* (Braunschweig and Wiesbaden, 1988); Werner Durth, *Deutsche Architekten: Biographische Verflechtungen 1900–1970* (Braunschweig and Wiesbaden, 1986).
7. Hartmut Frank, *Faschistische Architekturen: Planen und Bauen in Europa, 1930–1945* (Hamburg, 1985); Tilman Harlander and Gerhard Fehl, *Hitlers Sozialer Wohnungsbau, 1940–1945: Wohnungspolitik, Baugestaltung und Siedlungsplanung* (Hamburg, 1986).
8. *Informationen moderner Stadtgeschichte* appears twice a year. There is a group of scholars working in Berlin on reconstruction in that city; a number of essays on reconstruction have appeared in various publications celebrating the 750th anniversary of Berlin. On Munich, see Winfried Nerdinger (ed.), *Aufbauzeit: Planen und Bauen München, 1945–1950* (Munich, 1984).

9. For example, Werner Durth and Niels Gutschow, *Architektur und Städtebau der fünfziger Jahre*, Schriftenreihe des Deutschen National-komitees für Denkmalschutz, vol. 33 (Bonn, 1987), and *Museum der Gegenwart*, exhibition catalogue (Düsseldorf, 1987); Klaus von Beyme, *Der Wiederaufbau: Architektur und Städtebaupolitik in beiden deutschen Staaten* (Munich, 1987). Part of von Beyme's work is presented in the present volume (see Chapter 13).

10. For reasons of space it was not possible to include the papers by Teresa Zarebska, 'The Development of Concepts in the Reconstruction and Rebuilding of Bombed Cities in Poland'; Erik Lorange, 'The Reconstruction of the War-Damaged Towns in Norway, on the Outskirts of Europe'; Hartmut Frank, '3Mal Wiederaufbau' and 'Die architektonische Gestaltung eines Neubeginns'; and Fabrizio Brunetti, 'Sulla ricostruzione postbellica in Italia con particolare riguardo al caso di Firenze'. Gordon E. Cherry's paper, 'Britain in the 1940s: the Prelude to Reconstruction', was already committed to publication elsewhere, but he agreed to contribute a conclusion to this collection. All of the conference papers are discussed briefly in Jeffry M. Diefendorf, 'Urban Reconstruction in Europe after World War II', *Urban Studies*, 26 (1989).

11. In his paper, Erik Lorange also commented on his own personal participation in postwar Norwegian reconstruction, especially of housing (see note 10).

12. These insights were presented in the papers by Hartmut Frank (see note 10).

13. As reported by Gordon E. Cherry in his conference paper (see note 10).

14. See Jeffry M. Diefendorf, 'Berlin, Vienna, and Budapest: Rebuilding Capital Cities', in *Central European Capital Cities: Twentieth-Century Culture and Society in Vienna, Budapest, Prague, and Berlin*, ed. John Lampe (Washington, D.C., 1989).

15. The problems faced by preservationists in Poland were discussed in the conference paper by Teresa Zarebska (see note 10).

16. Carlos Sambricio has written on architecture and planning in Madrid under Spanish fascism, especially in the 1940s. See, for example, his essay in Frank (ed.), *Faschistische Architekturen* (see note 7).

# 2 Reconstructors' Tales: an Example of the Use of Oral Sources in the History of Reconstruction after the Second World War

## DANIÈLE VOLDMAN

Many of those who participated in the rebirth of towns destroyed during the Second World War are still alive today and quite willing to satisfy historians' curiosity. Because France had declared her intention of directing the entire reconstruction work from the moment of the first destruction in the spring of 1940, we can identify among the many participants in rebuilding a specific category of 'state reconstructors' appointed by the government to carry out its orders. Town planners, architects and civil engineers, both practitioners and theoreticians, formed a homogeneous nucleus, identifiable by the positions they occupied within the ruling classes during the years 1940–50.[1] This is why, apart from the abundance of written material available for the study of the period of reconstruction that followed the conflict,[2] a corpus of oral statements is gradually being formed, describing the beginnings of the big building sites and the creation at the Liberation of the Ministère de la reconstruction et de l'urbanisme (MRU) (Ministry for Reconstruction and Town Planning) for the purpose of conducting such an unprecedented operation. As a contribution to the discussion on the use of evidence in contemporary history, I should like to describe one way of using these oral sources for the period of reconstruction.[3]

## THE ORAL HISTORIES OF RECONSTRUCTION

The oral history collection currently contains about twenty interviews that vary in length and method of collection.[4] I have mainly used three sets of interviews. The first were collected for my Higher Doctoral thesis, *Reconstruire, la politique du MRU, ses antécédents, son application, 1940–1945*. My interviewees, working for or having worked for the MRU, were architects or 'decision-makers' who had helped to elaborate and put into practice the Ministry's policy. The second set stems from the interviews conducted by Rémi Baudoui when he was working on Raoul Dautry. And thirdly, the Institut français d'architecture and the Institut d'histoire du temps présent also recorded interviews with decision-makers and reconstructors. The different sets of interviews were used because, just as historians who work with oral sources sometimes hesitate to use interviews they did not themselves record, I wanted to test the hypothesis of the 'activeness' of a source, independent from the interviewer. And these sources are also incomplete in so far as the choice of interviewees was made according to their activity at the head of the MRU or at a relatively high level. They cannot be regarded as representative in a strict or sociological sense.

This is why written documentary material that could help describe the period will not be discussed here, nor will I analyse the building trades, whose members almost unanimously and without real cynicism considered this period to have been a kind of golden age, or the conditions under which the original institutions had been set up and which our informants enjoy describing.[5] These points have been touched upon elsewhere,[6] although they must be examined more carefully. I am interested here above all in the remarks directed by the reconstructors toward historians. And what interests me in these remarks are the means and motives they give for their past actions. François Bloch-Lainé, Directeur du Trésor from 1947 to 1953, suggested in his book *La France restaurée, 1944–1954* the importance of finding out who is the fairest chronicler of the battle of Waterloo, Fabrice del Dongo or the teacher of strategy.[7] He contended that 'it is right that historians, as the official clarifyers, should enable us to recognize with them, before we disappear, the crossroads we have passed. But we must take into account, both they and we, our respective tendencies in our efforts at analysis, in order mutually to correct them.' In spite of this warning, it is still the teacher of strategy's point of view that is deliberately adopted here.

Three causes for concern emerge from the reconstructors' remarks. Most of those interviewed insisted first of all on the continuity of their work during the period 1940–50, linking France's efforts to remove all traces of her first ruins with the measures taken after 1945. In their view, the Liberation made a break that was mostly of a political nature and of only secondary importance to town planning and the problems of space development. They then pointed out the climate of material constraint in which they were obliged to work, asserting that the requirements of reconstruction guided their actions and limited their initiative. Lastly, they warned their contemporary interlocutors against underestimating the specific temporal context of institutional and political life, essential in trying to appreciate under what conditions entire towns were recreated and revived in the devastated regions. They considered this to have been a decisive factor in explaining the delay in solving the housing crisis, which lasted longer in France than in neighbouring countries like Great Britain and Germany.

What are the arguments that structure the reasoning behind this discourse?

## 1940 – THE BEGINNING OF A DECADE

'By what unjustified and – after the event – laughable prudery do people want everything to have started in 1945?', exclaimed one of our informants at the beginning of an interview.[8]

As early as autumn 1940 the Vichy government had set up agencies to co-ordinate the first clearance of rubble and to examine the elements of a consistent policy of rural and urban development. The Commissariat technique à la reconstruction immobilière (CTRI) and the urban services of the Délégation générale à l'équipement national (DGEN) centralised all the issues connected with reconstruction. The latter agency, conceived with a view to the future, had two primary assignments, one practical and immediate and the other longer term. The practical task involved organising emergency measures. As early as summer 1940, but especially from the autumn, destroyed towns and villages received government aid. Newly appointed prefects watched over the evacuation of the debris, supervised the choice of building firms and public works that carried out the contracts, and took charge of the victims. For example, temporary bridges restored the traffic between the two banks of the Loire, huts were built for the homeless at Amiens, and the piers were repaired at Dunkirk. As part of the long term assignment, town planners and architects began to sketch on their drawing boards new plans for towns destroyed by the 1940 campaign, while other officials undertook the codification and organisation of reconstruction and town planning in legislative terms. After the war, most of these persons met again at the MRU as a result of the merging of the CTRI and the DGEN.[9]

This continuity, both human and institutional, justified the way in which the reconstructors linked the activities of 1945 to those of 1940 in the interviews. It is true that the unanimity of the remarks, more than the fact itself – for the State had indeed tried twice to reconstruct – is increased by the sample of informants interviewed. Almost all the architects were DLPG (Diplômés par le gouvernement) and had been educated at the École des beaux-arts; most of them were close to the École française d'urbanisme, having either studied at the Institut d'urbanisme de la ville de Paris or moved in that sphere of influence.[10] The civil engineers were often graduates from the Paris École polytechnique, having opted for the Ponts et chaussées.[11] Investigating reconstruction personnel enables us to follow the education and development of a system of knowledge, solidarities and affinities that explained the cohesion of the group. There were several superimposed circles that gradually melted and unified, fusing together into an *esprit de corps* personalities of diverse origins, professions and mentalities. In France, the social cohesion of the public service – apart from political convictions which, as a rule, need not be taken into account – generally prevented fragmentation into narrow groups. The criterion of belonging depends on the number of years of study and common attendance at 'The School', whether it be the Polytechnique, Ponts et chaussées, Beaux-Arts, or Centrale des travaux publics. In the present case, the community was based on involvement in the same adventure, one that mostly started during the interwar years.

There was, for instance, the circle of architects and town planners. Critical of the Beaux-Arts teaching, they did not completely reject its spirit, but tried rather to surpass it. They aimed at being technicians as well as artists, mindful of social issues and ideas on spatial development and planning. And then there were the people who worked on the Paris International Exhibition of 1937, an event glorifying technical skills and modernity at the service of art and the happiness of mankind.[12] Here again one finds the personnel of the town planning department of Paris, the very ones who formed part of the first circle of reconstructors. An ongoing study[13] should lead to the discovery of several circles: the 'planistes' of the 1930s, the polytechnicians among whom was Raoul Dautry; the people from the railway networks, those of the Comité d'aménagement de la Région parisienne; and, further, the proponents of the ideology of the Musée social and the Ligue rurale urbaine.[14] These varied groups had interacted before the war and were now joined together by their involvement in the two waves of reconstruction.

It is interesting to compare the stories about the recruitment of reconstructors in 1940 and in 1945. The newcomers had rarely solicited their positions; rather, they were 'summoned' by powerful personalities – former school friends, colleagues from previous functions, an admired superior, a master. Our informants enjoyed describing their feelings of those days, including the enthusiasm that accompanied each proposal and, in spite of the difficulties of their situation, the sense of being given an opportunity to accomplish a genuine mission, thanks to the exceptional circumstances of the Occupation. In 1940 it was a question of helping to restore the country or to save its dignity. In 1945 it meant pursuing the task of the Resistance, proving that the work done under the German Occupation had indeed been a preparation for the future.

Those who began their careers in 1940 laid more stress on the government's determination to use their technical competence to combat the disorganisation that followed the defeat; they liked to remember the errors of reconstruction made after 1918 against which they had protested in the 1930s. Their recruitment into the CTRI or the DGEN meant an opportunity to avoid making the same mistakes. The 1945 newcomers stressed their preference for public service and their desire to participate in their country's rebirth by applying their practical knowledge of their trades. They also mentioned how concerned the provisional government was to maintain an infrastructure of technicians from among those who had not too strongly compromised themselves. The advent of Raoul Dautry at the head of the MRU reinforced the merging of the circles. It was his policy to 'mix blood', that is to say, to appeal to all of the larger state agencies to help with reconstruction.[15] It was mostly Dautry who achieved a unity of views by drawing upon the reserves of the 'Conseil d'état', 'Inspection des finances', 'Corps des mines', 'Ponts et chaussées', 'Génie rural', and other offices.

## A PROFESSIONAL CONSCIENCE

Rare indeed were those informants who would give an ideological or political reason for having accepted the position they were offered. One exception claimed to have given up working in government departments during the German Occupation because of the oath which all civil servants had to swear to the head of state. He was recruited by the MRU as soon as the Ministry was formed. Similarly, another individual, a great figure in the Resistance, said that he wanted (among other reasons) to continue the struggle against barbarity by working for the MRU. Moreover, the stories of the Occupation are studded with allusions to acts of solidarity, mutual aid to the oppressed of the time: Jews who were saved by being recruited, opponents to the Nazi regime who were protected, Resistance workers who were kept informed. These acts were always presented within the scope of professional activities, never as acts of heroism – a clear conscience, as it were, confirmed by ulterior events. Only one of our informants was dismissed at the Liberation, and without otherwise experiencing any persecution. The political motive for the dismissal – a very real one, since it involved a high official – was minimized at the time by the new authorities. The political atmosphere after the war, and indeed France's official ideology throughout the 1950s and 1960s, in fact was captured perfectly in the 1946 French film *Mr Orchid*.[16]

It is interesting to see the extent to which this way of presenting 'the dark years' was taken up by the storytellers. Consider, for example, *Le Chantier 1425*.[17] In 1941, a wide-ranging survey on rural housing was launched at the initiative of George-Henri Rivière within the scope of research undertaken by the Musée des arts et traditions populaires. The Vichy authorities encouraged it, interested as they always were in traditions and regionalism. This is how the DGEN came to take an active part in it, under the joint direction of Urbain Cassan and Rivière. The research team was composed of some forty architects whose statements were to be used for an ethnological analysis of housing customs in the French countryside. Immediately after the end of the war, the promoters of *Chantier 1425* felt the need to justify their research and claimed that the scientific activity, far from serving Vichy's purposes, had provided cover for persecuted colleagues.[18] This version, the validity of which there is no point in verifying here, was taken as an example to reinforce the thesis of the continuity of the decade of 1940–50 or, to put it differently, to whitewash politically work done prior to 1945.

In fact, according to our informants, there was no doubt that the CTRI and the DGEN were preparing a postwar world in which France could once again be a sovereign power. Forty years later, not one of these informants can recall ever having imagined Europe's return to peace under German rule. All were convinced that the occupying forces would withdraw. Consequently, they directed their efforts towards the day of Liberation. Most of our informants laid little claim to political involvement during these years. Not one of them claimed to have been, even within the framework of his professional career, an active opponent of Pétain's regime, or admitted to having been a Nazi sympathiser or a collaborator. No one claimed to have been either an active Resistance worker or a militant supporter of Pétain. They tended rather to evade these issues and to reply reluctantly to questions about their attitudes and opinions of that time. This applies to those who had had no recognised political activity as well as to those known to have been politically involved, whether actively or intellectually. None the less, and this may well be a methodological weakness, we feel that the interviewers were haunted by the questions, perhaps barely articulated, that were all-important after the Liberation: what did you do during those dark years, did you behave well, and what have you to say in your defence?

This partly explains why, with regard to those who remained in office throughout the decade, the accent was placed above all on the short- and long-term importance of the 1943 regulations known as the 'Town Planning Code'. This was part of legislation that had remained in force since the 1920s, and it enabled us to pinpoint long-term phenomena not easily influenced by fluctuating political circumstances. Our informants commented in detail on the origins of the 1943 regulations, portraying them as a response to measures taken since 1919 to try and arrest the uncontrolled development of the suburbs and the anarchical growth of the towns. The wartime regulations thus represented an effort to form a rational, harmonious synthesis of previous laws and policies. 'Dautry received a very substantial inheritance', said one of them, adding 'it's crazy how hard we could work at that time'.[19] All of them considered the 1943 measures to have been the foundation of postwar town planning. When comparing the 1941 legislation on war damage with that of 1946, they showed the coherence of the first, its influence on the second, and the 'errors' which the postwar period was unable to avoid.

Similarly, the organisation of the CTRI and the DGEN foreshadowed that of the national and regional development services. The DATAR (Délégation générale à l'aménagement du territoire et à l'action régionale) was in fact not created until 1963, but our informants insisted that we see that its origins went back as far as 1943. One person remarked:

I like Olivier Guichard, but his group has led people to believe that national and regional development was an invention of DATAR. They expanded their organisation very well, better than we did, but they invented absolutely nothing. The whole structure was already set up. In the beginning it was Dautry, yes, Dautry who, as War Minister, was one of the promoters of industrial decentralisation. And that is the first concept of national and regional development.[20]

On this point our informants were unanimous. With the same assurance, both those who had identified with government authorities and those who had fought them from London or Algiers dated the birth of French town planning from these years. No one disputed the rightful legacy or paternity of the concept. On the other hand, there was general criticism of the territorial organisation of the country, and all agreed on the need to transform it. It is undeniable that many men (and a few women) in the CTRI had looked into the possibilities of renewed town planning. And the fact that others had also thought about it while underground or across the sea only confirmed the feeling of brotherly understanding that could unite people on opposite sides of the political spectrum.

Here again they were reflecting the ideology of the Liberation, which had decided to keep the administrative management of the Vichy regime in place, weeding out only those who had compromised themselves too far, and calling for a national reconciliation in the euphoric fiction of a country which had, on the whole, supposedly resisted the Germans. More important than the ideological justifications, however, was what the interviews revealed about the working conditions and accomplishments in the decade from 1940 to 1950.

## THE CONSTRAINTS ON GOVERNMENT POWER

Apart from the obvious issue of self justification, the frequency with which the reconstructors praised the town planning law of 1943 and the invention of national and regional development planning suggests the need for examination of bureaucratic and decision-making mechanisms. The reconstructors could not help wondering why so much time was lost between the proposal of a concept and its application. With the clear conscience of technocrats isolated from politics, many of them were not convinced that they had mastered the decision-making process or even that they had understood where their power really lay, even though they had been high up in government circles. Some who remained in office during the entire period blamed changes from one ruling party to another, the incompetence of ministers, government incoherence and the demands of political deadlines. They still thought that the relative stability of the group of technocrats (compared to the instability of politics) enabled their causes to advance and their ideas to take shape. In other words, ministers pass from the scene but directors remain. Thus real power was with the technocrats who had time and job security. To others, 1958 meant an important break. They had no strong Gaullist sympathies, nor had they demonstrated their opinions in the preceding period. They considered that the achievement of important projects was made possible not so much by the new economic circumstances as by the evolution of social structures. Another informant also placed the break in 1958, but for a different reason: he claimed that from that time onward, and contrary to the practices of the Fourth Republic, technocrats were 'pledged to a party'.[21]

None of them was convinced, however, nor could they convince others, of the reasons for the slowness with which town planning was implemented or for the delays in housing construction. This illustrates the contradictory position of our informants. In the professional and social hierarchy they were leaders, including, at the highest level, a former minister and directors of MRU departments. Yet they did not achieve their goals. What characterised this group of 'state reconstructors' was the gap between their intention to transform French town planning, impose reforms, instigate new procedures and even change mentalities, and the difficulties they encountered in obtaining tangible results. In retrospect they viewed their achievements with some reserve. They could talk with pleasure about the dynamism of their daily activities, but tended to consider that the results had not always been up to their ambitions.

So some of our information tends to show the weakening of power and sometimes its absence. The difficulty these men had in identifying decision-makers and defining their actual powers led to a vague theory on the multiplicity of power. Some did not rationalise quite so much and simply described their activities, without bothering to indicate what happened in reality. This was true mostly for those who wrote or prepared reports, legal texts or regulations. For instance, the team that originated the research on the plan for national and regional development presented to the government in 1951 by the Minister for Reconstruction, Eugène Claudius-Petit, stressed more the elaboration of the plan than its practical results.[22] Some who expressed their thoughts on the respective roles of economics and politics were sceptical about the real power of the administrative authorities and doubtful of the very idea of power. As they were none the less convinced of the reality of a power of decision at all echelons of the government structure, they expressed the idea that its weakening, multiplicity and dispersal slowed down and even hindered achievement. While the pure technocrats rejected the reasons put forward by the politicians to account for a certain backwardness, the latter called upon the entire social structure to explain their relative impotence. For instance, a former minister asserted that the effort to solve the housing crisis in the early 1950s was met with incomprehension by the population and its elected representatives. Contrary to the British, the French were, in his view, incapable of understanding that they must pay rather a lot for good housing. Similarly, the freezing of rents, a result of the 1948 law on rent, was not analysed as a misjudgement by its sponsors but as the result of electioneering compromises which the politicians could not avoid. Reading between the lines, the message was: if the technocrats had been able to act alone, neither the 1946 payment of war damages nor the 1948 rent system would have been organised as they were.

That being the case, how can we determine the real range of possibilities for the postwar elaboration of urban policies? Having emphasised the continuity between the Vichy government and the Fourth Republic, our informants could hardly describe themselves as having been traumatised by some shattering blow or dependent on an inheritance too burdensome to manage. On the contrary, claiming to have themselves initiated their actions, they stressed the *political* lack of preparation of the postwar years. It is as if they blamed the politicians for all the problems caused by chance and coincidence. Implicitly they held the government almost entirely responsible for the slowness of the reconstruction. It was the government, as an entity outside of themselves, which should have foreseen the rapid population increase and the consequences of the baby boom, the government which had not taken the appropriate steps to check the housing crisis, the government again which had not immediately replaced all the slum dwellings. The technocrats felt themselves more or less blameless. Describing only this aspect of their testimony, however, would grossly misrepresent their thoughts.

Indeed, they never forgot to mention the financial difficulties and shortages that upset all their projects. They all mentioned the catastrophic condition of the country, both in 1940 and in 1945, and the extent of the ruins. How could they anticipate long-term developments, they argued, when victims were homeless and immediate relief was urgently required? Thus they all pointed out the contradiction between short-term emergencies and long-term requirements. Architects, town planners, civil engineers, administrators and politicians, none underestimated the fundamental opposition between the obligation to reconstruct rapidly and the needs of good quality town planning, which was slower to carry out because more demanding of materials both in quality and quantity. Thus, in the reconstruction of Le Havre, in order to justify giving up an innovation suggested by Auguste Perret, shortages were blamed: 'Perret wanted to raise the city on to a platform, with all the fluids running below; the project was much discussed, but it would have used up all the cement provided for reconstruction. So we did not go through with it. We couldn't . . . '.[23] Similarly, with regard to the lukewarm reception of Le Corbusier's ideas, the reasons given were very down-to-earth. The material difficulties seem to have carried more weight than disagreements on style or dissension between factions. One of our informants believed that the reason why Le Corbusier constructed so little in 1947 was that he had used too much of the good material that was still available that year.[24] While it is true that oral evidence should not be used by historians in accordance with a methodology different from that used for written sources, this kind of evidence suggests court proceedings.[25] Here we cannot help noticing how skilfully our interlocutors mastered the arts of sidestepping and justification. We do not in the least hold it against them, but we do want to show how changes, rejections and transfers of responsibility came about. In the eyes of our interlocutors, it was always from the outside that obstacles arose to the coherent implementation of their plans. Some put forward the impatient demands of the homeless, or the narrowmindedness of reconstruction societies; others pointed to the rapid turnover of leadership or the politicians' concern over elections; and everyone stressed the boundless needs of a country exhausted by war, privation and political upheaval. This is a usual phenomenon which François Bloch-Lainé had already pointed out:

> Commentators on past events are more likely to be right than the protagonists. But although they have the advantage of

hindsight over the inconveniences of the future and the lucidity of the present, they are induced into other errors by their liking for doctrines. Personally I am prepared to admit that practitioners are inclined to exaggerate the constraints to which they are subjected, the complications and fatalities of daily life, and to minimize their real freedom of action.[26]

But in the last analysis, what was brought into play was the importance of time more than disappointment with politics or the requirements of political economy. In order to build, one needed a spirit of decisiveness, money, intelligent ideas and the desire to do things well. But all this was useless without sufficient time. After sketching an analysis of the limits – or rather the unreality – of their powers, our informants reverted to an appreciation of the irreplaceable value of time. The real time they had spent in their offices mattered little. What emerges from these statements is a vision of the inexorable march of time: governments change too quickly, people are in too much of a hurry, concrete splits as soon as it is dry. This explains the failures. Time was also too short to advise the population to be patient, to compensate for the restricted electioneering of political leaders, to insist on careful work from building firms. In fact, there was time only to consider, organise, legislate. This, no doubt, is why the interviewees repeatedly insisted on the 'intellectual' and pioneering aspects of the work accomplished.

What results from these few interviews with reconstructors, who often spent several years of their working lives with the MRU, is not only a critical look at postwar town planning. All these interviewees were more or less influenced by nostalgia for the days of youth and enthusiasm. They also took a stand on the nature of public service, which they felt should, in a democratic system, be independent of the political party in power. Even if one is hesitant about the legitimacy of a state such as the one formed after the 1940 armistice, is it not the duty of every state employee, aware of the value of his function, to remain at his post? For some, the decade of 1940–50 sharply highlighted the question of the relationship between public servants and the state that employed them. But questioned in the autumn of life about their activities during the reconstruction period, this was not what was closest to their hearts – at least, not explicitly.

Deliberately confining themselves to the technical and professional aspects of their activities, they were wary of shedding

light on their behaviour as citizens. Their justifications, and we
have seen how self-justifying their statements were, concerned
their work and not their involvement in it. Questioned in their
capacity as reconstructors, it is as reconstructors that they replied.
No doubt this is another weakness of this corpus of interviews,
where questions on 'the dark years' received little or no reply.
Our informants, approached as reconstruction professionals, showed
themselves to be, today, divided between satisfaction at duty done
and, for some, an unconscious sense of guilt that is not recognised
as such but is changed into pride at having done a long-range job
for the country. The honour and solidarity of the profession and the
artificial self-consciousness of any individual made to look back over
his past life encourages such behaviour.

In the end, the main contribution of this set of interviews is the
study of the mechanisms of memory construction of a group. The
historian is always dependent on his sources: his work consists in
finding the most reliable, the most diverse sources, those that will
stand up to criticism and any kind of verification and cross-checking.
In this sense, oral sources cannot be used by themselves. But now
that, in the history of mentalities, memory has become as much a
subject of history as odours and tears,[27] oral sources, although not
sufficient in themselves, have become indispensable.

**Notes**
1.    No study has yet been carried out on the different professional
      groups that participated in reconstruction. For general problems, the
      reference work is still Anatole Kopp, Frédérique Boucher and Danièle
      Pauly's *L'architecture de la reconstruction en France* (Paris, 1982).
2.    The sources for the history of reconstruction in France are very
      abundant and extremely varied. The MRU archives at the National
      Archives consist of several thousand archive files, enabling historians
      to approach all aspects of the question.
3.    On these problems, see 'Questions à l'histore orale', *Cahiers de
      l'IHTP*, no. 4 (June 1987), particularly Danièle Voldman, 'L'invention
      du témoignage oral'.
4.    This work summarises part of the hypothesis I developed in
      'Entretiens avec les Reconstructeurs, contribution à l'étude d'un
      groupe de décideurs', 5th Colloque international d'histoire orale,
      Barcelona, March 1985, multigraphed. At that time I had used only
      evidence I had myself collected. For this paper I used individual or
      collective evidence by Raymond Aubrac, engineer and member of
      the cabinets of Raoul Dautry and François Billoux, head of mine

clearance; Robert Auzelle, architect-town planner, inspector general of town planning; Paulin Biage, MRU administrator; André Brunot, engineer; Eugène Claudius-Petit, Minister for Reconstruction and Town Planning from 1948 until 1953; Paul Dufournet, chief Town Planner at the MRU; Jacques Garancher, engineer; Pierre Gibel, controller general for the development of the Paris region at the MRU; Jean Gohier, MRU administrator; Jean-François Gravier, official representative of the MRU; André Gutton, town planner; André Larieu, MRU administrator; L. Lissakovski, engineer; Jean Kérisel, engineer; Bertrand Monnet, architect; André Muffang, engineer, commissioner for housing reconstruction; Roger Puget, town planner; Pierre Randet, head of the national and regional development service at the MRU; Yves Salaün, MRU administrator; J. Sialleli, MRU administrator; Jules Verne, engineer. Some recordings were limited in time (about one hour) due to circumstances or the wishes of the informants. Others took place over several weeks. They were sometimes preceded by a written or telephoned questionnaire and were mostly semi-directive. In order to respect privacy I have minimised personal references in the text, giving the indispensable references in the notes.

5. On institutional history, see Danièle Voldman, 'Reconstruire pour construire ou de la nécessité de naître en l'an quarante', *Les Annales de la recherche urbaine*, no. 21 (1984).

6. For example, apart from the work by Kopp already mentioned, see *Images, enjeux et discours de la Reconstruction*, ed. Danièle Voldman, *Cahiers de l'IHTP*, no. 5 (July 1987).

7. François Bloch-Lainé and Jean Bouvier, *La France restaurée 1944–1954: Dialogue sur les choix d'une modernisation* (Paris, 1986). Both quotations in the paragraph are from the foreword, pp. 7 and 8.

8. Discussion with P. Dufournet by R. Baudoui, 17 December 1982.

9. Danièle Voldman, 'Aux origines du Ministère de la reconstruction', *Les Trois Reconstructions: 1919–1940–1945*, Dossiers et documents de l'Institut français d'architecture, nr 4 (December 1983).

10. On reconstruction architects, see Martine Morel, 'Reconstruire, dirent-ils', in Voldman (ed.), *Images* (see note 6), and D. Voldman, 'Les architectes reconstructeurs forment ils une génération?', *Effets d'âge et phénomènes de générations dans la société intellectuelle française*, ed. Jean-François Sirinelli, *Cahiers de L'IHTP*, no. 6 (Autumn 1987).

11. Gilles Jeannot, 'Les ingénieurs et la reconstruction, images et strategies', in Voldman (ed.), *Images* (see note 6).

12. *1937–1987*, catalogue de l'exposition du cinquantenaire (Paris, 1987). I am accepting without argument the idea of modernity put forward by contemporaries to describe this event.

13. This matter was already touched upon at the time of the comparative study of French and English reconstruction conducted by the IHTP jointly with the University of Sheffield. It should be published in Voldman, *Reconstruire: La politique du MRU*.

14. *Raoul Dautry*, Dossiers et documents de l'Institut français d'architecture, publication forthcoming.

15. Discussion with J. Kérisel by R. Baudoui, 25 September 1986.
16. 'Le Père tranquille', made in 1946 by René Clément with screenplay and dialogues by Noël-Noël.
17. Christian Faure, *Folklore et révolution nationale: Doctrine et action sous Vichy, 1940–1944*, University thesis for Lyon II, 1986, multi-graphed.
18. Ibid.
19. Discussion with P. Dufournet by R. Baudoui, 18 April 1986.
20. Discussion with P. Randet by R. Baudoui, 20 May 1986.
21. Discussion with R. Auzelle by D. Voldman, 4 May 1983.
22. On the plan for national and regional development, see D. Voldman, 'Reconstruire la France en 1945: des usines ou des villes?', in *L'Usine et la ville, culture technique*, special issue, 1986.
23. Discussion with P. Dufournet, see note 19.
24. Ibid.
25. Voldman, 'L'invention du témoignage oral', see note 3.
26. Bloch-Lainé and Bouvier, *La France restaurée* (see note 7).
27. Alain Corbin, *Le Miasme et la jonquille, l'odorat et l'imaginaire social, 18–20 siècle* (Paris, 1982); Anne Vincent-Buffault, *Histoire des larmes* (Marseille, 1986).

# 3 Between Regionalism and Functionalism: French Reconstruction from 1940 to 1945

RÉMI BAUDOUI

## PREFACE

Before any actual research was undertaken on reconstruction, French architectural historians, still dominated by the Modern movement from l'Esprit Nouveau to the Congrès Internationaux d'Architecture Moderne (CIAM), opposed the triumphant radicalness of the functionalism of the 1950s and 1960s to the multiplicity of aesthetic trends of the 1930s. For example, high-rise housing developments, considered for a time to be an embarrassing inheritance of functionalism and Le Corbusier's Charter of Athens, demonstrated *a posteriori* the success of modern architecture. From this antithesis between the interwar period and the 1960s, a singular history of reconstruction slowly developed, in which the beginning of this radical transformation in the aesthetic of French architecture might be found.

By challenging the prevailing explanations, the first research on reconstruction, carried out at the end of the 1970s, was bound to raise more questions than provide answers. For example, in keeping with the traditional political interpretation of the period, one that stressed rupture and discontinuity – a theme upon which the political and ideological projects of the revived French republic were based – the analysis of reconstruction after 1940 was kept apart from discussion of post-1944 developments. By shifting the starting point for a history of reconstruction away from the defeat of June 1940 to the moment of the Liberation and the restoration of a republican government, scholars were thus splitting the history of reconstruction into two separate and discrete histories.

Events themselves, however, argue for beginning the study of reconstruction in 1940. From an institutional viewpoint, it is significant that the creation of the first Ministry of Reconstruction and Urbanism on 13 November 1944 had been preceded by the creation of the Commissariat à la reconstruction immobilière on 11 November

31

1940. (The administrative apparatus of 1940 was supposed to provide men and equipment for the new ministry created by de Gaulle during his temporary government of 'national consensus'.) The destruction itself, which was compounded by the Anglo-American bombings in 1942, appears to provide a natural linkage between these two periods of reconstruction. However this was not sufficiently persuasive to architectural historians, even though the continuity in the process of destruction should inevitably have led to the recognition of continuity in architectural and town planning ideas.

It was with such difficulties in mind that at the first international symposium on reconstruction, held in Paris in 1983, scholars sought to place the reconstruction activities after the years 1919, 1940 and 1945 into the same genealogical framework.[1] All the investigators agreed on the need to study carefully the years of German Occupation from the point of view of architecture and town planning. This led to a great deal of research in which the Occupation was treated as the starting point of French reconstruction with regard to the Second World War, without systematically limiting research only to that period.[2] The research enabled us to make a great deal of progress, though we were not spared some misinterpretations, due sometimes to reading the evidence on a purely political level. Still, how could this have been prevented, since the period to be studied had already been defined by such political events as the armistice at one end and the Liberation at the other? How could the end of the Third Republic and the creation of the government of Marshal Pétain not also mean radical control of architectural aesthetics, as had happened in the totalitarian states of Germany and Italy?

Indeed, some investigators have discerned an ideological alignment of Vichy on the German pattern and influences of this cultural pattern on the architecture of French reconstruction between 1940 and 1944.[3] They point to legal changes that were introduced: in the control of architecture under the town planning law of 15 June 1943, which generalised the procedures for obtaining planning permissions and defined, with limiting constraints, the notion of reconstruction and development plans; in professional organisations under the law of 31 December 1940, which created the *ordre des architectes*; and at the level of municipal government, under the law of 16 November 1940, which divested the local authorities of their political responsibilities. In addition, a complete opposition between modern architecture and regionalist architecture was posited under Vichy. An official French aesthetics was supposed to have been based on the criticism of functionalism and on the glorification of historicist architecture, considered as the only style capable of integrating the perennial values of 'Maison France'.

If, following the German example, the Vichy regime discussed architectural matters using the logic of racial purification, Nazi influence in fact does not go much further than that. This is first of all due to the fact that the vague authoritarian impulses of the regime of the 'Révolution nationale' could not keep up the illusion and conceal its own contradictions concerning aesthetics. The wish to redefine a return to tradition did not mean that it could formulate a Maréchalist aesthetics. Recent research in the field of the arts under the Occupation has suggested that we should consider the possibility that reconstruction projects between 1940 and 1944 did not in the least define a proper Maréchalist style. Beyond the formal groups of picturesque buildings in the Loire Valley, did the French government merely attempt a literal reconstruction, or did it change the nature of architecture and town planning on the basis of some rational, modern design?

The scandals that emerged from the reconstruction after 1919 were too vivid in people's memories in 1940 to imagine that the French government would have ratified an architectural and urban reconstruction determined solely by the demands of the landlords whose property had been damaged. A sense of the common good necessarily produced the general rule underlying the 1940 reconstruction; it would not be based on mere architectural criteria but first of all on town planning criteria.

This paper attempts to show that it is fruitless to believe that ideological opposition existed, in terms of formal choices, between regionalists and functionalists. Such opposition would have to presume the existence of a clear division within the civil service of the French state, with the traditionalists on the one hand and modernising technocrats on the other hand. The division was not so clear cut. In fact, there was not a technocratic front in aesthetic matters, as can be seen from brief consideration of the efforts of Le Corbusier to work with Vichy.

The colonial administrator Marcel Peyrouton, a former resident-general in Tunisia and Morocco and Minister of the Interior to Marshal Pétain from August 1940 to February 1941, gave his full support to Le Corbusier's ideas. On the other hand, François Lehideux, named Commissaire à la lutte contre le chômage (Commissioner in the Fight against Unemployment) in November 1940, then Délégué général à l'équipement national (Delegate General of National Technical Facilities) in March 1941, refused to support Le Corbusier's demands for modern architecture because, as a Catholic, Lehideux believed that aesthetics – synonymous with Christianity and divine harmony – must take into account the elements of the past.[4] Therefore, in the same sweeping gesture, he dismissed Le Corbusier together with Auguste Perret. The journalist and learned historian Lucien Romier, who was Pétain's personal adviser before being named Minister of State from August 1941 to December 1943, knew Le Corbusier from the period of the Redressement français (the 'French Resurgance', a technocratic organisation formed in 1925), but at Vichy he does not seem to have shown him any particular favouritism.[5] Still, Le Corbusier was an overpowering figure for some Frenchmen under Vichy.[6] There could be no better proof of this than the elaborate praise published in the Pétainist press of his books. Here we are doubtlessly touching upon something that has long been interpreted as a paradox of the 1940s: the quest for a regionalist architectural identity co-existing with the presence of Le Corbusier within the administrative apparatus of the Vichy regime. And how can we explain the great success of his theoretical work published in the middle of the Occupation? Let us not forget after all that Le Corbusier successively published: in 1941, *Destin de Paris* and *Sur les 4 routes*; in 1942, *La Maison des hommes* (with François de Pierrefeu) and *Les Murondins*; in 1943, *Entretien avec les étudiants des écoles d'architecture* and *La Charte d'Athènes*, the last of which had been taking shape since the fourth CIAM conference in 1933.

All of this should warn us against any conclusion that Le Corbusier's supposedly heroic fight under Vichy was a solitary opposition to mediocre administrative ideas on architecture and urban planning that were leading to 'reconstruction à l'identique', a reconstruction of things as they had been before. If he stayed at Vichy from January 1941 to July 1942 and was able in the meantime to plan future work within the administration, it means above all that the French state was divided on the choice of a guiding theme for reconstruction.

Therefore, rather than systematically opposing regionalist architecture and the Vichy regime on the one hand to modern architecture and the Fourth Republic on the other, we must look upon these two periods as a single unit. Beyond the Liberation and the return to democracy, a unified history of reconstruction must be developed that rests largely on the continuity of the administrative structures that dealt with reconstruction from Vichy to the Fourth Republic. Without underrating the effects of the surrender of democracy or its restoration, we postulate that reconstruction after the Second World War poses, both for the Vichy period and for the postwar period, the question of an aesthetic norm of good taste in direct relation with the goal of rational modernism. It is only within the latter that architectural trends intervene. Typical here are the ideas of Gien, whose reconstruction plan dates back to 1940, and of Royan, whose reconstruction plan dates to the period after the Liberation. Although they presented radically different physionomies because of their disparate architectural characteristics, they make up the archetypes of the main trends of postwar town planning.[7]

## THE LOIRE VALLEY: A LABORATORY FOR THE RECONSTRUCTION OF 1940

The Second World War came to France in May 1940, and the destruction it wrought transformed the very image of the ruins of war inherited from the First World War. Whereas thirteen departments had suffered damage by 1918, there were sixty-four in June 1940. Although the density of the urban areas that had been damaged decreased as one moved from north-east to south-west, the great novelty – if we may put it in such terms – lay in the wide area of destruction caused by aerial bombardment, which greatly contributed to the German victory from a physical point of view as well as a psychological one.

It was in the context of military withdrawal and civilian exodus that the Loiret department suffered its devastation between 14 and 19 June 1940, making it the last department to suffer from the German attack. The aim of the German air raids was to cut communications between the banks of the Loire. Consequently they destroyed the railway stations and the bridges as well as the town centres of Gien, Châteauneuf-sur-Loire, Sully-sur-Loire and Orléans, as well as smaller urban areas. On 22 June the armistice was signed. Three days later, the reconstruction of the Loiret was already being planned, and the newly named Prefect Morane was settling in Orléans.[8]

The armistice agreement explains why the French administration hurried things so much in the Occupation zone. Article 13 obliged the French government to repair the communication and transportation network in all the territory that was to be occupied by German troops.

Hence it is clear that the situation in the Loire Valley cannot be regarded solely from the point of view of urban reconstruction. There were, in fact, two objectives: to repair the damaged infrastructure and to promote an architectural reconstruction along regionalist lines that accorded with the ideological orientations of the Vichy regime. Within this new rationality of reconstruction – the pre-eminence of the restoration of the communications infrastructure over the rebuilding of housing – a programme of modernisation and rationalisation that extended to town planning can be distinguished.

It would be wrong, however, to think that the reconstruction of the damaged infrastructure imposed by the occupying power can be dissociated from the second, aesthetic one. Despite German pressure to encourage work of strategic importance and consequently to give higher priority to communications than to town planning, they form a single process. Indeed, the same French technical teams worked on both of them. Moreover, since they felt that any technical job could further a possible restoration of French administrative authority in the occupied zone, they had no reason to dissociate the first sort of task from the second. Hence their eagerness to satisfy the German demands despite their coercive nature.

The primacy of rebuilding the transportation and communications networks in the Loire Valley also found expression in personnel choices. Prefect Jacques Morane was a graduate of the École polytechnique as well as a civil engineer. As soon as he was at his post, he obtained from the Germans the release of Jean Kérisel, a young Orléans civil servant with a similar educational background who was at the time a prisoner of war. Kérisel was given the task of organising the technical part of the preparatory work on Loiret reconstruction, and he also participated in the town planning study for Orléans. Jean Royer, who had founded the journal *Urbanisme* in 1932, was appointed head of the town planning department. On 26 July 1940, just after the arrival of Royer, the members of the departmental planning commission for cities and villages met at the request of the prefect and authorised the drawing up of a reconstruction plan for the five main towns, in conformity with Article 2 of the 1919–24 planning law governing town extensions and beautification.[9] On the same day, Prefect Morane assigned the execution of this project to the relevant local authorities: for Orléans, Kérisel and Royer; for Gien, Laborie; for Sully-sur-Loire, Royer; for Châteauneuf-sur-Loire, Royer; and for Saint-Denis de l'Hôtel, Coursimault.

The deep-seated unity of architecture and town planning in the reconstruction of the Loire Valley cannot be attributed simply to the choice of town planners who, although 'chosen among architects who had no bonds nor interests in the region', were nevertheless to display a similar passion for regionalism.[10] The order to demolish structures in the areas around bridge heads (what Roger Baschet calls their 'sad fate'[11]) was identical from one town to another. Orléans, Gien, Sully-sur-Loire and Châteauneuf-sur-Loire were all towns that had been built up around their river crossings and thus had seen their historical centres badly wounded by the German bombs. Despite differences in the number of destroyed housing units, the Loire Valley towns were alike in their pattern of destruction. The fact that their historical centres had been levelled raised the problem of urban identity. This was clearly defined by a resident of Orléans who, upon his return from exile, tried to assess the consequences of the war by listing the historical buildings that had been destroyed and those that had not:

> What was left of the Chancellery, of the rue Royale, of the rue Tabour, of everything that gave Orléans charm and honour? Thank God the front of the Chancellery stood up. That of the Jeanne d'Arc museum and the historical museum too. François des Franc's house was intact. The fronts of the houses next to Jacques Boucher's house had survived. . . . In this common tragedy the best works had escaped bombs and fire. The witnesses to the past survived, and we were ready perhaps to get down to work to finish the great task from which our ancestors had drawn back.[12]

All the ambivalence in the attitude toward the destruction is expressed here. Despite the irremediable loss of certain buildings, the rubble that resulted from the war was an occasion for rethinking the city in general terms and reviving its prestigious past as a regional capital embellished by the urbanism of the eighteenth century and renowned for the political history of Jeanne d'Arc and for the cultural monument of *Le Roman de la rose*. At the moment when France, shocked by the defeat and the humiliating territorial losses inflicted by the victors, was in search of a new identity, the Loire Valley reconstruction project presented itself as the ideal territory for formulating such an identity. This is what Roger Secrétain thought when he wrote:

This is what I am dreaming while walking through the bombed areas where the rubble has been cleared away and for the contractors' workers and materials are awaited. Purged of its rubble, the landscape of ruins has been reduced to a stage set of precariously propped-up fronts, of remnants emerging from disaster. At the heart of the city are great drafts of air and light. . . . The ruins are beautiful. Like all ruins they are surrounded by the nostalgia of things past. But they will disappear: they are fake ruins, they will be swept up and replaced by living things.[13]

Although one particularly audacious project was considered – a skyscraper for Orléans – the reconstruction of the Val-de-Loire was not an arena where supporters of regionalism would oppose supporters of functionalism. If the nature of the destruction facilitated the emergence of projects influenced by regionalism, it does not necessarily mean that this was due simply to the new ideological orientation of the French state. Many things militated against functionalist projects: the geographical and historical particularities of the destroyed sites, the importance of tourism in the Loire Valley and the legislation in force, especially the general framework of the 1919 law concerning town extensions which had to be used for lack of a special reconstruction law.

The staff who directed reconstruction were also regionalist in orientation. The architect Jean Royer had studied at l'École des hautes études urbaines, and, thanks to the influence of Marcel Poëte, appreciated the importance of history as a means of analysing the evolution of urban forms.[14] Of the engineers, both Jacques Morane and Jean Kérisel favoured regionalist architecture, perhaps because they had attended Gustave Umbdenstock's lectures on architecture at the École polytechnique. Winner of a second 'Grand Prix de Rome', a polemicist and strong adversary of modernism and Le Corbusier, Umbdenstock was militantly in favour of regionalism.[15]

In addition, a general theoretical agreement emerged during the reconstruction of the Loiret. Everywhere reconstruction planning had as its starting point a consideration of traffic problems. The destruction of the historic centres was first and foremost an occasion for rethinking the city in terms of urban organisation. The first task of the civil engineer was to set up a new traffic plan in the interests of technical rationality.

The case of Orléans is the best example, with smooth collaboration between a civil engineer, as head of the municipal utilities, and a chief town planner of international reputation. Jean Kérisel and Jean Royer thus proceeded to reshape drastically the town centre by widening the streets. Three parallel roads were introduced to relieve traffic on the rue Royale, which, as the only existing north–south axis, was infamous for its traffic jams. One on the eastern side carried the traffic that crossed the bridge towards the place du Martroi. A second was on the western side and was used by the cars that drove down from the place du Martroi to the bridge. The third was a widened rue Royale whose sidewalks had been replaced by pavement and were relocated as arcades under the buildings.

Rebuilding in other towns followed similar lines. The main street in Sully-sur-Loire, the rue du Grand Sully, was straightened and broadened by Royer in his reconstruction plan which also modified the line of nearby streets. In Châteauneuf-sur-Loire, he took advantage of the destruction of the principal church to resolve a dangerous traffic problem within the centre. In this case, it was no longer merely an instance of reconstruction. It was necessary for the planning of the town centre to continue what the bombing had begun by expropriating and destroying some undamaged buildings. In Gien, Laborie reorganised the traffic plan by adding a second major artery to the main Paris–Bourges or Paris–Orléans highway. These examples illustrate how the authors of the reconstruction plans went beyond reconstitution and even reconstruction. If they were not supposed to think in terms of more radical town planning and architecture, they clearly opted for a compromise between past and present and were thus at one with the ideas of most of their contemporaries, as a remark by Roger Secrétain suggests: 'One had to work both with the past and towards the future. To build something new without upsetting the harmony of a region, without affronting a mentality and a tradition that are summed up in a single word: moderation.'[16]

This first step in urban rationalisation shaped the nature of town planning and architecture during reconstruction. The modification of the urban fabric by cutting open dense blocks and bringing light and air to the city centre brought to the fore the issues of beautification and zoning. The proposals put forward by Jean Royer and Laborie are again good examples. In Orléans Royer put in a new circular open space which, being at the crossroads of several streets, was to open up historical and picturesque perspectives of the monuments of the town. In the centre of Sully-sur-Loire he modified a square that was soon named after Marshal Pétain. In Gien, Laborie opened up the area around the Château by planning a new square in front of it. In these cases, the assertion of public power was expressed by the refusal to rebuild exactly as things had been in the past, despite numerous complaints from the owners of affected property and the agency responsible for historical monuments. All the projects studied here assumed a need for centralisation that was expressed by bringing together in the city centre key government agencies. In Gien, for example, the town hall and its annexes, the covered market, the auditorium and various other public offices were brought together in the same project.

The problem of a regional architectural identity was clearly posed for these disaster-stricken urban centres. It was, however, not simply a question of restoring the destroyed façades; living conditions had changed, and it would have been criminal to deprive the population of the benefits of modern comforts and hygiene or to ignore traffic needs. However, the problem was first addressed from the point of view of aesthetics; namely, as the creation of an architecturally pleasing urban setting. To give 'the pretty little town' of Gien back 'its incredible colours', Laborie elaborated a stylistic programme that required the use of a mosaic of pink and black bricks and certain types of stone and tile. Such constraints were not appropriate, however, for every town. In fact, it was up to each town planner or architect to define the degree of regionalism he wished to achieve. This aspect of the architectural question had inevitable repercussions for rational planning. From this policy, oriented toward the rebuilding of town centres in a traditional style, emerged a general planning philosophy that in no way favoured those who wished for a return to a rural or agrarian tradition. To improve the quality of life, the factories were relocated to the outskirts of the urban districts in industrial areas especially created for that purpose. Similarly, entire programmes for urban renewal were drawn up by engineers in the name of hygiene.

Started in the summer of 1940, plans for the reconstruction of the Loire Valley were presented to the respective town councils and ratified during the following October. In the meantime, the administrative structures for reconstruction gradually took shape. On 12 July 1940, treasury inspector François Piétri was appointed Minister of Public Works and Communications. Two months later, although things seemed to be progressing, he was replaced by Jean Berthelot, a Polytechnic graduate and mining engineer. The new Minister of Communications was eager to substitute a vast building programme instead of the repair of the communications network which his predecessor had started[17] – not so much to reduce unemployment as 'to allow the country to recover', 'to gain its confidence back' and 'make it more powerful for the peace table'.[18]

The problem of destroyed and inferior housing had to be addressed, since it had been considered the main source of social disorder ever since the interwar period by the public health officers, the town planners, and the politicians. Some even believed this to be the real cause of the defeat of 1940. The law of 11 October 1940 concerning the reconstruction of blocks of partially or totally destroyed apartments gave birth to a special Technical Commission for Housing Reconstruction (the Commissariat technique à la reconstruction immobilière (CTRI)) which, placed under the authority of the Minister of Communications, had the power to direct and approve reconstruction and town planning schemes and to establish a general building programme.

Recruited by Jean Berthelot, André Muffang was made the Commissioner of the CTRI. Called by one reconstruction architect 'a veritable dictator of reconstruction',[19] Muffang was a fellow student with Berthelot at the Polytechnique and was currently chief civil engineer in the area of Amiens. This assured a common front on reconstruction. Jacques Morane and André Muffang not only came from the same school, they adopted the same ideas. For Muffang, who had had a lot of experience as a civil engineer in Valenciennes and Amiens, reconstruction was more a job for engineers than for architects. It had to be thought out on two levels: that of the transport facilities and that of urban rationalisation. Like others who had trained at Umbdenstock's school, Muffang argued in favour of an urban architecture integrated with the surrounding urban tissue, and thus he had reservations about Auguste Perret's reconstruction of Amiens.[20] The National Committee for Reconstruction, also formed under the law of 11 October 1940 and made up of like-minded architects appointed by Jean Berthelot, was also placed under Muffang's authority. This Committee included Pierre Remaury and Jean Marrast, chief architect for government buildings and national palaces. As commissioner of the CTRI, Muffang was responsible for the appointment of the reconstruction architects, and he named as his architectural advisor André Leconte, a childhood friend and supporter of regionalist-inspired aesthetics. For all these reasons, the success of the reconstruction plans for the Loire Valley was never in doubt.

## THE LOIRE VALLEY: A MODEL FOR VICHY RECONSTRUCTION

The visit by André Muffang and his director of technical services to an exhibition of reconstruction plans for the Loire Valley in Orléans on 23 November 1940, at the moment when these documents had been approved by their respective town councils, promised ministerial approval. Pierre Remaury, responsible on behalf of the national reconstruction committee for soliciting the plans of Orléans and the other towns of the Loiret, gave his endorsement.[21] On 3 January 1941 the members of the national reconstruction committee ratified the opinion of its spokesman after having made only minor alterations to the different projects. Signed by the Minister of the Interior and the Minister of Communications on 10 April 1941, the plan for Orléans was the first such proposal to receive state approval under the Occupation. On 4 August 1941 the designs for Gien and Châteauneuf-sur-Loire were accepted as well. Two days later the reconstruction plans for Sully-sur-Loire, 'the French town to have suffered the worst destruction', were approved, and 'following its terrible trials of the summer [it] was given the most valuable help it could get: the patronage of the Marshal, the head of state'.[22]

The successful rebuilding of Orléans, Sully-sur-Loire, Gien, and Châteauneuf-sur-Loire had an impact beyond the boundaries of the Loire Valley; it became the model that the central administration meant to promote. We can see the premises on which this model is based in two actions taken by the CTRI. First, its Paris agencies brought in the two main architects of the Loire Valley project, Jean Royer and Jean Kérisel, for top jobs. Frédéric Surleau, formerly director of technical services in the CTRI, was appointed Inspecteur général des services de la Délégation générale à l'équipement national, and Jean Kérisel took his place. Jean Royer was named Chargé de mission de la sous-direction urbanisme and made responsible for approving the town planning and reconstruction proposals submitted to the CTRI. Secondly, the CTRI instructions drawn up between its creation in October 1940 and July 1941 were modelled directly on what had been done in the Loiret. This went so far as to replicate the way in which tasks had been divided among the architects, engineers and town planners in the Loire Valley, which was now made official procedure.

Three procedural rules published at the beginning of 1941, at the time when the central administration was in charge of the work in the Loiret, were the product of this state of mind. The first was a charter for architects involved in reconstruction; the second concerned the drawing up of reconstruction plans; the third concerned sanitation projects.[23] The first document, drawn up by the architect André Leconte, took into account the aesthetic principles formulated during the reconstruction of the Loire Valley. The task of the reconstruction architect was defined in terms of a reconciliation between traditionalism and modernism and a rejection of all 'architecture without racial roots' and 'trite and superficial copies'. After having studied historical data and the typology of the surrounding houses, the architect should seek a synthesis that would give his work that 'spiritual element which, according to whether or not it is present, makes architecture human and alive, or, on the contrary, disappointing and dreary'. Similarly, from the reconstruction of the Loiret, André Leconte derived the terms for an aesthetic compromise that surmounted the conflict between regionalism and functionalism:

> Make sure not to ask yourself, has it got to be modern architecture or local architecture, because those who ask this question demonstrate that they have not understood the problem. . . . You should be looking to be modern, that is to say, to design and build houses that correspond to the actual way people live. But you should not limit yourself to a solution based solely on rationalism and ignoring all local and traditional factors. . . . This was the great mistake of those who believed that this was the basis of modern architecture. Conversely, you must not believe that solutions that would be mere imitations of the past would solve the problem. This would be an equally great mistake for those who would hope in this way to create a contemporary local architecture. In sum, you should build in a modern spirit, permeated with that which, in traditional architecture, has best resisted the passing of time and is best adapted to local conditions.[24]

In the same vein, the instructions for reconstruction planning and the programmes to improve the sanitation system resulted in an urban and technical planning programme, which, while respecting the original character of the town, resemble sensible, modern, postwar planning. All appeals to functionalism, however, were rejected; for example, the often boring straight street that opened up to 'meaningless architecture', and the clean sweep that destroyed forever 'some fundamental layout of the town'. The town planner should replace straight streets with 'curved roadways that offer constantly changing perspectives to the passer-by and add something picturesque'.

If these instructions harmonised perfectly with the urban aesthetics set out in *La Charte de l'architecte-reconstructeur*, they also fit in with the principles of urban rationalisation. In the first place, the improvement of urban sanitary conditions, necessary to the completion of reconstruction planning, would facilitate the development of public hygiene by linking the rebuilt apartments buildings to the new sewerage systems. The reconstruction programme also included a place for public buildings. Moreover, it took advantage of the destruction to establish a zoning system that distinguished between residential areas, unhealthy areas, natural parks or urban areas to which special preservation laws were to be applied, and isolated industrial zones where dangerous and polluting factories were to be built. These principles, all put forward by the agencies of the CTRI, derived from the planning experience of the Loire Valley.


CONCLUSION

It is important to outline the reasons why the reconstruction projects begun by the Vichy regime were not reversed later in the Occupation or after the war. Transcending the political rupture of 1944, the continuities in urban planning and architectural treatment, which cannot be said to have been the result of a cabal of academic architects directed against the functionalists, brings into question not only the behaviour of the project directors but also that of the political and administrative leaders. We can find the explanations only by examining the complex motives of the actors of the time.

The reconstruction of the Loire Valley, the first set of principles deduced from it by the CTRI, and the urban planning law of 15 June 1943 were perceived by building professionals as part of a homogeneous set of measures aimed at reforming the human geography of the nation. It might be because they saw in them the fruition of their own struggles during the interwar period that the architects welcomed these reforms with such enthusiasm. The lessons learned from the experience of the Loire Valley were immensely valuable. They testified to the success of a central planning administration – something that had long been argued by planners who had succeeded in overcoming local resistance to modernisation without at the same time ignoring the historical identity of the damaged towns. Jacques Gréber, professor at the Institute for Urbanism in Paris and president of the French Society for Urbanists, recognised a direct link between Lyautey's work in Morocco and the reconstruction of the Loire Valley, and attributed to the latter the primary elements of 'an entire Charter of National Renovation'.[25]

The enthusiasm for centralised town planning, with a strong trend toward technical modernisation, was carried into the post-Liberation period, but this did not mean a victory for modernism. Some modernist architects in exile, such as André Sive and Marcel Roux, had worked for the Resistance and supported functionalist principles within the congress of UNITEC (the Union nationale des ingénieurs et des techniciens). But while the resistance movement of the OCM (Organisation civile et militaire) had stood up for CIAM by appealing to the Charter of Athens, the French Liberation did not announce the hegemony of the modern movement in French reconstruction. Once again the career of Le Corbusier provides a good illustration.

If Le Corbusier's departure from Vichy in July 1942 seemed to mark the end of his collaboration with the Vichy regime, it did not mean that he was going to succeed in his postwar undertakings. During the years right after the war, Le Corbusier met with the most bitter of setbacks at Saint-Dié and La Rochelle-La Pallice. The latter, a grand reconstruction project, was never begun, and the most he could do was salvage one design for the building of the Unité d'habitation in Marseilles, which enjoyed the equivocal status, to say the least, of experimental architecture. This cursed label as an experimenter was so closely associated with him that Le Corbusier was never able to get a public position as a reconstruction architect, despite his nearly perennial nomination for the position of Minister of Reconstruction and Town Planning by Claudius-Petit, his ceaseless defender.[26]

Le Corbusier's failure in Vichy and his difficulties in the immediate postwar period testify to the refusal of the politicians to support a purely modern urban order, despite a complete change in political personnel between the time of the Resistance and the Liberation. By contrast, the failure to purge the technical services personnel associated with the wartime reconstruction effort and their integration into the Ministry for Reconstruction and Urbanism that was created in November 1944 meant that the pattern of reconstruction developed by the Pétain government would last beyond the return of a republican regime.Does not the participation of French functionalist architects in German reconstruction – Lods in Mainz, Pingusson in Saarbrücken and Menkès in Saarlouis – prove the inability of the modern movement to make a place for itself in its own nation?

Raoul Dautry, the first postwar Minister of Reconstruction, demonstrated in fact that urban reconstruction in France was compatible with all aesthetic trends. He refused to endorse the ideas of Le Corbusier, who wanted to obtain power to plan the whole Lower Seine valley. The Charter of Urbanism, a new town planning law prepared by Raoul Dautry's ministry, called on the architects of reconstruction to work in a modern fashion, but with respect for the past. French reconstruction would thus be moderate and seek a harmonious relationship between modern town planning and historic cities.[27]

## Notes

1. *Les Trois Reconstructions en France: 1919–1940–1945*, Institut français d'architecture, dossiers et documents no. 4 (Paris, 1983).
2. Anatole Kopp, Frédérique Boucher and Danièle Pauly, *L'Architecture de la reconstruction* (Paris, 1982).
3. The law instituting the *ordre des architectes* and regulating the profession of architects already stated in Article 2 that to be qualified to be an architect one had to have French nationality. A new step was taken with the decree of the 24 September 1941, which instituted discriminatory anti-Semitic measures.
4. Holder of a degree in political science and trained in the United States (he had worked for Ford in Detroit), in 1934 Lehideux became the administrative manager of Renault, where he made every effort to pursue and improve methods of scientific management.
5. Their participation was limited to the preparation of an issue of *L'Illustration* for spring 1941 (which was never published) entitled: 'For an introduction of the national policy on reconstruction'. Le Corbusier was to write an article on the theme of folklore and Lucien Romier on the new French tradition.
6. For more of the public's attitude toward Le Corbusier during this period, see Rémi Baudoui, 'L'attitude de Le Corbusier pendant la guerre', *Le Corbusier, une encyclopédie* (Paris, 1987) pp. 455–90.
7. Danièle Voldman, 'Du pastiche à la modernité. Reconstituer ou moderniser: les choix de la reconstruction', in *Monuments historiques*, no. 140 (August–September 1985) p. 59.
8. Yves Durand, 'Chantiers urbains et projets urbains sur les ruines de juin 1940. L'exemple des villes sinistrées du Loiret', in *Revue*

*d'histoire de la deuxième guerre mondiale*, no. 79 (July 1970).

9. Jean Royer, 'Le Reconstruction des villes du Val de Loire', in *Urbanisme*, no. 71 (January–May 1941) p. 18.

10. Roger Baschet, 'Les Bords de Loire', in *L'Illustration* 'Construire' (24 May 1941).

11. Ibid.

12. Louis d'Illiers, *Pour la résurrection d'Orléans* (Orléans, 1943) pp. 13–14.

13. Roger Secrétain, 'Des villes vont renaître', in *Urbanisme*, no. 71 (January–May 1941).

14. As soon as the École des hautes études urbaines was founded, Marcel Poëte, a historian and a former student of the École des chartes, gave a lecture on 'the evolution of towns'.

15. For teaching 'a sound distrust' of modern architecture, Le Corbusier attacked Gustave Umbdenstock in 1933. See Le Corbusier, *Croisade ou le crépuscule des académies* (Paris, 1933).

16. Secrétain, 'Des villes vont renaître' (see note 13).

17. François Piétri, *Mes années d'Espagne, 1940–1948* (Paris, 1958) pp. 18–20.

18. Jean Berthelot, *Sur les rails du pouvoir* (Paris, 1968) p. 94.

19. André Gutton, *La Charte de l'urbanisme* (Paris, 1941) p. 157.

20. Interview with André Muffang, 5 November 1986.

21. Pierre Remaury taught at the Institut d'urbanisme de Paris, then at the École des hautes études urbaines, and was a supporter of the planning principles current in 1940.

22. Jean Vincent, *La Reconstruction des villes et des immeubles sinistrés après la guerre de 1940* (Paris, 1943) p. 98.

23. *Charte de l'architecte-reconstructeur* (Paris, 1941); *Instruction concernant l'établissement des projets d'aménagement des agglomérations totalement ou partiellement détruites par faits de guerre* (Paris, 1941); *Instruction sur la rédaction des projets d'assainissement dans le cadre des programmes d'aménagement des agglomérations totalement ou partiellement détruites par actes de guerre* (Paris, 1941).

24. *Charte de l'architecte-reconstructeur* (see note 23).

25. Jacques Gréber, 'Urbanisme', in *France 1941: La Révolution nationale constructive, un bilan et un programme* (Paris, 1941) p. 489.

26. Interview with M. Eugène Claudius-Petit, 16 February 1987.

27. *Charte d'urbanisme* (Paris, 1945) p. 13.

# 4 Continuities in Belgian Wartime Reconstruction Planning

## PIETER UYTTENHOVE

Belgium's towns and countryside are striking examples of the omnipresence of modern progress. Their appearance bears testimony less to simple bad taste or naïve creativity than to an unbridled collective faith in modernity. Modernity seems, however, merely to signify a presence of forms and objects rather than a way of life which has remained traditional. Lifestyle has retained its traditions. Can we say, then, that modernity is an outside product, an imported thing, an exogenous form? If we accept progress as a universal human endeavour, then modernity must be seen as its rational systematisation.

Like other western countries, Belgium had its own rationalists before 1940, and yet their place in society had been relatively minor due to a general belief in individual liberty as opposed to systematic applications. We must return to the beginning of the century and to the First World War in order fully to understand the concept of modern rationalism. As for the mass acceptance of modernity's forms and objects, this is a phenomenon best explained by events of the Second World War, where reconstruction was characterised both by continuity in the application of rationalism and by discontinuity in the societal structure; in other words, the emergence of mass society. Rationalism continued along the same lines as in the prewar period, but due to its 'official' sanction during the German occupation, it broke through to modern mass society. The Commissariat général de la restauration du pays (CGRP) during the Second World War tried to promote a positivist organisation of daily life through increasingly large, concentric planning of matter and space. In attempting to be consistent with its own positivist system, reconstruction displayed the face of a narrow and oppressive modernity.

## THE CGRP AND THE LEGACY OF MODERNISM

Oddly enough, reconstruction was organised administratively almost immediately after the German Occupation in the summer of 1940, whereas reconstruction during the First World War had been plagued by inertia. Various reasons can be given to explain the difference: the novelty of the reconstruction problem in the First World War, the political circumstances, the dispersion of initiatives and the conflicting attitudes about the meaning of reconstruction. In the final analysis we might conclude that the First World War reconstruction had been an indirect preparation for what happened during the Second World War.

In 1914 the destruction caused by the German invasion reached an extent of material damage that surpassed all former experience. It spread over almost the entire national territory, and the damage to urban centres brought entirely new problems to the fore. There was simply no theoretical paradigm or operational know-how available at the outbreak of the First World War to help solve essential material and administrative tasks. There existed, however, strong national-istic and ideological movements in Belgium which contributed to rebuilding the nation in an international context, to the application of socio-biological ideas and to social reform in municipalities.

In the government in exile in Le Havre, minister Joris Helleputte and his collaborator Raphaël Verwilghen, together with other Bel-gian refugees in neighbouring countries, embraced progressive ideas, and they were well aware that something had to be done to preserve and enforce these ideas during reconstruction. Otherwise the middle-class ideology of private property would restrict reconstruction to the confines of nineteenth-century *laissez-faire* liberalism.

The political will of Helleputte and the unremitting study of planning and reconstruction by Verwilghen resulted in the progressive law of 25 August 1915 prescribing the elaboration of a general town plan and an extension plan for devastated cities. For Belgium this was a very innovative vision requiring a tremendous international contribution from England, France and the Netherlands. From the outset of the war, Belgian refugees in London were introduced to the recent developments of the new science of town planning; their apprenticeship was more or less successfully organised by the Belgium Town Planning committee in conferences, courses and workshops in London. Meanwhile, a group of Belgian refugees in Paris worked in close collaboration with young French town planners to establish courses, a documentation centre and the École supérieure d'art public for a new kind of professional education. Louis van der Swaelmen founded the Comité Néerlando–Belge d'art public in The Hague. He played an important background role by writing, in collaboration with prominent Dutch planners, the first book on town planning theory in the French language.

The new town planning law of 1915 was the result of the undaunted work of Raphaël Verwilghen, who travelled to Great Britain for his study and maintained a close correspondence with van der Swaelmen. Verwilghen started preparing for reconstruction as he travelled between his professional contacts in Paris and his work in Le Havre. He developed knowledge and insights about town planning, housing and land control in order to take up his work as secretary of the section for the reconstruction of towns and villages in 1917 and as director of the Service des constructions, under the authority of the Office des régions dévastées in 1919.

Since there was no national parliament during the war, laws were enacted by ministerial decree and royal approval, and the town planning law of 1915 was rapidly passed. There were, however, only a few town plans drawn up according to the law during the war. Outside Belgium reconstruction appeared to be a question of time, whereas inside the country, due both to the German Occupation and to a conservative spirit on the municipal level, it was often a struggle for independence. The new law, conceived so that a town's development would be treated as a whole, was perceived by city governments and by such conservative institutions as the Commission royale des monuments et des sites as too radical. Conservatives feared that the 'meddling' which modern progress represented would adversely affect their autonomous power in such diverse areas as aesthetics, housing and sanitation. The devastated country was compelled to live under the administration of the German Occupation but hardly accepted it, which resulted in isolated groups studying particular projects in many towns of the country. They perpetuated the planning system used since the last half of the nineteenth century: a combination of alignment plans, hygienic and aesthetic laws, building permits and expropriations of private property for public uses.

Thus there were two visions of reconstruction, just as there were two Belgiums – an exterior and an interior, a modernist and a traditional. On 8 April 1919, several months after the war ended, parliament voted for a new law to start reconstruction – directed by the State – of the devastated towns. Returning refugees like Huib Hoste, Jean Eggerickx, Louis van der Swaelmen and Raphaël Verwilghen were thwarted in their attempt to impose their modernist notions about rebuilding the country. The only realisation of their ideas about rational architectural construction and the functioning of towns were several garden cities on the outskirts of the reconstructed towns.

By the Second World War, the notions of the general town and extension plan and of planning in general had been cautiously accepted in the more progressive settings of both national and municipal governments, but no definite law had been passed. Projects for laws had been drafted by the Fédération des ingénieurs communaux de Belgique in 1921, and proposed by Emile Vinck from the Union des villes et communes Belges in the Senate in 1931, where it was voted in 1936. But until 1939 the law was still being studied by the Centre d'études pour la réforme de l'état (CERE), presided over by Baron Houtart. The proposed law grouped the three levels of urban regional and national planning in one hierarchical administrative system and brought about a revision in the powers of planners to dispose of privately held land. After its modification, the proposal had only to be voted on when the war broke out.

Although regional planning was already part of the law of April 1919 on town reconstruction, it was not until the 1924 congress of towns in Amsterdam that it became a real preoccupation of Belgian officials. After 1935 the economic crisis in the Borinage and the decline and the urban disorder of Spa and West Flanders demanded solutions on the regional level. In Antwerp, Bruges, Brussels and Ghent, commissions were set up to direct material or administrative actions on the planning of urban agglomerations. While special commissions studied the regional problems, an Office du redressement economique (OREC) was founded by the socialist prime minister Henri de Man in 1935 to study the general economic recovery of the country. The OREC created the Société nationale de la petite propriété terrienne to promote a transfer of small parcels of property to working people. The office also oversaw the activities of the Société nationale des habitations bon marché granting premiums for low-cost social housing construction. However, in the years preceding the Second World War, OREC, with control over a great deal of money, was accused of fiscal waste and eventually had to cease operation.

The Second World War presented an entirely different set of conditions in terms of reconstruction. Shortly after the German invasion and the surrender of the Belgian king in May 1940, the decree of 29 June 1940 established the Commissariat général de la restauration du pays (CGRP). German Occupation was made more palatable for Belgian administrators because a semblance of self-government was maintained. As opposed to the situation in the First World War, the country was administered by general commissioners in the absence of the king and the government. Other institutions functioned normally even though there were no longer political parties.

The CGRP was by far the most important institution in the Belgian war administration because of its central position. It directed the co-ordination of four sorts of activities: the resumption of labour for workers, economic recovery, the restoration of transport and the reconstruction of towns and houses. Charles Verwilghen, former general secretary for labour and social security, was made General Commissioner, and his brother Raphaël became director of the Service de la reconstruction. This office was composed of the departments of planning, urbanisation, architecture and conservation of monuments.

The Service de la reconstruction consisted of a group of technocrats and experts at the top of its hierarchy, most of whom were either university professors, professors at the Institut supérieur des arts décoratifs (ISAD) in La Cambre, engineers or members of prewar ministerial cabinets and OREC. The architect Henry van de Velde, who had been a counsellor at the Ministry of Public Works before the war, was made artistic counsellor for architecture, and Stan Leurs was named as counsellor for the archaeological section of the conservation of monuments. In sharp contrast to the First World War example, the CGRP was an extremely centralised hierarchy conceived as a pyramid structure at the base of which were provincial commissioners and urban surveyors, with sectional directors and a general commissioner above them. Most of the participants were carefully chosen from the modernist circles of the interwar period. In the section for the conservation and restoration of historical monuments, for instance, the General Commissioner selected modern architects such as M. Winders, I. Hintjens, Jos. Viérin, V. Vaerwyck and V. Acke to fulfil the roles of provincial counsellors. Members of progressive, more theoretical circles from the specialised periodical press were also involved, such as Pierre-Louis Flouquet from *Bâtir*, Raphaël Verwilghen from *La Cité* and others from the newly founded *Urbs Nova*. Henry van de Velde, former director of the Weimar Kunstgewerbeschule and of the ISAD, was well suited to the philosophy of the CGRP.

*Reconstruction*, a new semi-official review set up by the CGRP for documentary and propagandist purposes, continued along theoretical lines similar to those of the architecture and town planning reviews prior to 1940, and drew from the work that had been done by the OREC and by the planning offices of the bigger urban agglomerations from the prewar era.

## THE MAIN ISSUE OF RECONSTRUCTION

Reconstruction was conceived differently during and after each war in part because of variations in concentration and extent of physical destruction. The damage of the First World War may have been far worse than that of 1940, and yet the social, economic and financial situation of the country was much more precarious during the Second World War. The destruction of the First World War affected numerous public buildings, churches, monuments and private houses, whereas the Second World War destroyed primarily technical equipment, roads and factories, affected a larger proportion of towns and villages, and greatly hindered national activity by paralysing transportation. Needless to say, German Occupation weighed heavily upon the Belgian economy.

In the First World War, destruction was perceived by the Belgians as barbarous vandalism committed against Belgium as a nation in order to erase its culture. In rebuilding, people consequently called for a restoration of national values. The notion of nation-building dominated the first reconstruction, and it can therefore be understood as a sort of sentimental reconstruction of history. The restoration of monuments, the restoration of former townscapes (artificial or not) and the imposed *vieux-neuf* style for the architectural façades of urban buildings illustrate to what extent the reconstruction of the First World War was conceived as the personification and formalisation of the national urban community. It was essentially an urban project which visually symbolised the living past and was close to the notion of a civic centre.

Reconstruction during the Second World War was, quite to the contrary, a reaction against history and against the symbols of its failures (the architecture and the towns) and the failings and errors of past reconstruction. A lesson had to be learned from the mistakes of the past. The result was a reaction against the recent past, against the impotence of politics, against the ignorance of the prewar study-commissions and against a pervasive individualism. This reaction had to be transformed into positive action. Both Belgian history and her culture were denied. This, in fact, matched German plans nicely. In their initial decisions about national redevelopment, the Germans may well have considered Belgium as an autonomous state, but they none the less planned for the annexation of the country to the Third Reich.

This attitude shows the degree to which Belgian national identity was suppressed and replaced by an anonymous and neutral representation of the State. Historical symbolism was rejected in favour of a pragmatic symbolism stressing, for the present period, 'virility' and 'action', and for the future, 'youth' and 'motherhood'. This symbolism did not allow for any individuality or local autonomy. The German centralist ideology inspired by the romantic ideal of Roman imperialism seems to have taken hold of Belgian administrators. They entertained a vision of a 'Prince' in the form of public powers and of the State both as the inspiration of all economic and productive activities of the country and as the guarantor of all social order.

## THE IDEOLOGY OF WORK AND COLLECTIVITY

Work was seen in economic and social terms as the organising principle of society. Only work could create a functional society, and only a functional society could create work for everyone. Professor Reyntjens, director of the Department for Employment, maintained that the existence of large public works requiring a large work force was, first of all, a socially therapeutic means to fight inactivity and, secondly, a move toward economic revival. This philosophy is reminiscent of the 1850s, when the Belgian economy was saved by the construction of canals and railways.

A good many schools and churches were rebuilt in 1941 because the construction required large numbers of skilled workmen and because buildings materials were available locally, thereby reducing transportation costs. Modern facilities were encouraged as well: for example, water distribution networks, the extension of greater Antwerp which necessitated the demolition of the city's fortifications, the sanatorium of Aalst, and municipal equipment for public services in Courtrai. Some of these projects had been started prior to the war, but most were continued by the CGRP.

The only justification for construction was its public utility.

This was the guiding principle of Joz. L. Custers, Adjunct General Commissioner. In other words, only massive projects such as road, railway, waterway construction and other transport and infrastructural building begun shortly after the war's devastation were authorised and financed by public officials. The decrees of 15 October and 15 November 1941 had stipulated that all other construction had to be authorised by the reconstruction commissioner of the directly affected province. This was the means by which the CGRP attempted to prevent the private use of materials and to fight speculation which could prove injurious to the prosperity of the nation. Speculation and individualism had been the despised consequences of the reconstruction of the First World War, and therefore, in the second reconstruction, they were to be avoided at all costs in favour of a new exemplary and symbolic collective utility.

According to the CGRP, the exceptionally modern character of the problem of economic and material reconstruction was contrary to prewar traditionalism. The switch from an individualistic society to a more collective one did not, however, bring about a rupture with popular traditions. The modern orientation of a reconstruction leading to a positive collective future was a kind of experiment not only in architectural but also in judicial terms. Meanwhile tradition had to be maintained. The CGRP ideology compressed the two conceptions of work and collectivity, while the notions of modernity and (popular) tradition stood respectively for the (technical) means and the (moral) aim of reconstruction in a larger sense.

Full employment was assured by legislation and the so-called 'work-regulating programmes', which were to be established in the event of massive lay-offs during economic crises. Legislation restricted individual profits in favour of the collective good. The work-regulating programmes – basically public works programmes – included the expansion of the merchant marine, sanitation of agricultural land, canalisation, sewerage and water purification, demolition of urban neighbourhoods in their entirety, electric equipment for railways, urban heating, synthetic treatment of coal, roads, afforestation, and generalised water distribution. Thus a totalitarian utopia of a society at work was to produce an energetic, healthy future and therefore break radically from what was considered an 'unhealthy' past.

The same preoccupation with a collective future was expressed by the special attention shown in matters of the physical and moral education of youth and of the conservation of nature. The educational project included the intention to provide tourists easy access to both urban centres and natural landscapes which embodied these values. In fact, the programmes to establish and regulate physical education, sport and recreation facilities for youth were never realised, and the few projects for sports facilities which did exist were a carry-over from the 1930s. The drafting of a special 'Statut de la Jeunesse', intended to create 'a sane, strong, disciplined, happy army for the struggle of work and life', pointed to the ultimate stage of a discipline-forming work service. Examples of playgrounds and sports facilities were directly taken from Germany, as well as the model of a necessary national policy for physical education.

Tourism was seen as being not only a moral and didactic cause, but an economic and social one as well, and measures were to be taken to gain a maximum profit from the nation's tourist resources. Policy focused on three main areas: the protection and conservation of town and landscapes, propaganda, and increased tourism. In practice, however, measures to encourage tourism remained under the direction of the prewar Commissariat général au tourisme of 1939, and only a small co-ordination committee with delegates from both Touring Club and Vlaamse Toeristenbond was established in conjunction with some officials of the CGRP. Finally, in an effort to follow the example of other developed nations and maintain their lands in their natural and uncultivated state, the CGRP planned to create national parks and natural reserves.

## PLANNING AND TECHNOCRACY

Town planning and economic planning became parts of a larger conception of the national interest. The crucial problem from a collectivist point of view was the limitation of private property. It was thus foreseen that individual compensation claims resulting from damage to property sustained in the war would be restricted by subordinating them to the assessments of official surveyors belonging to the Commission d'estimation des dommages de guerre. Each case would be investigated in terms of financial, economic and town planning exigencies. During and after the First World War, restitution was based on prewar property values and material reconstruction costs. This had resulted in maintaining the pre-1914 property lines and the old system of urban land distribution. To counter a similar evolution and to re-establish the civic sense of property, the CGRP pinned its hopes on urban planning, which could introduce the notion of zoning and land redistribution. Raphaël Verwilghen, director of the Service de reconstruction (architecture et urbanisme), expected that the new decree of 12 September 1940 concerning damaged towns would inaugurate a new period of methodical planning. This new law was intended to help Belgium join the other European countries in the same way as the first town planning law of 1915.

The law of 1915 had appeared very abruptly in the Belgian context. The decree of 1940, in a certain way, had been announced and studied for several years, but had not been officially approved before the war. After the beginning of the war its passage was prepared in a few months by a commission headed by Baron Albert Houtart. The decree had repercussions on public finances, private rights and the future of towns. It outlined five stages in the elaboration of plans, one of which was a public examination of a project prior to approval by the General Commissioner. This provision was actually less radical than the law of 1915.

Reacting against earlier planning systems, the decree of 1940 foresaw two kinds of planning documents: a general plan first and then a detailed area plan. It also stipulated the possibility of setting up aesthetic (architectural) and functional (land use) laws to structure a zoning scheme, with effectiveness guaranteed by the municipality's control of building licences. During the war plans were made for Nivelles, Enghien, Bouillon, Andenne and many others, most of them in response to design competitions organised by the CGRP.

In general, these competitions emphasised three aspects of the problem of reconstruction: the layout of the street pattern, the restoring or reconstruction of characteristic buildings and the reallotment of land. In each case, the main reconstruction focus was the old town centre. A good project was supposed to reproduce the existing local character and at the same time satisfy the needs of contemporary architecture. Tradition and modernity, ostensibly opposed but both inherent in reconstruction, were explicitly accepted by simultaneously stressing the visual character of the town and the needs of a rational construction. The visual images of the urban projects all recreated a regional atmosphere of traditional forms, while road building, the layout and organisation of traffic and so on, were supposed to be technically very modern. Even the most modernist architects, such as Renaat Braem (for Enghien) and Sta

Jasinski (for Nivelles), complied with this dual role. Once outside the urban centres, however, the most progressive and gigantic projects for (social) housing neighbourhoods (for example, the urbanisation of Flémalle-Haute by the architectural group of L'Equerre in Liège, designed in 1938) were considered acceptable. From 1940 until October 1943, twelve town planning contests haʲ been organised and 535 town planning projects had been completed under the new degree.

The real innovation in the 1940 decree on urbanisation was the introduction of planning on a supra-municipal level; namely, on the level of agglomerations and regions. Collective well-being depended on a social vision with an impact on the entire territory and on different administrative levels. The Service d'urbanisme engaged fully in this process of centralisation by subsuming other administrative offices, such as the Service spécial d'urbanisme of the OREC and the prewar Voirie communale (Ministry of Public Works).

The decree of 1940 proposed a quite simplistic vision about the content of spatial planning, which was summarised by Pierre-Louis Flouquet in the words 'analysis, synthesis and aesthetics'. A methodical preliminary survey had to precede the making of all plans, in the same way as had already been conceived by H. V. Lanchester before the First World War, and as had been scientifically developed in a classification system by van der Swaelmen in 1916. All possible data about the history and the existing features of a town and its inhabitants were thought useful. By this means the qualitative knowledge of local historians, artists, functionaries, doctors and so on, would be replaced by data compiled by a professional surveyor. Verwilghen himself developed a system of symbols and colours to serve as a uniform legend for all plans, and he drew up very detailed explanatory notes for the municipalities and provincial commissioners to guide the survey and planning activities. Planning required the production of new precise plans and maps of all cities concerned, because this had never been done before. The survey information was to serve as a synthesis, which for people like Verwilghen had a resonance of magic power. It symbolised the total interrelation of all levels of local, regional and national plans. For this he went back to van der Swaelmen's ideas and to those of other planners who had thought organically, like Patrick Geddes, Paul Otlet and Gaston Bardet. These theories illustrate the effort to substitute geographically based entities like big agglomerations and regions for administrative units (like provinces and arrondissements).

On 1 September 1941 the Commissariat du royaume aux grandes agglomérations was founded. Planners then began projects for the unification of the urban agglomerations of Antwerp, Brussels, Ghent, Liège and Charleroi. In the following spring this movement was furthered by the decree of 18 May 1942 which created other big urban complexes like Bruges. The study of big agglomerations was based on a prewar report of Baron Holvoet in 1937, which posed the problem in terms of a conflict between the central city and growing suburbs consisting largely of independent municipalities.

Regional planning started slowly. The country was divided in 'organic' regions which, unlike the big agglomerations, consisted mostly of numerous small towns and villages. Real regional planning, as it existed in Germany or Great Britain, did not occur, probably due to the circumstances of the war. Most of the time regional commissions were concerned with re-establishing full employment and with the restoration of public buildings and other utilities damaged in the war in accordance with the policy of the CGRP. In a larger perspective, regional planning attended only to the rebirth of crafts and the installation of tourist industry. It seems that the same duality of tradition and modernity appeared once again in the opposition of regional planning and *planologie*.

The word *planologie*, originally coined by the Dutchman van Eesteren in the 1920s, had been used for the first time in Belgium by Verwilghen in a report of 1938. The ultimate goal of *planologie* was to establish a national plan based on the economic geography. In 1941 the geographical, demographic and economic analyses of the nine provinces were finished, while other studies about communications and about the configuration of planning regions were started. According to René Soetewey, *planologie* was to be the global science delineating the relations between localities, regions and the nation in a technical but creative way. He believed that under a rational territorial arrangement it would be possible to preserve both economic rights and natural beauty. Yet Belgian *planologie* remained during the Second World War in an analytical stage. The dichotomy between data about spatial relationships and abstract economic theories was far from being resolved. From the beginning, the discordance between the organically fixed relations in space and time and the imposed administrative structure of towns and regions were a fundamental obstacle to planning.

The last stage of planning, referred to by Verwilghen as *la phase virile*, was the transition from the abstract plan to concrete reality. An aesthetic or synthetic moment, this transition was a mission of creation and of decision making, requiring skilled and qualified professionals who had to be products of new kinds of education and experience. The intervention of the State had to be visually manifest, and toward this goal the State emphasised uniform typological examples. Plans of cemeteries, green spaces and small public buildings were drawn by the CGRP and distributed to the city governments. For this typological way of thinking and for the overlapping of different planning levels, Verwilghen relied largely on his prewar town planning courses at the École nationale supérieure d'architecture of La Cambre and on his experiences with his colonial projects for Bukavu and Uvira (Congo) in the 1930s.

In the opinion of Verwilghen, the task confronting planners in 1943 was the accomplishment of the work already started but still incomplete. He complained about the absence of culture among the population and about the deficiency of experts. In his eyes, the uneven progress of *planologie* and town planning was due only to theoretical and administrative but not to technical failings. However, real social planning would only be attained when full adaptation to the new conditions of national collectivity was achieved. Besides legislation, the main obstacle was administrative. This reveals the main issue in this period of reconstruction: technocratic domination. The lack of comprehensive town planning in the sense of organisation for higher national efficiency could only be compensated for by the rational contribution of technicians. Among other things, this required strong professional status, good remuneration and a close collaboration of engineers and architects.

Technocracy, in order to have real meaning, could not tolerate traditional administration, much less bureaucracy. Verwilghen warned against confusing political action with urban reform that could only consist of technical and practical (professional) acts. He contended that 'town planning can not be realised without a strong power'. Here the big difference with the First World War reconstruction emerges: the script of reconstruction had been rewritten for a new cast, namely for the 'Prince' and his technocrats. The reconstruction during the Second World War was a legitimate *putsch* by an oligarchy of technicians who maintained their power behind a façade of rigid knowledge, but without any guarantee of real change in terms of social improvement.

## THE STRUGGLE AGAINST UGLINESS

Convinced in his struggle against ugliness, against nineteenth-century decadence of taste, against incoherence and fantasy, Henry van de Velde, in his role as general counsellor for architecture, was probably one of the most important protagonists in the CGRP's ideological visualisation of a new order. He had himself been an instigator of modern architectural style at the beginning of the century, and he wanted to impose a discipline and an aesthetic formula corresponding to the mentality and to moral law which was to transform the world after the chaos of the Second World War. Reconstruction had to be education. The legacy of the prewar OREC direction of aesthetic and artistic matters must be taken into account when examining the relationship between the notion of 'reconstruction' and the revival of the public's taste. During the war this moral heritage became reality and constituted for van de Velde an absolute *fait nouveau*. Thanks to aesthetic control by the Service de l'urbanisme et de l'architecture and the personal consultations of van de Velde, Belgium was catching up with other countries where the idea of a new style had long since been in vogue.

According to van de Velde there was no absolute rule for the *Esthétique de la Reconstruction* to follow. Only specific cases existed. He liked the very modernist architecture of Max and Gaston Brunfaut, Sta Jasinski, Jean Moutschen and others, but he valued regional styles as well and even recognised the importance of *vieux-neuf* architecture in certain rare situations.

The real foundation for a new architecture had to be, however, the system of rational construction. By means of rationalism both modern architecture and regionalism became products of one philosophical source. One had to return to the love for the (building) material, to standardisation, to sobriety, truth, dignity, honesty and tact, which were the ingredients of a 'judicious building system'. It appeared to van de Velde that municipalities had understood this message better than the national government.

A real danger lay, however, in the possible agreement between the outrageously decorative desires of individual clients and architects whose modernism was too recent to be penetrated by the dogma of purity and functionalism. A unique and unified direction from the CGRP was therefore necessary. Although rationalism united the entire new architectural movement, there hardly existed a global consensus about its symbolic meaning. Regionalists, as for example

Emile Henvaux and Jean de Ligne (delegate at the regional commissariat of Tournai), were against any international influence because of
their fear of losing the material and spiritual values of ancestral, local
and cultural contributions to their regional consciousness. Reacting
against the myth of total prefiguration of urban decor, arguing that
a town lives and changes continuously over time, du Ligne conceived
a piece-by-piece integration of individual works of architecture following a global order. His proposals for the reconstruction of the
Grand'Place of Tournai go back to a very elaborated scheme of
volumes, gables and roofs dominated by the cathedral. It harked
back as well to the same principles of the traditional urban art of
city-building which had ruled the reconstruction after the First World
War. In a kind of vicious circle, rationalism thus reconnected with
a formal past. (In 1943, in disagreement with the general intentions
of the German Occupation, Henry van de Velde resigned from his
office in the CGRP.)


## POSTWAR REALISM

At the end of the war pressing social problems came to the
fore again. The reconstruction of social housing had dropped to
one-tenth of prewar rates during the war. Slum clearance was
extremely urgent. After the war the problems of small individual
land holdings, housing co-operatives and private home ownership
were discussed once again, whereas they had been eliminated during
the CGRP administration.

    After the Liberation the activities of the CGRP were taken
over by the new Ministry of Reconstruction under Jean Terfve.
The centralised supervision of the CGRP in aesthetic and planning
matters was transformed into a more liberal administration. Several
members of the CGRP joined the Conseil supérieur des cités
indigènes and later the Office des cités africaines in the 1950s
in order to apply their ideas on the colonial urbanisation of
the Belgian Congo. Others returned to their prewar activities in
education. Postwar reconstruction was characterised by the very
quick economic recovery of Belgian industry. After 1947 Belgium,
to which other European countries were indebted for the purchase
of her products, was financially aided by the American Marshall
Plan. This strengthened her position at an economic turning point in
Western European history. The massive aid disrupted, of course, all

economic and regional planning started during the war. Nevertheless, despite all the changes after the war, wartime planning legislation, including the formal structure of town and regional planning and even the *planologie* of 1940 were maintained until 1962, when finally a new law was enacted.

## Sources

Due to Belgian privacy law, research on official sources from the last fifty years is not permitted. Thorough study of the Second World War is impossible at present, though general works, printed documentation, contemporary publications and reviews, and some private archives are already accessible at the Centre de recherches et d'études historiques de la seconde guerre mondiale (Brussels). Also notable is the important Legacy Raphaël Verwilghen at the University of Leuven which contains his personal archives concerning his role as director of the Service de la reconstruction (CGRP).

For reconstruction during the First World War, see *Resurgam: La Reconstruction en Belgique après 1914*, with contributions from M. Smets (ed.), G. Bekaert, J. Celis, R. de Meyer, G. Geenen, R. Gobyn, J. Maes, H. Stynen and P. Uyttenhove (Brussels, 1985). This also contains an extended bibliography.

During the Second World War, a few works were published, such as Emile Henvaux, *Aspects de l'urbanisme* (Brussels, 1944), and Jean de Ligne, *La Reconstruction de Tournai, le plan d'aménagement et ses servitudes urbanistiques* (Brussels, 1945). *Reconstruction (urbanisme-architecture-génie civile-industrie)* was the official review published by the CGRP to legitimise its policies.

To date, two studies have been published concerning the problem of reconstruction: Emile Henvaux, 'H. van de Velde dans l'oeuvre de la reconstruction de la Belgique (1940–1943)', in *Cahiers Henri van de Velde*, 8 (1967), and a special issue of the *Cahiers de La Cambre. Architecture* (3 May 1986) devoted to 'Le contrôle esthétique en '40'. One should also refer to the chapter 'La Cambre pendant la guerre 1940–1945', in Jacques Aron, *La Cambre et l'architecture* (Brussels, 1982) pp. 93–103.

Special thanks go to Lisa Neal for her assistance in editing this article.

# 5 Planning the Impossible: History as the Fundament of the Future – the Reconstruction of Middelburg, 1940–4

## J. E. BOSMA

### THE NEW TASK

The old town centre of Middelburg, situated in the south-western part of Holland on the island of Walcheren, was renowned as a treasure-house of Dutch architectural history. Hence, after this jewel was badly bombed on 17 May 1940, its reconstruction was considered so important that it was placed under the direct authority of the central government in The Hague. 'At that moment we were convinced, the most radical spirits among us were convinced, that we must hold on to and protect our architectural heritage: we were all determined to preserve it.'[1]

After thorough preparation, the reconstruction was carried out in accordance with 'vernacular' norms. Both the rebuilding of streets and squares and the restoration of the historical monuments were being governed by what was considered to be the 'typical Middelburg atmosphere' and by the symbolic effect of deeply cherished Dutch architecture.

The reconstruction of the town centre in accordance with a traditionalist scenario was seen by both the Germans and the Dutch as a model for the reconstruction of other bombed towns in Holland. Moreover, it offered scope for widely differing interpretations. The Germans, the occupying power, saw it as a move away from British traditions or 'ein Brennpunkt des Reichsgedankes', while to the central reconstruction office in The Hague, reconstruction in the best Dutch tradition was a gesture of resistance. To the designers of the reconstruction plan it was an expression of the vernacular style. All these layers of meaning with which the reconstruction architecture in the war period was invested came together in the flexibility and political feasibility of traditionalism.[2]

The following discussion describes how, from a traditionalist viewpoint, the aid of history, in terms of forming a 'better' past, was evoked to create the future image of a resurrected Middelburg.

In the postscript this conception of reconstruction will be examined again in order to explain why it was jettisoned immediately after the war.

## THE CENTRAL RECONSTRUCTION ORGANISATION

The reconstruction of Middelburg (20 000 inhabitants) was regarded as exceptionally important and thus became the direct responsibility of the central government in The Hague. The centralisation of the reconstruction machinery created during the war and the resultant government intervention in the building industry were completely unprecedented. The powers of the new Government Commissioner (later General Deputy) for Reconstruction, Dr J. A. Ringers, were regulated by the reconstruction decrees of 18 and 24 May 1940. These regulations covered the granting of approval to projects, co-operation with government departments, the power to expropriate land, rubble and buildings, and the finalisation of reconstruction plans, the execution of which had to be allowed by all.

Expropriation was expressly meant not to make the land the permanent property of the municipality but rather to restore it to private ownership again after it had been reallocated in accordance with the reconstruction plan. The legal obligation to carry out the reconstruction was placed on those who benefited from it. Financing of reconstruction was seen as a matter for the whole community, and those whose property had not been damaged were expected to contribute as well. Damage-investigation committees went around the country so that the payments to be made could be settled on the spot. Since it was felt that the damage indemnification ought not to bring about any 'unmotivated movements of capital', it was decided to indemnify property owners for their losses without taking account of the financial strength of those affected. The basis chosen for the payments was not the present value of the property, but the value it had the day before the beginning of the war, on 9 May 1940, and payment was only to be made when the rebuilding of each of the premises actually began, in order to discourage delays in rebuilding.

All in all, the working out and putting into practice of the reconstruction decrees placed the central reconstruction organisation in a unique position; Ringers and his staff, who escaped German

influence for the most part, ultimately controlled the whole of the
building industry. In this constellation there were no time-consuming
approval and professional procedures and the establishment of direct
lines of communication between the central offices in The Hague and
the designers of the reconstruction plans was supposed to guarantee
successful planning. What the centrally organised administration
meant to Middelburg in concrete terms was that the development
of reconstruction plans was not impeded by local resistance, lengthy
procedures or existing patterns of ownership.

The reconstruction came to a halt half-way through the Occupation period because, among other things, the scarcity and severely
inflated prices of building materials made the true rebuilding costs
of individual premises much higher than the indemnifications based
on their value on 9 May 1940. Furthermore, the Germans imposed
a ban on building in 1942. Nevertheless, we can still determine what
was planned.

## THE TRADITIONALIST ADMINISTRATION

The groundwork for wartime reconstruction was done by traditionalist architects who represented the prevailing ideas of that time in
the fields of architecture and town planning. The skirmishes at the
beginning of the war had taken place along the lines of communication and in and around the centres of towns and villages, and this
type of warfare damaged the inner cities and severely mutilated the
hearts of villages. The structures in these areas were usually small
in scale, and buildings consisted of a type which mixed shops and
business premises with dwellings above or behind them. In fact,
there was every reason for restoring the old situation again, as long
as some contemporary planning corrections could be introduced into
the reconstruction plans, particularly in respect of traffic flow.[3]

The reconstruction of bombed inner cities was something new in
the Netherlands. Town-planners had gained their earlier experience
primarily from urban expansion plans, and there were no methods
available for the rebuilding historic town centres. In this situation
the task of drawing up reconstruction plans was put into the hands
of traditionalist town planners, men who knew the local situation
and had a firm grip on the municipal machinery.

The traditionalist administration of reconstruction was geared to combating the lack of definition and order in city building. Planners were not afraid, however, of massive interventions in the historic hearts of cities. From the traditionalist viewpoint, the reconciliation of these modernising interventions with the historic image of the city took place in a broad hierarchical ordering – capable of infinite variation – of the cornerstones of town planning:

- church and town hall as dominant features of the townscape;
- squares as meeting places, enclosed by buildings;
- cultural and other institutions built into the walls of public space;
- dwellings and housing facilities as the basic vernacular elements and a focal point for family life;
- concentration of handicrafts at given points in the city and a relocation of industry outside the city.

On the basis of the clear demarcation of urban functions, a planning synthesis came into being through an ordering in which each element acquired its appropriate place in accordance with its position in the hierarchy. Social relationships could be deduced from the structure of the urban environment.

This planning framework was complemented by a striking architectonic compositional scheme, which united extremes or opposites, created transitions and clearly brought out relationships of size and scale. This compositional scheme was founded on the syllogism, a method employed in Aristotelian logic, whereby two extremes or opposites are united by a mediating mean. For example, a column ends at the bottom in a base, which indicates the surface supporting, and at the top in a capital, and thus it mediates between supporting and being supported. This purely architectural principle could be transferred to town planning. Between extremes like suburb and town centre, dwelling and street, some form of transition had to be created by means of added elements such as pavements, walls and hedges, which could at the same time make it possible to measure the relationship between their scales. This did not sublimate such mediating structures, but actually gave them more significance, since their existence became comprehensible through their siting and scale. This ordering was at once architecture and town planning. Hence it fixed the image of the city.

## THE RECONSTRUCTION PLAN

The bombing on 17 May 1940 killed 22 people and damaged or destroyed 253 private houses, 320 business premises and 18 public or semi-public buildings, including a large number of historical monuments. The central question was, of course, what the city would look like in the future.

Middelburg had originated in the ninth century as a fortress, and the town had always been of fluctuating economic significance. During and after the French Occupation of 1795–1812 it had lost its most important function, that of a port, and since then it had been a provincial town with an administrative function as a seat of the provincial government. It also served as a market for the agricultural island of Walcheren, and its many historical monuments made it a tourist attraction. Its economic development was as small as its population growth, and there was no prospect of industrialisation. The basic functions and structure of the town had thus remained unchanged for centuries. The street plan could not take much intensification and motorisation of traffic because access and traffic flow were hindered by the lack of a north–south link and by the fortification walls which constituted an obstacle (see Figure 1, p. 221). In addition there was a desperate shortage of housing for the lower income groups.

In preparing the plans for the reconstruction, there was a continual tension between the traditional townscape that was being aimed for, with the Town Hall and Abbey as focal points, and the interventions that had been opted for in order to fit modern traffic and housing into that townscape. The results of a regional survey carried out in 1939 were crucial for the reconstruction plans. These plans declared that in the future, Middelburg should concentrate on improving its ability to function as a tourist attraction, the market town for Walcheren, and the centre of government of the province Zeeland. Middelburg should be restored to its old glory without the negation of present-day requirements like traffic and housing.

The central figure in the traditional administration of the rebuilding of Middelburg was P. Verhagen, who set himself the aim of recreating its characteristic atmosphere around the focal points of the reconstruction plan, the Town Hall and the Abbey.[4] Verhagen made some massive interventions in the town's structure on the basis of traditionalist opinions. The historic centre had already existed for some 850 years as a circular fortress with a diameter of about 180 metres. Its circumference, now Lange Delft, acted as an inner ring road, and this was intersected by a straight south-west to north-east diameter line about 350 metres long. Precisely in order that the dominants in the town plan, the Town Hall and Abbey (by reason of their volume and height), should be completely encompassed in the town centre, Verhagen replaced this straight diameter by a bayonet. Series of squares, linkages in the form of small free-standing buildings and a sophisticated injection of sightlines subordinated the circulation of the traffic to the administration of the townscape. The curves and narrowing of the streets needed to create the image of an enclosed image of the town made long wide streets and big breakthroughs impossible.

## THE TOWN HALL AND THE ABBEY

Just as the reconstruction plan allowed room for modern require-ments such as traffic, so the restoration of the badly damaged Town Hall and the burnt-out Abbey offered scope for adaptation to con-temporary functional needs. The size and shape of the sites, as well as the forms of the buildings, were determined on the basis of the reconstruction plan, and it was on this premise that the restoration architects had to draw up their designs, a process that was naturally not always devoid of friction.

Verhagen saw the Town Hall and the Abbey, focal points of church and state, as symbols of spiritual and temporal authority which merited appropriate places in the spatial framework of the plan.

A space, a marketplace, is defined by the surrounding volumes, the walls of the market. . . . Space exists of its own volition, a margin of that volume. . . . Church and town hall belong among the primary volumes, the square is the primary space with which a town planner has to work [see Plate 1]. Church and town hall should be allotted the most perfect volume form in the town plan as a whole, that is, with their own margins, and the square the most perfect spatial form.[5]

Verhagen elevated the Marketplace and Abbey into two relatively autonomous fragments with a self-evident cultural symbolism; these in turn would draw the public to the Marketplace and the Town

Hall and to the residential areas around the Abbey complex and the churches. In order to insure the dominance of the Town Hall and Abbey, he made use of surprising little vistas, numerous enclosures and rich contrasts. The logical consequence of this decision to centre the town plan on the two dominants was that the greatest possible sobriety, anonymity and monochrome tonality had to be sought in the architecture of the individual private buildings (see Plate 2).

In Verhagen's eyes, the only attractive feature of the original Marketplace was the placing of its walls around the Town Hall. In his plan he changed it from an irregular trapezium into a rectangular widening of the circular ring-road. The southern funnel of this road was lengthened in such a way as to afford a surprising oblique view of the Town Hall, which brought out the effect of its Late Gothic architecture to best advantage. Thus the Marketplace was laid out at an angle to the Town Hall and made a vista from the Plein 1940. The projection of the north-east wall, which has a subtle kink in it to mark the transition from Marketplace to Town Hall Square, is such that twice as much of the side of the Town Hall can be seen from the Lange Delft. 'The spatial effect of the old Marketplace was very seriously impaired by its convex floor, behind which the Town Hall seemed to sink away. The highest point of this floor has been lowered by about a metre!'[6]

The splendid Abbey had developed out of the monastery, founded around 1100, which lay inside the original fortress. During the Reformation it had passed into lay hands and had been used for ever more prosaic purposes. At the same time, a process of decay had set in, which was only halted by the radical restoration of the end of the nineteenth century. The mostly superb monumental buildings surrounding parts of the Abbey were either badly damaged or completely destroyed during the bombing in 1940. The possibility this offered for providing the seat of the provincial government with sufficient accommodation was immediately seized upon, as was the idea that the Abbey could be made freestanding. It proved possible to extend the complex on the east side, where the Hotel de Abdij had fallen victim to the flames. The immediate surroundings of the Abbey were kept sober by the projection of houses, offices and a smaller hotel, the volume and scale of which enhanced the majesty of the Abbey buildings.

The ideas governing the restoration of the Abbey and the Town Hall did not call for the complete reconstruction of their mediaeval forms. Because too much had been destroyed to make a complete reconstruction feasible and because it was now desirable to meet new demands on space, the prime aim in this reconstruction too was a 'Middelburg atmosphere'.

## SUPERVISION

The close bond between town planning and conservation was naturally also present in the architecture of the streets. After the design of the definitive town plan had been completed at the end of 1940, the Stichting Herbouw Middelburg (Foundation for the Reconstruction of Middelburg) was set up, with Verhagen as its director. This Foundation directed the clearance of the rubble after its expropriation, the restoration of old or the planning of new streets, sewers, mains and cables, the preparation of plots for building, and the drawings of the individual premises for initial cost estimates.

Verhagen's decisions to give precedence to the restoration of commerce and industry and to use the expropriation ruling for traffic interventions had very concrete consequences. As a result of the widening of a number of streets and the creation of small squares and the like, 46 undamaged buildings in the town centre were demolished in addition to the remains of the 456 buildings destroyed in the bombing. Moreover, because the rebuilt premises were allowed to have slightly wider frontages, only 250 of the 502 buildings would be rebuilt. This meant a loss of 50 per cent, so the reconstruction plan was complemented by a plan for expansion outside the town walls, with housing mainly for the lower income groups.

Although the tradespeople were disappointed in general at the depth of buildings to be allowed behind the façades, the reallocation of land in the town centre had been worked out in broad outline by the end of 1940. The methods of the reconstruction organisations drew sharp criticism from the interested parties, because they were based on haste and extreme economy. What the critics were mainly alluding to here was the rigorous limitation on space: the rebuilding was to cover at most only 80 per cent of the original parcel of land belonging to each of the premises. On the other hand, they pointed out the danger of an 'architectural lie', namely that Middelburg would be decked out with street frontages that gave a false impression of what lay behind them. The priority of the façade, which had to be attuned to the town planners' decision to assign priority to the 'Middelburg atmosphere', led to the production of extremely minimal, dilettantish ground plans that did not correspond to the image of these façades. This was not just an aesthetic question, of course. What the victims feared was that the loss of space and harmony in buildings that were too small behind their large façades would lower the value of the premises.

The townscape had now been fixed two-dimensionally in the reconstruction plan, but how was it realised architecturally? The directive from The Hague was that committees must be appointed in each region to select architects, the underlying idea here being that each region had its own character and matching architecture. For Middelburg, too, a list of architects was drawn up. Apart from criteria such as qualifications and total dedication, the most important requirement for the elect was that they must be prepared 'to adapt to the spirit of the town of Middelburg: in other words not to reveal their own personalities too much, but to build up the townscape in close accommodation between themselves'.[7] The role of co-ordinator was reserved for Verhagen, the supervisor and director of the Stichting Herbouw Middelburg. It was he who had to ensure that each building was suitable for the region and who in each case chose the architect and assessed the plans, the estimates, the method of construction, the choice of materials, the colour and the execution.

In order to produce the image he was after, Verhagen insisted that the work of the architects selected should be 'anonymous' and geared to achieving the 'Middelburg atmosphere'. Architects from whom too much individuality or self-conceit could be expected were turned down. The street image that Verhagen had in mind was a highly personal one. He was not particularly interested in the architectural history of the town, because he realised that it would be senseless to aim for a specific Middelburg style, so he confined himself to an idea of the Middelburg atmosphere which was actually strongly conditioned by his own preferences. In a correspondence in which it was pointed out to him that a case could be made on historical grounds for the predominant use of brick, he precisely emphasised his marked preference for a Middelburg with white plastered and painted façades: 'I have advocated the incriminated façade finish not as a historical fact, but as the vehicle of today's townscape. . . . The plain fact is that I am afraid of a brick town. In the long run it is sombre and heavy and all too soon monotonous as well. And it is not Middelburg. . . . I do not want to be stifled by brick walls.'[8]

Verhagen tried to emphasise the individuality of each building by preventing any one architect from designing two adjacent houses. Moreover, he himself supervised the composition of the façades in a highly energetic manner. He wielded his red pencil vigorously in making corrections on façades, the pitch of roofs, and in the positioning of windows, doors and fanlights, and he insisted that the architects should aim at vertically articulated street walls with gutters at staggered heights. This could be achieved by keeping to a fixed width of six to seven metres for each building and accentuating its individuality. In addition, he drew up architectural guidelines for the size of windows and the arrangement of their panes. His aim here was to prevent shops from having large display windows, so that their façades would lose the wall effect and, because of being divided in two, acquire a horizontal rather than a vertical articulation.

It can be concluded that, thanks to the war situation and the special problem posed by the rebuilding of the centre of Middelburg, Verhagen had a unique opportunity as designer of the reconstruction plan and in his role as supervisor of the architecture to safeguard the townscape. He further had a planning scheme designed in accordance with his own ideas, while, as the designer, he himself was able to fit any necessary changes into his original concept. In this unity of architecture and town planning the architects were manoeuvred into playing second fiddle.

Several moments are to be found in his supervisory work in which Verhagen changed his rather intuitive approach and did not shrink from having façade designs he had already approved done all over again for the benefit of the townscape. In September 1942, when he studied the combined street wall drawings, he concluded that less picturesqueness and arbitrariness and a greater strength in detail ought to be demanded of the architects. The variation in the façades made the street walls too busy, and that detracted from the beauty of the broad lines of the street image and the vertical effect of the façades of which he was such an ardent defender.

In fact, we see Verhagen confronted here by the consequences of 'anonymous' architecture. A number of architects had taken their cue from the forms of the past without a proper understanding of the essence of the public architecture of Middelburg, namely the relationship of the old buildings to the spaces around them in respect to scale, structure, rhythm, handling of material and the tonality of their façades. The parroting of motifs, elements and details precisely missed that essence. The more docile architects complied with Verhagen's typical Middelburg atmosphere, but his

idea of what was 'typical' underwent several changes. Since the
reconstruction or continuation of the Middelburg style was no
longer considered possible, 'atmosphere' was a neutral concept for
which Verhagen himself had to supply the definition – the task of
the supervisor, after all. And here the traditionalist administration
came face to face with itself: the gap left by the lack of historical
justification for the desired townscape was filled by Verhagen's own
preferences. He did not find this easy, for later he complained that
he really would have liked more individuality from the 'anonymous'
architects: 'Atmosphere is something different from style. It was
conceivable that by means of personal work the architects might
have supplied more atmosphere and less tradition.' 'I really do
feel a need for something more individual than the tradition pure
and simple which is quite often presented to me here.'[9] Within the
traditionalist framework Verhagen was striving for a contemporary
style, but he failed to perceive it. It was precisely through the
maximum exploitation of the traditionalist repertoire that he became
aware of its limitations. Anonymity and tradition, focused on a
Middelburg atmosphere, mixed poorly with a contemporary style.

## POSTSCRIPT

Chronicling the history of the reconstruction of Middelburg leads to
an unequivocal conclusion. Although the designers were not afraid
to make radical corrections in the plan of the town and to drive
the majority of the non-tradespeople out of the town centre for
the benefit of an improved townscape and a better traffic flow, the
resurrected Middelburg must be interpreted first and foremost as a
significant traditionalist product of five years of Occupation and as
an open-air museum for the cherishing of Dutch culture and the
vernacular.

As stated in the introduction, the planning and architectural
substance of the open-air museum allowed all sorts of ideological
interpretations, but what is more important is that the designer of
this museum became aware of the limitations of the traditionalist
scenario during its construction. Traditionalism proved to be nothing
more than a hodge-podge of notions about the past – subjective
preferences, which Verhagen as supervisor passed on to the architects as the 'typical Middelburg atmosphere'. Only in an artificial
manner did the traditionalist viewpoint link up with the historical

architectural tradition of the town, and it was unable to latch on
to a contemporary style. It is precisely this hybrid character that
makes the reconstruction of Middelburg as interesting as it is dated:
an incident explicable by history.

Immediately after the war Verhagen saw Middelburg not as
a recipe for the reconstruction of other destroyed town centres
(Arnhem, Groningen, Nijmegen), but precisely as a unique vernacular chapter which was now closed. In 1946 and 1947, when
he co-operated on an expansion plan for Middelburg, he strove
for a contemporary style of which the contours were visible. On the
basis of expected future developments, he demanded for this plan
a modern design that took account of the industrialisation of the
building trade, the de-emphasis of the vernacular, the replacement
of the enclosed block by free-standing buildings and the use of lively,
animating green spaces and self-sufficient suburbs – in short a fresh,
rejuvenated Middelburg around the old pearl.

The reconstruction plans for damaged cities in Holland during
the war differ fundamentally from those carried out afterwards.
That difference lies in the reaction to the German Occupation and
the view to the future. Whereas during the war the aid of history
was evoked – in vain – to shape the future, after the war renewal
took pride of place, and history could retire again. Traditionalism
had served its turn.

**Archives**
Ministerie van Volkshuisvesting, Ruimtelijke Ordening en Milieuhygiëne
(Ministry of Housing, Town Planning and Environment) in The Hague.
Gemeentearchief Middelburg (Municipal Archive of Middelburg).
Rijksdienst voor de Monumentenzorg (State Service for the Conservation
of Monuments) in Zeist.
Rijksinstituut voor Oorlogsdocumentatie (State Institute for War Docu-
mentation) in Amsterdam.
Stichting Herbouw Middelburg/Walcheren (Foundation for the Recon-
struction of Middelburg/Walcheren) in Middelburg.

**Notes**
1.  J. F. Berghoef, 'Stedebouwkundige en architectonische aspecten
    van Middelburgs wederopbouw' ('Architecture and Town Planning
    Aspects of the Reconstruction of Middelburg'), *Bulletin KNOB*, 6th
    series, 9 (1956) p. 143.

2. For a detailed analysis see K. Bosma, 'De wederopbouw van Middelburg' ('The Reconstruction of Middelburg'), *Plan*, 2 (1984) pp. 6–22.
3. C. de Cler, 'De wederopbouwperiode' ('The Reconstruction Period'), in F. de Jong (ed.), *Stedebouw in Nederland* (*Town Planning in Holland*) (Zutphen, 1985) p. 210.
4. On Verhagen see K. Bosma, 'Ideeën over wederopbouw: P. Verhagen en de stedebouw' ('Ideas about Reconstruction: P. Verhagen and Town Planning'), *Plan*, 3 (1984) pp. 35–42.
5. P. Verhagen, 'Kerk en samenleving' ('Church and Society'), *Bouw*, 21 (1948) p. 168.
6. B. Abspoel, 'Hoe zal Middelburg herrijzen?' ('How Will Middelburg Rise?'), draft for an article in a regional newspaper, Christmas 1945.
7. Letter from Verhagen to G. Hamerpagt, 18 June 1942. Municipal Archive, Middelburg.
8. Letter from Verhagen to A. Siebers, 21 April 1941. Archive, Stichting Herbouw Walcheren (Foundation for the Reconstruction of Walcheren).
9. Letters from Verhagen to A. R. Wittop Koning, 10 June 1942 and 10 March 1943. Archive, Stichting Herbouw Walcheren (Foundation for the Reconstruction of Walcheren).

# 6 Warsaw: Destruction, Secret Town Planning, 1939–44, and Postwar Reconstruction

## STANISLAW JANKOWSKI

### THE DESTRUCTION OF WARSAW

Warsaw is situated on the Vistula River, at the crossroads of ancient trade routes running from the east to the west and from the north to the south. The trade routes contributed to the development of the town, but from time to time they changed their character to become routes of war and destruction. Warsaw is 700 years old, and for nearly 400 years it has been the capital of Poland, the centre of its science, culture and industry. On the eve of the Nazi invasion of Poland, Warsaw with 1.3 million inhabitants counted among the quickly developing European capitals.

Warsaw takes a special place among Europe's cities destroyed during the Second World War, both in terms of the extent of its destruction and the mode in which it was effected. Whereas the other cities were destroyed in the course of war operations, in Warsaw the Nazis carried out a previously prepared plan for total annihilation, something that went far beyond war damage.

On 1 September 1939 the first bombs were dropped on Warsaw; a few days later the three-week-long siege began. As the first big city to offer bitter resistance to Nazi forces, it sustained heavy losses. The number of killed and wounded amounted to some 60 000. About 12 per cent of all buildings were destroyed. Then followed five long years of brutal Nazi Occupation. In his diary, Hans Frank, the Nazi Governor for occupied Poland, wrote on 4 November 1939: 'the Führer has discussed the whole situation with the Governor General, informed him of his plans, and approved the actions undertaken by the Governor General in Poland, particularly the decision to demolish the Royal Castle in Warsaw, and not to rebuild the city'.[1] Dr Ludwig Fischer, the Governor of the District of Warsaw, wrote: 'When, on 26 October 1939, I assumed the post of Governor . . . , the Governor General gave me the order to do everything possible

77

to deprive Warsaw of its character as the main centre of the Polish Republic.'[2]

Nazi town planners prepared the implementation of these ideas. For centuries past the task of the town planners had been to design and to build towns, but in 1940 Nazi town planners from Würzburg prepared the so-called Pabst plan for annihilation of an existing city in order to build 'Warsaw – the new German city' (see Figures 2 and 3, p. 222). The Pabst plan included fifteen maps and two photographs of a model. It called for a new Nazi town for 130 000 inhabitants to be built on one-twentieth of the area of Warsaw, a town of 1 300 000 inhabitants. This was made quite clear by map 13, entitled 'The demolition of the Polish city and the construction of the German city'.

The years 1942–3 marked the second stage in the destruction of Warsaw, namely the tragedy of the Jewish ghetto. When the Nazis entered Warsaw in October 1939, the Jewish population of the capital exceeded 360 000. From the very first days of occupation, the Nazis proceeded to carry out a planned liquidation of the Jews. In the northern part of the town, behind a high brick wall, the 'Jewish residential district' was established. In July 1942 the Nazis began the 'Final Solution of the Jewish Question'. They started the 'resettlement' of the Jews eastwards, and 320 000 persons were deported from the Warsaw ghetto to the gas chambers in the extermination camp of Treblinka. At dawn on 19 April 1943, SS and police detachments started the final liquidation of the Warsaw ghetto. An uprising flared, led by the Jewish Fighting Organisation, and dogged, heroic fighting lasted till 15 May. The extermination of the ghetto was completed, resulting in the loss of over 350 000 human lives and the complete destruction of the northern part of the town's central area.

The third stage in the destruction of the town was the Warsaw Uprising which broke out on 1 August 1944. For the first time since October 1939, the Polish Home Army, 40 000 men strong, began regular, open warfare against the Germans. The fighting lasted sixty-three days and resulted in the loss of 150 000 human lives, in the ruin of rest of the town and the deportation of the remaining population from left-bank Warsaw. But even during the Warsaw Uprising, the soldier-architect did not stop being an architect.

In September 1944, during the Uprising's final days, we knew that we could not count on help from the Soviet army stationed across the Vistula. Among ruins, ashes and graves, knowing about preparations for capitulation, we were getting ready to leave Warsaw, a difficult decision after sixty days of combat and hope. It was less difficult for the Home Army soldiers who were to become POWs than for the hundreds of thousands of civilians who stayed with us till the very end. People were hastily gathering medical supplies, remains of food stocks, warm clothing.

While on a patrol mission as a Lieutenant in the Home Army I met Second Lieutenant Stanislaw Dziewulski, a town planner. He asked me to visit him. When I went there the next day, I met the architect Kazimierz Marczewski. Both of them were preparing to leave Warsaw. On a piece of carbon paper Marczewski had just finished a drawing of a housing district, Muranów, situated on the remains of the Ghetto. Dziewulski also handed me a document entitled 'Directives – Warsaw's Reconstruction', dated 16 September 1944. No one knew what fate awaited us, or that the typed note, blending precise planning language with an undefeated faith in the prompt reconstruction of Warsaw, could someday become important. It seemed impossible that the memorandum was written amid the burning rubble of the city.

After the Warsaw Uprising the town was in ruins and the Nazis proceeded to the final settlement of accounts. The basis for action was provided by Hitler's order: 'Warsaw has to be pacified, that is, razed to the ground, while the war is still on, unless military necessities connected with fortifications prevent it.'[3] This is probably the only document in history that did not even attempt to justify destruction by arguing military necessities. On the contrary, it ordered the destruction of an entire city with the exception of military installations. The order was carried out with precision. A special staff composed of experts and scientific advisers was in charge of the operation. Warsaw was divided into areas for destruction. Corner houses were numbered. On selected buildings and statues special inscriptions were made indicating the proposed date of demolition. Special detachments known as demolition and annihilation squads proceeded to destroy the deserted city – house by house, street by street.

The Nazis were particularly fierce in the destruction of everything that represented Polish history and culture. Out of 957 buildings classified as historical monuments, 782 were totally destroyed and 141 partly destroyed (see Figure 4, p. 223). General Eisenhower, who visited Warsaw shortly after its liberation, said: 'I have seen many towns destroyed during the war, but nowhere have I been faced with such extent of destruction executed with such bestiality.'[4] The losses which were borne by Warsaw during the five years of war and Nazi Occupation amounted to about 700 000 killed (60 per cent of the prewar population) and the destruction of 80 per cent of the town's buildings and its technical equipment.

## PREPARATIONS FOR WARSAW'S RETURN TO LIFE

On 17 January 1945 Warsaw was liberated by Soviet and Polish forces. A nation that had lost six million of its inhabitants – one-fifth of the population – and 38 per cent of its national property now faced the task of the reconstruction of its capital. Two decisions were of momentous importance for the future: the decision taken by the Polish government before the liberation that Warsaw would remain the capital of Poland, and the spontaneous return of Warsaw's inhabitants to the destroyed city. Both decisions were heroic. In January 1945 the left bank of Warsaw (80 per cent of the prewar city) had scarcely a single undamaged building; it had no water, no light, no telephones, no public transport. The railways were not functioning; there was no means of communication with the rest of the country. Both of these decisions were farsighted, too. The fact that Warsaw was to remain the capital made its reconstruction a key task of national significance. The return of the population mobilised a priceless reservoir of enthusiasm, initiative and perseverance.

In view of the fact that the Nazis had mined the ruins of the city, the military authorities prohibited entry to the area on the left bank until the mines were cleared. Indeed, in a sense the first words in the history of Warsaw's reconstruction were written by sappers on the walls of demolished and burnt out houses: 'Cleared of mines'. These words, hastily scribbled in the frost, spelled safe access to the ruins of one's own home; they bore the promise of reconstruction. Between 17 January and March 1945 sappers dismantled and removed from the ruins about 100 000 mines and unexploded shells. However, neither the danger from mines nor collapsing buildings nor shortages of food and shelter were able to stop the returning Varsovians. They were driven to Warsaw by a powerful inner urge to raise their city from ruins. They came in masses, in spite of the temptation to wait elsewhere through the most difficult period, in spite of the fact that easier conditions of life and work were to be found outside Warsaw. They were returning home. On the day of Warsaw's liberation, the population of the city, including the right-bank district of Praga which had already been liberated in September 1944, amounted to 164 000, of which 20 000 lived on the left bank. Four months later, in May 1945, the population of Warsaw had already reached 366 000, including 185 000 on the left bank.

The reconstruction fo the city began immediately after its liberation. On 14 February 1945 a Capital Reconstruction Bureau (Biuro Odbudowy Stolicy, or BOS), with the architect Roman Piotrowski at its head, was appointed by the President of Warsaw. Over 1400 town planners, architects, engineers in various fields, sociologists, economists and lawyers applied for jobs, the result being a large centre for research, design and implementation of reconstruction and development plans for a fatally ruined city. In those days the BOS employees were the happiest of all Varsovians. They were given a loaf of bread, a coupon to get a pair of shoes and a chance to fulfil their most magnificent dreams! Some drew up plans, while others were sent to do field work – depending on what shoes each of them had. From the very beginning, BOS was the leading centre working to bring the city back to life and rebuild it. BOS was one of the organisers of the exhibition 'Warsaw Accuses', which opened on 3 May 1945 in the National Museum in Warsaw; it also edited the *Skarpa Warszawska* (*The Warsaw Escarpment*), a weekly journal devoted to 'the reconstruction of the capital, the town, and its people', as the subtitle read. 'What were those BOS people like? Were they far-sighted realists or visionary dreamers?' Roman Piotrowski asked twenty-five years later, and he replied: 'I believe they were just ordinary people who happened to experience an extraordinary adventure, for on a small part of their lives, of only a few years duration, history had left an imprint of greatness'.[5]

What made possible the rapid beginning of reconstruction planning was the fact that clandestinely conducted studies on the social and spatial development of Warsaw had been undertaken during the German Occupation. This conspiratorial town-planning activity, carried out in conditions of terror unleashed by the Gestapo, implied awareness that planning itself constituted a form of struggle against the invader, and it also expressed the need for continuing professional work and for making preparations for new tasks that were to come.

Three main centres conducted semi-legal, semi-conspiratorial town-planning activity. The first of these was the Planning Department of the Warsaw Municipal Council, headed by Stanislaw

Rozanski and unofficially associated with a Studio for Regional Planning (led by Jan Chmielewski and Kazimierz Lier). It included a secret Commission of Town Planning Experts chaired by Professor Tadeusz Tolwinski. Throughout the occupation period, the Planning Department and specialists associated with it worked on various ideas for the future redevelopment of the main communication routes and squares in the city centre.

The second centre was the Faculty of Architecture of Warsaw Technical University. Though its role was officially reduced by the Germans to that of offering secondary education in the building trades, it operated illegally as a higher education institution and a centre carrying out research with a view to the future rebuilding of Warsaw and the whole country. Of particular significance was the work conducted in the Department of Town Building, headed by Professor Tadeusz Tolwinski, and in the Institute of Polish Architecture, led by Professor Jan Zachwatowicz.

Clandestine education was provided for over 150 students under the guise of draughtsmen's classes. Twenty-three graduate papers, nine doctoral and eight post-doctoral works were completed here. Several town-planning and architectural competitions were held, and in case they were discovered, the submissions were ante-dated to the prewar period. Part of the architectural documentation concerning the cataloguing of historic monuments in the city was hidden in a monastery in Piotrków, and after the war it served as a priceless source during the reconstruction of the Old Town.

Finally, the third, largest and most radical centre for underground architectural and town planning work was the Studio for Architecture and Town Planning (Pracownia Urbanistyczno-Architektoniczna), which operated clandestinely at the Co-operative Building Enterprise (Spoleczne Przedsiebiorstwo Budowlane.) The Studio for Architecture and Town Planning, headed first by architect Szymon Syrkus and, following the latter's imprisonment and subsequent deportation to Auschwitz, by Roman Piotrowski and Helena Syrkus, was interested in two basic planning problems: the place of residence (especially social housing projects) and the place of work (especially zoned industrial districts). The Studio enlisted the services of a large group of architects, planners, economists and sociologists, all of whom were later to constitute the core of the BOS staff.

In addition to the three organised centres, autonomous groups of architects and town planners worked independently and secretly. For example, Zygmunt Skibniewski, Stanislaw Dziewulski and Kazimierz

Marczewski prepared a general concept of the plan for Warsaw and a project for the redevelopment of the area along the old high bank of the Vistula in the city centre which became a point of departure for town-planning work undertaken after the liberation (see Figure 5, p. 224).

## POSTWAR RECONSTRUCTION

The law which laid the basis for the systematic planning and rebuilding of the city was the Decree of October 1945, which made all land within the administrative boundaries of Warsaw municipal property. Only the buildings continued to belong to their previous owners. This decree was particularly important for the reconstruction and development of the city centre and the other densely built-up prewar areas. Since more than 90 per cent of all buildings had been completely destroyed, it meant that all central areas of the capital could be immediately taken over by the city. There were no legal obstacles to changing land use, laying out new major streets or putting up large housing estates under a comprehensive plan. It took, however, some time for the town planners to realise that communalising land, while it removed private ownership, did not eliminate the meaning of land value.

The first draft plan of reconstruction was prepared as early as March 1945 (see Figure 6, p. 225). Architect Zygmunt Skibniewski, the first head of the Town-Planning Department of BOS, recalled that on his way to a Cabinet session, where the plan was presented to the President of the Republic, he was halted by an air-raid warning. The war was still on. Successive versions of the plan were prepared in May 1945, October 1945 and February 1946. The final outcome of these endeavours was the 'Plan for the Reconstruction of Warsaw' of September 1946, drawn up by the Town Planning Department of BOS. It constituted a complete town-planning project, containing both a general plan and a specific programme for rebuilding.

In view of the significance of the general guidelines included in the plan, some prominent Polish and foreign specialists were invited to Warsaw to review the plan critically. They were S. Y. Chernyshev and Professor V. B. Baburov of Moscow, André Lurcat of Paris, Paul Nelson of the United States, Professor Hans Bernoulli of Basel (before the war he had been asked to give his expert opinion on the 1931 plan of Warsaw), C. van Esteren, the chief town planner of Amsterdam, and Professor Tadeusz Tolwinski, the head of the Department of Town Planning in the Faculty of Architecture of Warsaw Technical University.[6] The response of the experts was highly favourable and worth citing: 'Characteristic features of the other capital cities have been analysed. The results of these studies have been adapted to the specific conditions of Warsaw. The problem has been treated in a way that is new to me' (Baburov). 'I consider the plan of Warsaw one of the best plans that I have seen since the end of the war' (Lurcat). 'For the first time in 150 years we have seen a town-planning project that can be implemented. . . . This imposes an enormous responsibility on its authors' (Bernoulli). The famous American sociologist Lewis Mumford, who saw the plan of the reconstruction of Warsaw during an exhibition held in Chicago in February 1946, wrote: 'In the new plans of Warsaw, the facts of modern social life constitute the backbone of the whole structure. . . . In the plans of the Warsaw Bureau for the Reconstruction of the Capital, the architects begin at the foundations, and basing themselves on nature and man's essential needs, find an expression of the epoch.'[7]

The enthusiasm of the critics was echoed by the participants in the planning process and the city's citizens, but Varsovians were also well aware of the difficulties ahead. 'If the Warsaw community is to be reborn', the outstanding sociologist Stanislaw Ossowski recalled, 'if its core is to be constituted by former Varsovians, then they have to be given back their old rebuilt Warsaw to some extent, so that they can see in it the same city, though considerably altered, and not a different town on the same spot. One must take into consideration the fact that individual attachment to old forms is a factor of social unity.'[8] 'Were we to adapt ourselves to the difficulties of the moment and think only of rescuing the surviving remnants of Warsaw', the town planner Waclaw Ostrowski argued, 'we would have to abandon those projects that aim at directing the city's development on to new paths, to give up the idea of eliminating the errors committed in the past and taking account of the demands of the present day in the construction of Warsaw.'[9] The architect Stanislaw Dziewulski, one of the authors of the plan of Warsaw, later said:

In Polish town planning, and hence in Warsaw's town planning, the year 1945 was a unique moment, one that would never occur again. . . . This was reflected in the first versions of the plan, in their boldness and radicalism – which was even excessive, as it later turned out. That radicalism, which marked town and country planning as well as political and economic planning, gave a powerful impulse for the rebuilding and at the same time the transformation of the city – in spite of all mistakes that were unavoidable at the time.[10]

Determining the proper proportions between recreation of the historic city and transformation of that city, however, was a very difficult and controversial problem – especially so when it turned out that the underground installations and the basic network of streets were largely preserved, a fact of enormous significance. A conflict thus arose between the immediate effect of localised reconstruction or repairs and the complex programme of radical transformation. The story of 'Trasa W%Z', the East–West Thoroughfare project presented in 1947, showed that the dispute was not merely a theoretical one.

When floating ice demolished the temporary bridge on the Vistula, a second northern river crossing became indispensable for the functioning of a city situated on both banks of the river. The preliminary decision to rebuild the bridge (it had been blown up in September 1944) was followed by another, namely to reconstruct the partly damaged Panzer Viaduct that connected the bridge with the historic central district situated on the high bank of the river. This decision, which would have restored the prewar spatial and communication layout and consequently precluded any radical transformation, was of particular significance for this area of the city. A proposal counter to this decision was prepared in the Town Planning Studio by J. Knothe, J. Sigalin, Z. Stepinski and the author. It called for an East–West Thoroughfare, a seven-kilometres-long communication artery with a bridge, a tunnel under the historic district, and a newly designed housing project for Mariensztat (see Figure 7, p. 226). This plan required the dismantling of the Panzer Viaduct and the buildings that stood along it. Who knows what was more shocking about the plan, the intention to demolish the existing housing or the suggestion that completion of the whole project should be within two years?

The Ministry of Transport, which was responsible for all road building ventures, challenged the idea of the East–West Thorough-fare, while the journal *Przeglad Budowlany* (*The Builder's Review*) wrote: 'Let us leave the construction of the East–West Thoroughfare to the future generations and for the time being let us do what is indispensable and what we can afford.' In the BOS Studio, many hours of discussion of the model and project of the thoroughfare took place. The planners finally appealed to the President of the Republic who approved the project and schedule, and the whole venture was carried through as proposed.

As suggested above, my own initial contribution to reconstruction consisted of work on this project. When I returned to Warsaw in September 1946 (after German captivity and having earned a town planning diploma from Liverpool University), I offered to work on the reconstruction of Warsaw and started work under Stanislaw Dziewulski, who then headed the General Planning Office. Kazimierz Marczewski managed the City Centre Department. After the collapse of the Uprising I had taken with me the 'Directives' they had typed out, and I managed to protect the document during numerous searches in POW camps. I did not imagine then that I would help apply these directives in practice.

Compared with contemporary town planning institutions employing hundreds of specialists and administrative staff, ours of 1947 was very modest. Initially, we were thirty strong, working in the afternoon's 'second shift'. Instead of computers and portable telephones, we were equipped with a thick notebook – a 'Construction Journal' – where we entered notes while travelling between the site and our office. We observed one principle: answers were to be given the same day to questions asked. Decisions were made quickly and urgently needed drawings submitted. We worked on location and had to keep up with its rapid pace. In spite of our best efforts, we did not manage to steer clear of errors. Zygmunt Stepinski recalled one of them.

In April 1948 we issued the first plans for the Mariensztat residential district. Zygmunt was asked to go to the construction site because 'something's gone wrong'. The problem was that the first storey was built on top of the ground floor of a neighbouring building that happened to have been equal in width. I also committed the 'crime' of changing plans previously approved for execution. A roundabout had been designed for the East–West Thoroughfare overpass. I was responsible for the urban planning aspect of the project, and something 'just did not fit there'. I stayed at the office all night and the following morning showed my colleagues the altered roundabout which incorporated the Mariensztat Square – a design that still exists unchanged. They agreed that my proposal was better and the plans were forwarded to the site. Józek Sigalin, the site's manager, joked and asked me 'to sign a statement' that I would not introduce more changes in the plans.

On 26 April 1949, just eighty-seven days before the promised completion date of the project, and at a time when work was most intense, we read in the 'Construction Journal' a note that could endanger not only the completion deadline but the entire social and architectural achievement of the East–West Thoroughfare. The entry simply read: 'Cracks appeared on dome of St Ann's Church' – the historical church towering over the tunnel's entrance. The next day the Journal noted that the 'cracks in dome and floor are growing'. A geological survey proved beyond doubt the threat of a disaster: 'Sudden slope landslip, north-eastern part of the church breaks off from the mass.' From then on, the reports reached our emergency headquarters every 12 hours. Night and day for a month we struggled to apply new technology to save our work.

To rescue the church we tried, among other things, Professor Cebertowicz's method of electro-osmosis for petrification and water drainage, the first time this method was used so extensively; erection of an additional supporting wall at the base of the slope; and reinforcement of the inside of the church with steel and the construction of a steel grid to bind its foundation. On 2 May, however, the journal still noted that 'the church and earth movement continues, the disaster can happen within two weeks', and the next day's comment was that the 'upper part of the belfry bends one centimeter per day'. An emergency staff met every twelve hours, while work and tests at the site continued around the clock. The first good news came on 12 May at half past six in the evening: 'No change in church's apse cramps in the past three days.' On 27 May, fifty-three days before the completion date, the journal entry read: 'Landslips slows down, slopes consolidation progresses, the process has not been finished yet.'

On 22 July 1949 – as planned – the East–West Thoroughfare was opened (see Plate 3).[11] Its construction was a breakthrough, demonstrating the feasibility of carrying out large, complex and difficult town-planning projects in ruined Warsaw. In a survey conducted in 1970 by the weekly *POLITYKA*, the Thoroughfare was recognised as the greatest architectural and town planning achievement in Poland since the war.

With the northern part of the city returning to life, it became possible to begin the large-scale restoration of Warsaw's historic districts. As early as February 1945 a Department of Historic

Architecture was set up at BOS. Its first head was Jan Zachwatowicz, who was succeeded in 1946 by Piotr Biegánski. In 1947 Biegánski was appointed Conservator of the Capital City of Warsaw, with overall responsibility for the restoration of Warsaw's historic quarters. Moreover, it became apparent that the conservation of historic ensembles was closely related to the general programme for the city's rebuilding; rebuilding historic monuments thus required officials to take modern town planning criteria into account.

To start with, surviving architectural fragments and details were catalogued and preserved, and iconographic material was amassed. In many cases, old and long-obliterated arrangements of houses and streets were restored. In some places, previously unknown fragments of mediaeval architecture and frescoes were uncovered. Authorities could then move on to larger projects. On 22 July 1953 the so-called Old Warsaw Route connecting the Old and New Towns was opened after its complete restoration. Its extension, the Krakowskie Przedmiescie Street, with its predominantly palatial architecture, churches and monuments, was restored next, followed by Nowy Swiat Street, the layout and architecture of which dated from the early nineteenth century. The crowning project in the restoration of the Old Town was the rebuilding of the Royal Castle in 1974 as a Museum of National Culture (see Plates 3–6).

The reconstruction of these historic ensembles played a particularly important role in shaping Warsaw's unique spatial character and in forming the emotional ties of its inhabitants with their city. Despite full awareness that these quarters had been rebuilt or occasionally virtually recreated from nothing, they have gained unreserved social approval and play an important part in Polish culture. In 1980 UNESCO entered Warsaw's Old Town on the official list of the World's Cultural Heritage.

The bulk of the expenditures for the reconstruction of Warsaw came from state funds allocated under the national investment plan. However, there was also another important source of funds, one that revealed the special atmosphere which prevailed during the first years of the reconstruction. This was the Civic Fund for Warsaw's Reconstruction (Spoleczny Fundusz Odbudowy Stolicy), supported by voluntary contributions from all over Poland. This fund made an outstanding contribution both by mobilising a vast capital of social support for and assistance to this cause, and by providing considerable financial resources which in the years 1946–64 amounted to as much as over 4.5 million zlotys, at that time an equivalent of 100 000 rooms in new housing. Thanks to this fund it became possible, for example, to rebuild the Poniatowski Bridge, to complete the East–West Thoroughfare, and to restore the Old and New Towns as well as numerous monuments and cultural facilities.

Varsovians had thus to start their new life after the war with housing of little value. In fact, most of the remaining dwellings ought to have been altered or replaced long before the war. By the irony of fate, those parts of the capital which would least be missed had escaped destruction [recalled Adolf Ciborowski]. At the beginning of Warsaw's reconstruction there was a two-fold task: to build new residential districts with all conveniences and to redevelop old and neglected city outskirts. Warsaw builders concentrated on the first part of this task. New districts had to be put out as soon as possible, to give people somewhere to live.[12]

In housing construction, architects drew on the progressive traditions of the prewar Warsaw Housing Co-operative and the secret studies conducted by the Town Planning and Architectural Studio during the Nazi Occupation. In 1948 a special housing office within the Ministry of Reconstruction was formed. The Department of Workers' Housing Estates (Zaklad Osiedli Robotniczych) existed until 1967 and supervised the construction of some 150 000 flats (see Figure 8, p. 226). In particular, the years 1949–52 saw the construction of the Marszalkowska Street Housing Project (MDM), laid out on the ruins of the central district and including the first new square to be built in the city centre.[13]

The implementation of a plan which established the guiding principles for the rebuilding and development of the city, especially one which would change its social and spatial structure for many decades to come, naturally encountered obstacles and unleashed conflicts. Thus the demand for housing conflicted with the needs of central city and state institutions. Her metropolitan status, which in this period constituted the most important element transforming Warsaw into a large, modern town, threatened those projects that served to satisfy the immediate needs of the city's inhabitants. In view of very limited resources, it was not easy to decide what merited the highest priority. In practice, the interests of metropolitan Warsaw took precedence over all others, which meant that in the destroyed central areas of the town, new edifices for various central institutions and offices were required. The central districts were cleared of rubble at a rapid pace; by 31 December 1947 about a million cubic metres of rubble had been removed. Architectural competitions brought in their wake a number of new buildings to house ministries and other offices. The reconstruction effort also encompassed the buildings of the National Theatre, the Philharmonic Society, the National Museum, Warsaw University and the Academy of Fine Arts. Thus the foundations were laid for a modern city centre.

In 1953–5 the city centre acquired a new feature, the Palace of Culture and Science. A gift from the USSR, it was designed and built by Soviet architects. It combined many different functions in the fields of learning and culture, and housed congress and exhibition halls, scientific institutions, theatres and cinemas. However, it is an alien element in its architectural form and grand scale, towering as it does above the town, and it continues to provoke many reservations among the public.

Rebuilding and improving the street systems was a relatively easy job because the most densely populated districts, which usually present the most difficult problems, lay in ruins. Moreover, as Warsaw's town planners learned in the first years of the reconstruction work, it was advisable to follow as far as possible the pattern of water and sewerage mains which were preserved in part under the old streets. The plan to rebuild and improve the layout of Warsaw's street system had the following aims: (1) to widen the main streets in the city centre to suit the needs of a modern city; (2) to channel through- and interborough traffic away from the city centre; and (3) to create thoroughfares for direct traffic between the centre of Warsaw and the new strip of outlying districts. Accordingly, the main arteries in the city centre, Marszalkowska and Swietokrzyska streets, were widened and extended in length, areas for future thoroughfares and parking spaces were marked out, and all bridges which had been blown up in 1944 were rebuilt.

The reconstruction of the ruined city also provided an opportunity to expand the areas of greenery. The old parks in the city centre, the Saxon Garden and Lazienki, were restored to their former appearance, while the old industrial part of the Powisle district by the river was turned into an expansive complex of parks and gardens. An important achievement was the preservation of the so-called Mokotow Fields (formerly an airstrip and a racecourse) bordering the city centre, which were turned into a vast park with the buildings of the National Library in its centre and various branches of Warsaw's higher education institutions along its edges. Along the old high river bank in the centre a three-kilometre-long green belt was laid out. It includes old and new parks joined together by a system of footbridges built over busy thoroughfares.

Important elements in the structure of every town are those sites that constitute a record of its past, such as monuments and commemorative plaques. The treatment of such sites received special attention during reconstruction. In a city like Warsaw, virtually razed to the ground and reconstructed, many of these places conjure up memories of the years of war and Occupation. They are referred to as places of 'national remembrance', and they perform a particularly significant function in shaping the city's symbolic space and the consciousness of its inhabitants. They include, for example, the Tomb of the Unknown Soldier in the only preserved fragment of the classicist colonnade of the no-longer-existing Saxon palace; the Monument to the Heroes of the Ghetto; 220 commemorative tablets on the sites of public executions carried out by the Nazis; the cemetery of soldiers fallen during the Warsaw Uprising, where each year on 1 August, the anniversary of the outbreak of the Warsaw Uprising, crowds of Varsovians gather to lay flowers and light candles; the memorial tree with plaques bearing the names of those who were murdered in the Pawiak prison; fragments of the Ghetto wall; and traces of bullets on the walls of old houses.

Many places and symbols of remembrance are still under construction, such as the Museum of the Warsaw Uprising in the preserved ruins of the National Bank, once an insurgent outpost; the Monument to the heroes of the Warsaw Uprising in Krasinski Square, where heavy fighting went on in 1944; and the Monument Wall on the site of 'Umschlagplatz', where in 1942 the Nazis herded 320 000 Jews from the Warsaw Ghetto to dispatch them to the extermination camp of Treblinka.

## SUCCESSES AND FAILURES

More than forty years have passed since the war, and I would argue that, on balance, there were more successes than failures in the rebuilding of the city. The most notable successes include: (1) the birth of a plan for reconstruction and development of the city and its agglomeration which, in so far as its basic assumptions were concerned, has stood the test of time, has made it possible to introduce indispensable modifications in the urban structure, and continues to provide the main guidelines for further growth; (2) the rebuilding and, in many instances, complete reconstruction of historic districts and their incorporation into the structure of a modern city; (3) efficient implementation of complex tasks connected with the reconstruction effort, conducted under difficult technical and economic conditions; (4) restoration and expansion of public parks and gardens that form the basic element of the city's ecological system; and (5) creation and consolidation of strong emotional links of the inhabitants with their city, their 'place on earth'.

And what about the failures? When one is trying primarily to evaluate the years of reconstruction, these seem to boil down to one basic question: Could more have been accomplished? It would have been much easier to put the railway lines underground using an open-excavation method amidst the ruins than to resort to costly and difficult tunnelling, as is necessary today. An expanded system of shopping facilities could have been built. A considerably greater number of parking spaces could have been constructed in the city centre.

The list could go on, but we should compare these omissions with some of the failures of present-day urban policy: the insufficient quantity and bad quality of new housing, which to many young families means having no home of their own for many years; insufficient efforts and funds for preserving and improving existing housing; the threat to the ecological system from the contamination of the air, water and vegetation; the absence of efforts to adapt various town facilities to the needs of handicapped people. All these problems, listed here by way of example, rarely have their origins in the errors committed in the postwar period. Severe criticism of current shortcomings, moreover, must not obscure the unquestionable achievements in the years of reconstruction, and those years can and should be a source of optimism for the future.

**Notes**
1. Archives of the 'District Warschau'.
2. Ibid.
3. Ibid.
4. Ibid.
5. Ibid.
6. The following quotations are from *Warszawa jej dzieje i kultura* (*Warsaw: Its History and Culture*) (Arkady, 1980).

7.   Lewis Mumford, 'Warsaw Lives Again' (1946).
8.   *Skarpa Warszawka (The Warsaw Escarpment)*, 1946.
9.   Ibid.
10.  *Rocznik Warskawski (Warsaw Yearbook)*, vol. 7 (Warsaw, 1966).
11.  Ten days prior to this date, with tears in our eyes, we had assisted
     with the re-erection of King Sigismund's III monument, destroyed by
     Nazis during the Warsaw Uprising.
12.  Adolf Ciborowski, *Warsaw: A City Destroyed and Rebuilt* (Warsaw,
     1964).
13.  The architects were J. Knothe, J. Sigalin, Z. Stepinski and the author.

# 7 People, Politics and Planning: the Reconstruction of Coventry's City Centre, 1940–53

## TONY MASON AND NICK TIRATSOO

In November 1940 much of central Coventry was destroyed in a large-scale German air attack.[1] Subsequently, the city's Labour Council vigorously campaigned for a certain type of reconstruction, one that would provide the focal point for their wider vision of a new kind of socialist society. The following paragraphs trace the evolution of this aspect of local authority thinking from the moment of the blitz in 1940 to the initial phase of actual rebuilding some ten years later. The aim is to highlight the relationships between the City Council, its local electorate and the national administration in London. How and why did the City Council opt for one particular type of central reconstruction and to what extent did decisions over such questions reflect the wishes and aspirations of local people? On the other hand, how did government ministers and civil servants react to an avowedly socialist local Council's plans, and was the climate of opinion different after Labour replaced the Coalition at Westminster as the war ended in 1945?[2]

In order to begin to unravel the answers to such questions, it will be necessary briefly to recapitulate certain aspects of the local scene in the years immediately before Labour's capture of city power in 1937. For the specific nature of Labour politics in Coventry during the 1940s, it seems clear, was shaped as much by a particular set of urban problems experienced in the preceding decades as by the canons of a broader ideology.

In the 1920s and 1930s, as is well known, Coventry's population grew at an exceptional rate, so that the total in 1939 – 224 000 – was 75 per cent up on the 1921 figure. Much of this growth was due to immigration, prompted by the attractions of the city's buoyant motor and general engineering sectors. Yet if Coventry was thus increasingly very proletarian in terms of its class structure, it was also abnormally deficient in terms of some of the kinds of working-class organisation found elsewhere. For the specific character of local industries, the historic weakness of the Left and the impact of migration all combined to

94

weaken the appeal of union membership and radical politics. Instead, the city developed something of a 'Klondike' atmosphere, with low rates of overcrowding and high rates of popular house-ownership and personal consumption. The rearmament boom reinforced these trends and drew more away from the insecurities of unemployment and ill-health. The city thus became remarked upon for its affluent and self-confident working class, both used to, and desiring more of, a widening range of comforts.

In contrast to this growing private prosperity, the civic amenities of the city were unusually deficient. Physically, Coventry had simply grown too fast, so that a centre still based on mediaeval scale and plan was now required to satisfy a whole range of modern needs. Shopping streets were thus congested by traffic and increasingly dangerous for pedestrians. At the same time, there were fewer and fewer open spaces since land was simply too valuable to leave undeveloped. Yet new building was as likely to be for industrial use as any other, so that the city suffered not only from poor zoning (with factories and houses mixed together in the centre) but also from a relative dearth of shops. Finally, and for the same reasons, there were insufficient Council facilities, symbolised by the gross overcrowding in the local authority's own offices.

These problems prompted considerable local comment and a growing concern, from the mid-1930s, with reform. The Tory–Liberal Coalition, which had dominated Coventry politics for nearly a decade, attempted to answer its critics by using existing planning legislation, but this approach proved inadequate both in terms of scope and speed. Labour, on the other hand, as the party of opposition, was untainted by these failures and so could credibly present itself as the agent of action and efficiency. Helped by good organisation and the lassitude of its opponents, this strategy finally paid off at the local elections of 1937. If the radical content of the party's campaign was fairly modest, its emphasis on the need for a more efficiently planned and run city was emphatic. The aim was certainly not to soak the better off but, within a rate stabilisation policy, to use resources to better ends and thus reverse the worrying trends of recent years. In the event, just enough were convinced, and Labour scraped home with 51 per cent of a 47 per cent turn-out.

In office, the Labour Party rapidly began to construct an agenda for reform, and its first five-year Capital Works Programme promised among other things new streets and more open spaces. Attention was given to the problem of how these developments could be carried out coherently and after some debate it was decided, during 1938, that in future all architectural work would be handled by a newly created department headed by a City Architect.

The first official appointed to this post, Donald Gibson, perhaps appeared an unlikely choice, since he was both young and relatively inexperienced. Yet in terms of outlook, Gibson's views certainly had much in common with those of his new employers. For example, his experience at the Liverpool University School of Architecture had clearly led him, if not to out and out modernism, at least to a strong belief that good architecture was desirable not just in terms of aesthetic improvement but also in terms of social reform. At the same time, he also vigorously believed in the need for, and efficacy of, trained experts who could operate free from bureaucratic niceties, views which again closely matched those prevalent among key local Labour activists.

To put these ideas into practice, Gibson was allowed to form a small department. Indicatively, he began by recruiting a number of more self-consciously radical architects, so that the Association of Architects, Surveyors and Technical Assistants soon had a strong Coventry presence. With its establishment settled, the department then began to consider the skeleton of the city, and the particular form a new civic centre should take.

But Gibson also clearly recognised the value of public relations work and so, spurred on by press debate and current developments in the city centre (particularly a 'classical style' bank and a mock-Tudor office building), a campaign was launched to spread town planning ideals. Efforts were made to involve members of the Council (for example, by distributing among them – on its publication in 1940 – copies of Lewis Mumford's *The Culture of Cities*) and also interest and educate the general public through lectures and an exhibition on the 'Coventry of Tomorrow'. This latter event, held over a week in May 1940, was significant, not only because of its impact (it was seen by 5000 people, including nearly all the senior school children in the city) but also because of its decidedly modernist content (which sprang, in part, from the heavy involvement of the Modern Architecture Research Group).

As the impact of the war began to bite, this work was somewhat curtailed, and Gibson found his department weakened both by the call-up and by the need for ARP planning. Then, quite suddenly, priorities changed again, as Coventry found itself on the receiving end of the first major Luftwaffe offensive against a provincial British city. In all, the raid of 14/15 November affected 50 000 of the city's 75 000 rated properties, but the impact was especially serious in the central core, 90 per cent of the which was irreparably damaged. More than one observer, visiting the centre in the next few days, was reminded of Ypres in the First World War.

At first, the Council's response to this disaster was necessarily framed in terms of crisis control. But as the immediate dangers receded, attention was focused on the question of how damage should be repaired. Gibson was characteristically quick to point out the potential:

> many citizens had despaired of the possibility of having a dignified and fitting city centre. High land values, the delays involved by town planning legislation, together with a lack of plan for the central area, made it seem impossible. Now, in a night, all this was changed . . . like a forest fire the present evil might bring forth greater riches and beauty.[3]

The diffusion of this kind of messianic zeal clearly influenced the Council, and prompted the establishment of a City Redevelopment Committee ('to secure . . . worthy re-planning and re-development') in December 1940. As a first step, Gibson and Ford (the City Engineer) were asked to prepare a new central area plan while the Town Clerk was to approach the government about the possibility of special enabling legislation.

This latter initiative led to a deputation from Coventry being invited to meet Sir John Reith, the recently appointed Minister of Works. Here the city's representatives were urged to adopt a broad outlook on the situation and not aim merely at conservative schemes of reconstruction. Furthermore, Reith strongly hinted that finance would not be a problem, since the government was coming to the view that individual councils could not, and indeed should not, bear the burden of blitz repair. Finally, the Minister made known his intention to regard Coventry as one of a few test cases, which would inform his future actions regarding legislation. To meet this requirement, he promised to send an inspector to the city to identify possible problems.

This interview, together with the inspector's subsequent appearance in Coventry, convinced the Council that swift action was essential, and pressure was applied to Gibson and Ford to complete their plan. However, the two officials could not agree

about basic principles – Ford wanted limited new building and the
retention of the existing road pattern, against Gibson's wholesale
redevelopment – and so the Council was eventually asked to choose
between competing schemes. On 25 February 1941 a large majority
agreed with the Redevelopment Committee's recommendation that
the City Architect's plan be endorsed.

The inspiration behind Gibson's plan came from a number
of different sources. Mumford's *The Culture of Cities*, already
mentioned, had certainly impressed the Architect's Department,
no doubt partly because of its apocalyptic tone and anti-Fascist
rhetoric, but also because of its cogent argument that future reform
would have to be sweeping in character and centrally related to
social need. Le Corbusier's *The City of Tomorrow* was apparently
'the main theoretical source',[4] though the works of a number of
British architects and town planners, such as Abercrombie and Alker
Tripp, may have exerted a considerable influence here too. Gibson
himself, more practitioner than ideologue, wished to copy some of
the successful features of locations he was familiar with – for example,
Chester's historic two-level shopping rows. Above all, he was keen
to respect Thomas Sharp's prognosis that good town planning would
succeed or fail on the basis of what the buildings looked like – the
third dimension.

The plan presented to the Council began by emphasising the
scale of the choice that faced the city and the national repercussions
of local decision-making:

> Now is the opportunity, and [sic] opportunity which may never
> recur, to build a city designed for the future health, amenity and
> convenience of the citizens. . . . The city is being made a test case,
> and its solutions will form a guide to the other cities which have
> been similarly devastated.[5]

Subsequent paragraphs then outlined a number of key elements
in the planned reconstruction. The circumference of the new
central area was to be marked by a simple ring road system,
designed both to ease traffic flows and facilitate access to a public
transport terminal. Within this boundary, Gibson proposed a number
of discrete zones based on function: houses in neighbourhood units,
a civic centre (grouping together all the different local and national
government operations), a light industrial area. Particular emphasis
was placed on the shopping zone, which the City Architect saw as a

series of traffic-free arcades, with galleries overlooking the central precincts.

The originality of this scheme lay not so much in any of the discrete elements (indeed some were common to other ameliorative proposals) but rather with the way in which they were combined. Gibson began from the user, grouping sets of functions together for safety and convenience. The different zones were then co-ordinated in order to frame existing natural or architectural features and thereby provide a number of aesthetically pleasing vistas, for example, the highlighting of the Cathedral. This gave the Architect's proposals a distinct feel and marked them off from other schemes (notably Ford's) which *started* from the remnants of the historic city.

Gibson's ideas, as a perceptive critic in *Reynolds News* suggested, were not so much a plan as an 'enthusiasm'.[6] Because of this, early judgements on them tended to be somewhat polarised. In Coventry, as has been indicated, the Council were heavily in favour of their Architect's scheme, with opposition being confined to one or two Tories and a maverick, if vocal, Labour alderman. The unifying thread here, expressed by both political parties, was a sense of civic destiny. As one self-confessed 'bloated capitalist' put it in the debate on the plan:

> Coventry has faced crises and difficulties previously. . . . We have surmounted obstacles in the past, and if we are really to conquer the despicable tyrant who has caused us all this damage we must erect a monument that will be a blessing in disguise.[7]

Outside the Council Chamber city views were more diverse. Careful enquiry revealed that public opinion in general was strongly in favour of a bold scheme of redevelopment. Nevertheless, observers noted a definite cleavage between immigrants and a Coventry-born, more traditional, minority. Much of the latter's discontent was channelled through the professional associations with, for example, all those canvassed by Reith's inspector declaring some degree of reservation. Time and again criticism focused on Gibson's (and the Council's) very sketchy estimates of cost. As a prominent member of the Warwickshire Law Society put it: 'The economic point is a very important one on this job. It is very nice to be idealistic, but to carry it out, if it is to be done on an economic basis, it has to be attractive to the people who are going to put their money down.'[8]

This refrain was fairly quickly taken up by the conservative *Coventry Standard*.

At a national level there was also divergence of opinion. The specialist architectural press generally reacted positively, agreeing that the scheme had considerable intrinsic merit. Left-leaning newspapers, such as the *Daily Herald*, the *News Chronicle*, and *Reynold News*, emphasised the social importance of the Gibson plan and depicted his vision as a model for the 'New Britain'. Centre and right-wing coverage was more muted, with the exception of Sir Ernest Benn's *Truth*, which called the scheme 'the first notable product of all the Priestley and other nonsense about the millennium after the war'.[9]

In the four years after the Council's adoption of the Gibson plan, a range of interests and agencies sought either to modify or confirm the details of the scheme. To some, the city's 'martyrdom' and subsequent resolution to rebuild with vision seemed to symbolise a new hope for the postwar world. As the direct threat to British cities receded, however, so government concerns with reconstruction in general tended to diminish. Indeed, after the creation of the Ministry of Town and Country Planning in 1943, Coventry found itself at the centre of a concerted and forceful campaign aimed at undermining confidence in its objectives. Ironically, if this intervention failed, it did so on the basis of the enthusiasm and cohesiveness engendered during the earlier phase.

The pressures which tended to confirm Coventry Council in its own judgements about reconstruction were of various kinds. National (and international) media attention in the immediate aftermath of the blitz certainly reinforced the view that Coventry was indeed a special case, an impression that gained further credence from the numerous references that were made to the city in official or quasi-official propaganda. Subsequently, Coventry found itself at the centre of complimentary discourses celebrating planning and anticipating the shape of an improved postwar world. Frequent discussion of the plan on the BBC, again in some official pronouncements, and in the voluminous popular pamphlet literature of the war years, created the idea that Coventry's example was very much one that all should follow.

More specific judgements tended to confirm this picture. There was, for example, growing endorsement among architects for some of Gibson's central ides. More significantly, King George VI himself was apparently a supporter, as he disclosed during a brief visit to Coventry in early 1942:

he was particularly satisfied at finding incorporated in the plans for the new Coventry an idea for arranging central shopping facilities under the arcading principle. . . . the King . . . expressed the opinion that in all schemes of re-planning towns and cities which had been badly bombed, the future amenities for the citizens were of supreme importance. The King expressed the hope that his visit . . . would help to make such plans materialize.[10]

In the world of hard government policy and civil servant machination, however, opinion was much less sympathetic to the thrust of Coventry's plans. Initial official evaluations – for example, the report of H. R. Wardill, Reith's inspector – were fairly non-committal. However, after Reith's dismissal from the cabinet in February 1942, attitudes began to harden. Over the next two years, in fact, pressure for modification was rarely relaxed, so that the city found itself subject to almost endless exhortation and investigation, orchestrated from the new Ministry, and using such channels as the Advisory Panel of experts on blitz reconstruction.

Two aspects of the problem particularly concerned Whitehall. Firstly, civil servants noted with shock that the financial side of the plan had barely been considered. Gibson's original formulation contained only vague references to costs, while subsequent Council statements, encouraged both by Reith's early advice and the Uthwatt recommendations on compensation and betterment of September 1942, simply repeated the local conviction that the problem should be solved by national legislation. Yet when the City Treasurer was finally persuaded by Advisory Panel pressure to make a full financial evaluation, Coventry's plan was revealed as being unusually expensive, largely because of the scale of the civic facilities proposed. At the same time, the amount of 'dead' land (parks and other open spaces) in the scheme seemed to undermine the possibility of adequate future return.

In parallel with these financial considerations, Ministry officials were also struck by the way in which certain interests in Coventry were voicing more open criticism of the Gibson scheme. Some city officials – the Town Clerk and the City Treasurer, in particular – made little attempt to hide their lack of confidence in what was proposed. The Chamber of Commerce, too, had begun to express more public opposition, recording, for example, that it was totally opposed to the precinct idea.

However, in their dealings with the city, the civil servants were also conscious of a number of potential political pitfalls. There was some general public concern about the way the national government was moving on town planning legislation anyway, and the terms of the new Act proposed in June 1944 further disappointed those who had expected radical change. In Coventry, this kind of unease was all the greater because of the city's predicament, and considerable antipathy towards the government continued to lurk just beneath the surface of public opinion. The Ministry was worried that too much of the wrong sort of pressure on the Council – for instance, against the civic centre *per se* – would provoke a backlash. It was advised that in any trial of strength the Council might receive backing from two-thirds of the local electorate.

Given these constraints, any vaguely political criticism of the Coventry plan became unacceptably risky. The Ministry therefore decided to concentrate on a range of technical points – the need for an adequate survey of future user requirements, for example – and thereby persuade the Council that it needed the advice of expert, 'responsible' interests. At the same time, every effort would be made to support disillusioned local officials and court any town councillors who might be susceptible to influence.

However, if the Ministry initially had high hopes for this kind of approach, the period of optimism was not to last. For the Coventry Council proved adept at playing the Westminster game, and enquiries on the technical points were either shrugged off or answered by counter-questions which frequently embarrassed the civil servants concerned. At the same time, hopes of developing local pressure through the Chamber of Commerce also quickly faded: meetings between that organisation and Coventry's administrators achieved little, while the Chamber's long-awaited alternative on the shopping centre turned out in the end to be, in the Town Clerk's words, 'just as much "a prairie plan" as was the City Council's'.[11] The Ministry therefore approached the winter of 1944 on a note of frustration as far as Coventry was concerned; despite considerable effort it had been unable to make any real breach in the Council's plans.

The Town and Country Planning Act of November 1944 at first seemed to promise the possibility of resolving this deadlock. Councils were now offered some guidance as to their legal powers and a possible agenda to follow in the prosecution of reconstruction schemes. But while this degree of clarification was generally welcomed, local authorities were much less impressed by the financial provisions of the new legislation. In fact, a number clearly decided to continue a policy of prevarication on certain key issues, in the hope that a return to electoral politics at the end of the war might lead to a more benevolent set of terms. In Coventry, the Council's ability to pursue this strategy was founded upon its close identification with popular reconstruction enthusiasms.

One clear implication of the 1944 Act was that progress on planning schemes would not be officially recognised until consultations with local interest groups had been adequately pursued. Consequently, over the course of 1945 the tone of negotiations between Coventry Council and the Chamber of Commerce became very much more constructive, with both sides plainly interested in compromise. Attention was once again focused on the precinct idea and its various merits and disadvantages. The Council, following Gibson, stressed safety and convenience. The Chamber, on the other hand, emphasised the importance of custom and practice in shopping patterns, and argued for the necessity of vehicular access. In the end both views were incorporated into a modified scheme: one axis of the proposed cruciform shopping precinct would be constructed as a normal road, while the other would remain for pedestrians only.

If local negotiations thus proceeded fairly smoothly, relations between city and Ministry continued much as before, with the emphasis on bluff and manoeuvre. Government officials were deeply dissatisfied with the lack of progress, since they feared bad publicity if Coventry, still in the national eye, was seen to be less advanced in its reconstruction plans than other blitzed cities. And they also could not ignore the widespread local enthusiasm for reconstruction, nor the success of various organised talks, films and displays on planning. In this situation there seemed to be no other choice but to continue with the policy of technical criticism and discussion over detail. By mid-1945, then, Ministry officials were coming to the view that no major progress would be likely until the political uncertainty accompanying the cessation of hostilities was fully resolved.

Over the following months, a number of developments interacted to strengthen the position of the City Council. The election of a Labour government at Westminster seemed to auger well for town planning in general, since the Labour Party – guided by the Barlow, Uthwatt and Scott Reports – was ostensibly more committed to an interventionist approach than the Conservatives. Hopes were raised further when the new Minister, Silkin, let it be known that he wished to expedite the rebuilding of the blitzed cities. In Coventry, meanwhile, reconstruction enthusiasm had reached new levels, with 57 500 visitors, for example, attending a municipally organised 'Coventry of the Future' exhibition over a two-week period during October. Further confirmation of the popular mood came at the local elections towards the end of the year, when Labour was returned with an increased majority.

In these circumstances, confidence about Coventry's city centre plan increased, and the Council began a more serious consideration of how best it could proceed under the 1944 Planning Act's machinery. The objective was to move along a prescribed path, involving official scrutiny and a public enquiry, to obtain a Ministerial Declaratory Order – the measure which would allow the Council the right of compulsory purchase within a given area. Nevertheless, on close examination, it was by no means clear in the statute what kind of land could or could not be permissively included in any specific proposal, and so local opinion was somewhat divided about optimal boundaries. Should the Council endorse the 1941 scheme (basically the city centre and the run-down Spon Street neighbourhood) or should it press for a much larger area, including further central slums, as some radicals suggested?

A number of factors counselled caution here. The first, perhaps surprisingly, was the complexion of the local political situation. Labour was no doubt gratified with the 1945 election results, but activists also recognised that the Party's success probably had most to do with its commitments on welfare and housing, issues that had been prominent during the election campaign. Attitudes toward the plan for the city centre were harder to gauge. While the Gibson plan no doubt did have a strong degree of bipartisan support, there were also continuing undercurrents of scepticism about its real viability. Central redevelopment could therefore no longer be regarded as the simple popular talisman that it had been in 1940–1.

The Council had also to take account of a whole number of procedural and logistical uncertainties about its precise role in reconstruction. There was, for example, the problem of the forty manufacturing enterprises owning sites within the central area. These would have to be relocated if the plan was to succeed, but it was by no means clear how this process would be financed, nor was it even certain that the government would sanction industrial relocation on surrounding 'greenfield' sites, since the official belief tended to be that the city was already too large.

A related problem concerned the fate of the 150-odd firms that had had shops in the central area before the blitz: while the Council publicly recognised its moral responsibility to include these retailers in any new development, few were confident about how easily this pledge could, in fact, be realised. Given the tangle of leaseholds and the very different sizes of undertaking that were involved, it was legitimate to suppose that hardly any firms would be even able to consider simply rebuilding their own premises.

In fact, it was this latter problem above any other that taxed the local authority most. The Council had never really explicitly decided who would be responsible for redevelopment, but an implicit assumption, encouraged by Gibson, was that overall control could not be left to market forces, since private developers appeared unlikely to be able to guarantee aesthetic co-ordination. Yet the 1944 Act was, once again, ultimately rather unclear as to how much redevelopment a Council could undertake itself. Furthermore, even if a local authority was allowed to play a major role, it would still have to traverse the so-called 'dead period' – the years of rebuilding when considerable outgoings (on servicing reconstruction loans) might substantially exceed income from a fairly restricted revenue base. Coventry was not disadvantageously placed here since the concentrated nature of the damage at the centre and the general affluence of the local populace had allowed the total rateable value of the city to remain relatively buoyant. But even allowing for this, the situation was hardly encouraging, since the 1944 Act implied that central government grants (equal to charges on the cost of purchase and clearance) would only normally run for two years. The Council began, therefore, to glimpse the terms of a rather unwelcome choice: they might either have to opt for a smaller, cheaper, more revenue-orientated scheme or call in private capital and thereby jeopardise the aesthetic and co-ordinated nature of the development.

In the end, the Council concluded that, given these conditions, it would be unwise to move too fast too quickly and more prudent to stick with existing plans, in the hope that lobbying from all the blitzed authorities would eventually persuade the Labour government to change the overall legislative framework. The 452-acre 'Area of Extensive War Damage No. 1' submitted for the Minister's scrutiny in the application of April 1946 therefore closely followed the original configuration outlined by Gibson five years earlier.

At first, things looked as if they would move very much in Coventry's favour with this application. The Minister, for example, underlined his desire for progress in the city, and assured Council

representatives that his interpretations of the 1944 Act's rather confusing statutes would be as liberal as possible. The public enquiry,
held in Coventry during the summer of 1946, also went well. All
told, 259 objections were raised to the scheme, representing 1000
of the probable 10 000 interests in the area. The great majority of
objections (177) were in 'common form' and dealt with precise legal
interpretations of the 1944 Act. The substantive criticism of the
planning scheme as such (limited to six objections) tended to be
based on more conservative aesthetic sensibilities. Anti-modernism
was given a clever ideological twist by one 'planning expert', who
argued that Gibson's plan was 'diabolically German and Fascist in
character'. But the prescription that he offered turned out to be
rather more prosaic: 'If the matter were put to someone like Sir
Giles Scott, he would take up the atmosphere of Coventry itself and
while he would interpret it on modern lines, it would be very different
from what you have there [that is, Gibson's scheme].'[12] In fact, the
opposition faded markedly as the enquiry proceeded, partly because
of the convincing performances of the Council's officials, and partly
because of the strong degree of overall public support for the scheme.
The *Standard*, indeed, noted a definite change of heart amongst some
erstwhile objectors: 'However aggrieved some of the businessmen in
the centre of the city feel, they realize that the bombing of the city
has made new planning inevitable. Moreover, many of them know
that in a problem of such magnitude, private interests are bound
to be affected.'[13] The enquiry therefore ended on a high note for
the Council, in that public acceptance of its plan 'uninformed as to
detail . . . but nevertheless weighty', was now incontrovertible.[14]

Within the Ministry of Town and Country Planning, opinion
remained very much less favourable. Officials continued to reiter-
ate their general belief that 'Lord Reith's "plan boldly" . . . [had]
been worked to death in Coventry';[15] and that the need over the
coming years was, rather, for a major injection of realism. To
this end, Coventry's submission was handed to a Reconstruction
Area Technical Examination Committee for detailed assessment.
The results were predictably damning. The Committee began by
noting the application's lack of substance – it was 'little more than
a description' which did not explain either the need to acquire the
area or the principles upon which reconstruction was to be based.
Following on from this were a series of detailed criticisms, involving
the alignment of the ring road, the layout of the shopping centre (too
many big units), the provision of office space (too much), and the

industrial and residential zones (inappropriate for an inner area). The proposals for the civic centre once again received especially withering comment. The Committee concluded that their examination could only suggest 'a considerable reduction in the area of land enclosed by the inner ring road'. The application ought therefore to be granted, but redevelopment should be on a reduced scale.[16]

It is not clear how far this report influenced the Minister. But more pragmatic reasoning was certainly leading him in a similar direction, since his fairly liberal judgement over an application by Plymouth under the 1944 Act had been successfully challenged in the King's Bench Court. In the end, therefore, the Declaratory Order for Coventry, legalised in July 1947, covered only about 280 acres of the central core. The aim, it seems, was to ensure that the first stages of reconstruction would be exclusively concerned with shops and businesses, in order to maximise possible financial returns to the local authority.

Over the following months, the Council began to consider how best to pursue development in the Declaratory Order area. One encouraging factor was the new Town and Country Planning Act, which passed into law at the end of 1947, for the administration now found itself provided with wider powers to initiate direct development and a more liberal grant environment than had existed previously. Hopes rose further when the city managed, in the face of civil service opposition, to lay out and plant a garden in the square at the top of the precinct, with bulbs presented as a gift by the Dutch people. Symbolically, it was felt, this marked a real turning point, since the city could not now be turned back from its plan.

Yet against this, the Council was also faced, once again, with some profound difficulties. Its central problem now stemmed from the statutory mechanism of land acquisition. If the 1947 Act had generally tilted the balance in favour of local authorities, it had not altered the principle of piecemeal purchase through a series of compulsory orders. Consequently, the possibility of 'betterment' – land increasing in price because of development around it – remained very real. A Council might therefore find itself having to find larger and larger sums in order to service the kind of loans necessary for a programme of rolling reconstruction.

This problem was all the more serious in Coventry because the Council was now beginning to feel somewhat threatened by a wider set of budgetary constraints. Labour had always stressed its commitment to financial orthodoxy anyway, but in the postwar years this was buttressed by a belief that rates were a key election issue. But if the Council's revenue-raising capabilities appeared inelastic, expenditure on welfare provision would be likely to rise steeply, as the municipal programmes for houses and schools began to be realised. The room for financial manoeuvre over central reconstruction therefore seemed to be narrowing. Feelings of vulnerability here were further magnified by a rather lacklustre (if not disastrous) performance at the 1947 local elections.

In these circumstances, the Council decided once again on a somewhat cautious approach. The first phase of reconstruction was to involve five blocks in the precinct – a hotel and four large stores with inset shops. In each case, the largest prospective tenant was to act as developer, on the understanding that they would then be offered ground leases by the Council. Overall control of the aesthetic side – design, elevations and materials – was to remain with the City Architect. As an extra safeguard, the Council reserved the power to act as a developer in its own right, if the circumstances were held to warrant it.

The building phase began with a burst of optimism. Logistics were obviously a worry given the general conditions of shortage in the country, but the Council was reassured when its plan to complete the five blocks over a three-year programme from 1 January 1949 was judged 'reasonable' by the regional representatives of the controlling Ministry. There also seemed to be no shortage of possible takers for precinct sites: according to the *Standard*, by the end of 1947 applications for shops had already exceeded the space likely to be available.

Such enthusiasm was, however, rather short-lived, as a whole range of problems – to do with each stage of the programme – began to make themselves felt. The initial phase of the project involved negotiations with suitable developers. Agreements were signed quite quickly in two cases, but for the remainder progress was uneven, with the Council having special trouble over the proposed Blocks 'B' and 'C'. The authority wanted the latter to be a hotel, but negotiations with a succession of local and national developers proved unsuccessful. This put some pressure on the Council, as it was recognised that the abandonment of the hotel idea, and the substitution of a shops-and-offices development, would lead to increased income. Nevertheless, civic pride finally proved more important than commercial gain, with the controlling committee of the Council concluding that 'the loss of potential income involved in the siting of the hotel in Broadgate would be offset by the asset to the City in having its major hotel in the ideal position offered by the site overlooking the Broadgate garden island'.[17] Eventually a lease was signed with Ravenseft (a London-based firm that had been active in other blitzed cities). In all, negotiations had dragged out over four years from Coventry's initial approach to a developer in 1949.

Block 'B' (opposite Block 'C' at the top of the precinct) provided similar kinds of problems. The central difficulty here was that development companies initially involved (principally Burtons) would not agree to build a connecting bridge over an adjoining street, which the Council insisted was part of the overall package. Again, the issue was commercial return versus civic requirement, since the bridge was adjudged locally to be 'an architectural feature of the first importance to the redevelopment scheme as a whole'. In the end, the need to get reconstruction started persuaded the council to act as developer itself, and a loan of nearly £400 000 was obtained from central government to cover building costs.

However, agreement to build and actual construction were very different things, as the Council soon found out. For Coventry was not exempt from national capital and raw material shortages, so that allocated quotas to the city were usually highly restrictive, despite special pleading. In addition, building operations were hampered by a purely local factor – the continuing flow of building labour into the engineering industry.

In the late 1940s and early 1950s, capital spending for all purposes each year was decided by central government through a series of allocations (initially of essential raw materials, later of actual monetary sums). In general, out-turns reflected immediate government priorities – exports and then rearmament. Some Ministers in both the Labour and Conservative administrations favoured reconstruction, but they were always in a minority. Consequently, actual expenditure in the eighteen blitzed cities remained paltry – £2.3 million for 1949 and 1950, £3.5 million for 1951 and £4.5 million for 1952, out of a total programme which annually ran into many thousand million pounds.

Coventry's strategy in this situation was to maximise what chances it had by advancing the argument that it should be viewed as a special case. Emphasis was placed on the scale of its predicament and the export potential of local industries. On occasion, this kind of lobbying paid off in that the city was apparently granted some measure of preferential treatment, but overall, results were disappointing. Thus, actual allocations never came near to satisfying annual applications. At the same time, constant pressure was unable to influence the somewhat unpredictable timing of official decisions over capital expenditure, so that local planners were constantly having to change their building schedules. The end product was akin to a juggling act, in which relatively small sums – £118 000 for 1949 and 1950, £317 500 for 1951 and £400 000 for 1952 – had to be used to their best advantage.

Coherent programming was made all the more difficult by the chronic shortage of building labour in Coventry. Numbers in this sector had in fact fallen postwar, from 5788 in August 1946 to 4249 in May 1949. Efforts to improve this position constantly floundered on the magnetic attractions of the engineering industry. In this situation, actual expenditure could easily undershoot even the allocated figure (as it did in 1951), to the embarrassment of all the parties involved. By 1952, the problem had become acute enough for the government to intervene, and arrangements were made for more building craftsmen to be brought into the area.

The three-year programme adopted in 1949 therefore proved to be completely unrealistic. In fact, over the scheduled period substantial building work was confined to only two sites – Block 'B' and a large department store. The scale of the problems encountered is illustrated by the fact that the first completion (the Council's Broadgate House) did not occur until March 1953, some four years after the start of construction.

The delay in rebuilding the city centre caused considerable comment among the local population. In the immediate aftermath of the war some experts had predicted a fairly quick reconstruction. But this kind of optimism was difficult to sustain in a climate of shortage and delay, and as a consequence there was a growing feeling of bewilderment and frustration. A *Standard* editorial of late 1949 could thus comment: 'The Shopping Precinct so glibly foretold two or three years ago is still a dream and so are the other central buildings. If it has taken . . . many months to produce a garden of flowers, how long may it take to build a real city centre?'[18] Coventry's predicament was all the more severe because it had continued to grow at some speed – its population increased by 15 per cent between mid-1945 and mid-1951 – largely because of the attractions of the engineering industry. Evidence of the strain on facilities was everywhere, but it was especially noticeable in a shopping area which had suffered so much damage.

Yet by and large, popular frustration did not rebound on the Council. In fact, Labour's performance in local elections, with the exception of the low point of 1947, remained fairly satisfactory, certainly sufficient to guarantee a continuing majority. More specifically, *direct* criticism of the city centre plan was very rare in this period, and usually only expressed by isolated figures on the political fringes. Significantly, even the conservative *Standard* continued to support the Gibson proposals. How was this consensus maintained?

One part of the answer to this question has to do with factors that inhibited criticism. At a general level, of course, reconstruction maintained its somewhat apolitical character, largely because Coventry's wartime image as a symbol of national regeneration and hope retained its potency in the media. But particular Council initiatives were also important in denying opponents grounds for valid criticism. For example, conservative financial policies meant that the rates were kept reasonably low, so that accusations of irresponsible spending were hard to sustain. At the same time, the Council was also clearly very careful in its sites allocation policy – time was spent in consulting local interests and satisfying their claims – so that criticism by the commercial lobby was minimal. Furthermore, the purchase of land on the city boundaries provided some leeway for any necessary resiting of industrial users. Finally, though a policy of allowing the construction of some temporary shops in the centre (Irst adopted in the war) could not assuage the popular pressure for new facilities, it did at least mean that Coventry was not, as many other blitzed towns were, just a collection of bomb sites and roadworks.

On the other hand, consensus was no doubt in part actively constructed by the Council. Labour had been conscious from an early date of the need to provide information – the need to keep 'the citizen . . . in day to day contact with the activities of the local authority' – and in the postwar years a variety of measures were introduced to aid communication. At a formal level, for example, initiatives included the appointment of a public relations officer, the maintenance of an Information Bureau in the town centre, and the publication and distribution of a broadsheet on civic affairs. At the same time, councillors were always ready to address any gathering about the plan and its application. In these ways, the camaraderie and civic pride engendered by the blitz were, to a certain extent, preserved into the peace.

Coventry's early efforts to rebuild its city centre were not therefore, as has been implied on occasion, simply shaped by central government. Limitations were no doubt imposed, with the aim of promoting commercial development. But there was no wholesale abandonment of the Gibson proposals, and in fact, what little building there was during this period tended to be as originally envisaged. The Council's ability to deflect pressure over such matters was to a large extent founded upon its continuing local popularity. Coventry people had little chance to shape rebuilding in any detail, but they seem to have clung more closely than might have been expected to the vision of 1941. In this sense, they, as much as Whitehall, provided the parameters for reconstruction.

**Notes**

1.  The argument and information in the following paragraphs has been compiled as part of a larger investigation comparing the post-1945 reconstruction of Coventry and Bochum. This project, which is financed by Stiftung Volkswagenwerk of West Germany, involves teams based at the University of Warwick (Coventry) and the University of the Ruhr (Bochum). We would like to thank Louise Campbell, Junichi Hasegawa and especially our colleague on the Coventry team – Bill Lancaster – for help with the material presented. We are also very grateful to Mr David Rimmer and his staff at the Coventry City Record Office for their help in locating Coventry Council records.

2.  The sources used to underpin what follows will be fully cited in the final joint report on the Bochum–Coventry project (to be completed in late 1988). Major series consulted include files in the Public Record Office (particularly BT 177/26; HLG 52/1509; HLG 71/13,600, 610, 617, 1287 and 1570; HLG 79/125–7 and 130–3; HLG 88/9; HLG 102/186; T 229/520–1) and the Coventry City Record Office (especially those collected by the Town Clerk); the minutes of the Coventry City Council and its Redevelopment (subsequently Planning and Redevelopment) Committee; and local and national newspapers and periodicals (including *Midland Daily Telegraph*, *Coventry Evening Telegraph*, *Coventry Standard*, *Architects' Journal*, *Architect and Building News*, and *Town Planning Review*).

3.  Reported in *Coventry Standard* (7 December 1940).

4.  P. Johnson-Marshall, 'Coventry: Test Case of Planning', *Official Architecture*, 21 (1958) p. 225.

5.  The Gibson plan is included as Appendix Five in HLG 79/130: report on 'Bombed Areas – Redevelopment of Coventry' by H. R. Wardill, 23 January 1941.

6.  Montagu Slater in *Reynolds News* (2 March 1941).

7.  Reported in *Midland Daily Telegraph* (26 February 1941).

8.   HLG 79/130: report by H. R. Wardill, 23 January 1941, Appendix 3 (iii) p. 8.
9.   *Truth* (7 March 1941).
10.  Reported in *Midland Daily Telegraph* (26 February 1941).
11.  This judgement is reported in HLG 79/131: letter from E. H. Doubleday to B. Gillie, 16 May 1944.
12.  Quoted in *Coventry Evening Telegraph* (28 June 1946).
13.  *Coventry Standard* (20 July 1946).
14.  *Coventry Evening Telegraph* (25 June 1946).
15.  HLG 79/127: letter from E. H. Doubleday to A. M. Jenkins, 1 October 1945.
16.  HLG 71/13: 'Technical Dept. Reconstruction Areas Technical Examination Committee. City . . . of Coventry . . . Report' [n.d., but 1946].
17.  Planning and Redevelopment Committee, 10 January 1951.
18.  *Coventry Standard* (1 October 1949).

# 8  Hamburg: the 'Catastrophe' of July 1943

## NIELS GUTSCHOW

### PRELIMINARY REMARKS[1]

After a long period of neglect, Fascist town planning in Germany has become a favourite topic of research scholars since the early 1980s. No doubt, this 'new discourse' adds to the manifold books and articles about every facet of Fascism. Saul Friedländer analysed this new discourse in his *Reflets du nazisme*[2] and pointed out a tendency to neutralise the terrible aspects of Fascism through a reinterpretation of symbols. Friedländer described how the fascination with death played a very important role in German Fascism. Death rituals were indeed the main focus of the Nazi party congresses, and the later redevelopment plans (*Neugestaltungspläne*) made the death memorials the very heart of the new centres. In summer 1944, Friedrich Tamms wanted to replace the high-rise party tower planned for Hamburg with a death memorial, and Hans Bernhard Reichow wanted to grow a grove there in memory of Germanic gods. Thus German Fascism formed its urban centres as stages for a religion of death. What might this have meant for the planning of the bombed urban centres? And how might our reflection on these plans change our perception of the reconstructed towns?

Let us first remember that planners favoured the reorganisation of the modern metropolis, which was considered to be the cancer in the social body. The new town of the future would be the town of a eugenically valuable race. The design and visual form of the town would reflect a sober society, with the Jews and the disabled annihilated, the heterodox in concentration camps, and the asocial in education and working camps. Adolf Hitler's speeches always reflected this intolerance of other people, and town planners proved willing tools in his hands.

After the destruction of Warsaw and Rotterdam, after thousands of towns and villages in Belgium, France, Holland and Norway were destroyed, Hitler signed a decree on town planning on 25 June 1940 – on the occasion of the capitulation of France. According to that decree, Berlin was to be prepared for the final victory.[3] The new

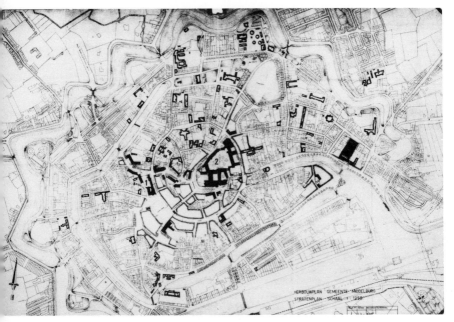

Middelburg: reconstruction plan, 10 December 1940

2 Middelburg: reconstruction plan for the town centre

3 Warsaw: the East–West thoroughfare, 1949

4 Warsaw: the Old Town Square, rebuilt 1953

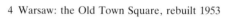

5  Warsaw: the Old Town Square, Piwna Street, 1944

6  Warsaw: the Old Town Square, Piwna Street, rebuilt 1953

7 Hamburg: the medieval core and the Cremon Island after the air raids in August 1943

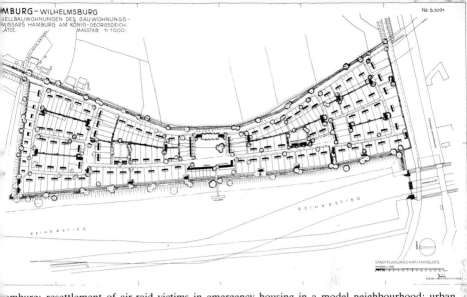

Hamburg: resettlement of air-raid victims in emergency housing in a model neighbourhood; urban design by the town planning office, landscape design by Heinz Paulus, Autumn 1943

Hamburg: design for so-called war-homes with two flats which were to be converted after the war into a single home; design by Hans-Dieter Gropp and Karl Friedrich Fischer for civil servants of the Sanitation Board, November 1943

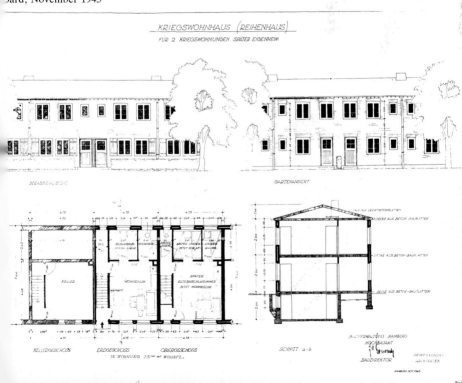

KRIEGSWOHNHAUS (REIHENHAUS)
FÜR 2 KRIEGSWOHNUNGEN SPÄTER EIGENHEIM

STRASSENANSICHT                    GARTENANSICHT

KELLERGESCHOSS     ERDGESCHOSS     OBERGESCHOSS
1E WOHNUNG 25.00 m² WOHNFL.

SCHNITT a-b

BAUVERWALTUNG HAMBURG
HOCHBAUAMT
BAUDIREKTOR

HAMBURG NOV 1943

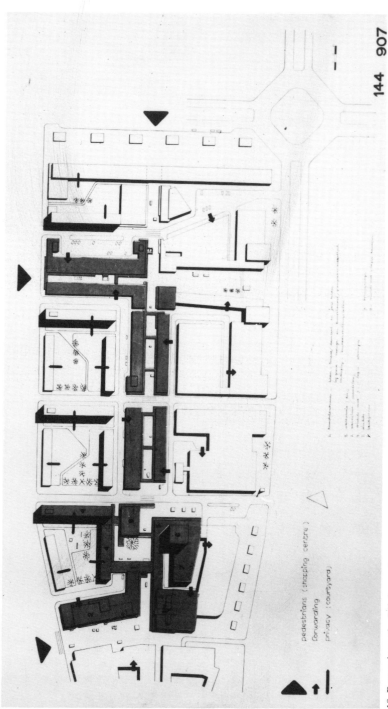

pedestrians (shopping centre)
forwarding
privacy (courtyard)

144    907

10 Rotterdam: the Lijnbaan plan

11 Rotterdam: the Lijnbaan under construction, with high-rise apartments and low shopping area

12 Budapest: Uri Street in 1945

13 Budapest: the 'White Dove' restaurant on the corner of Uri Street

Uri utcai kép

A háztömb földszinti alaprajza

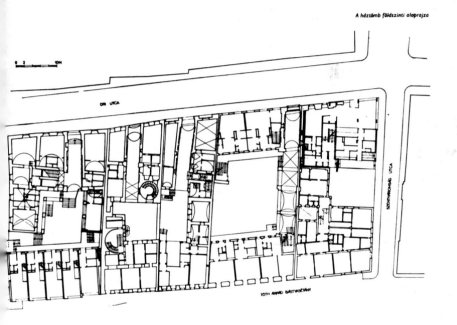

ORI UTCA

SZENTHÁROMSÁG UTCA

TOTH ARPAD BÁSTYASÉTÁNY

A Bástyasétány felöli homlokzatok

...lapest: Uri Street – façades from the Bástya Promenade, a block of buildings with new layout, and ...w of Uri Street's rebuilt façades

15 Dresden: river front, c.1930

16 Dresden: design for buildings on north side of new Altmarkt and the magistrale, competition entry by Schneider architects' collective (1952)

17 Dresden: Altmarkt – new buildings on the east side beside Kreuzkirche, begun 1953

18 Dresden: Altmarkt – façades of new buildings on the west side, begun 1953

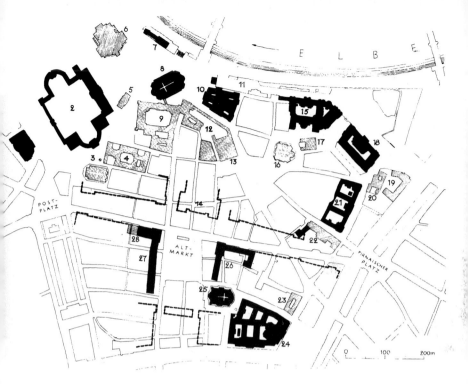

esden: outlines of new Altmarkt and magistrale (Ernst-Thälmann-Strasse) drawn over the street plan
fore destruction

esden: plan of city centre with completed buildings and projects (1959); architect: Hans Hunger of
e municipal building department

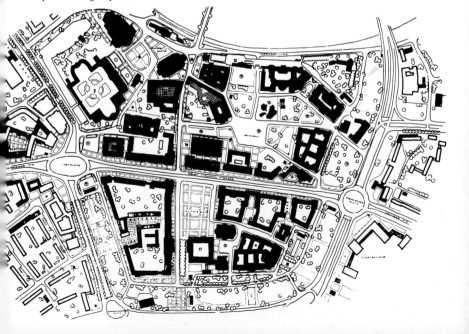

21 Dresden:
project of Zentraler
(Altmarkt) with tow
house (1953);
architect: Herbert Sch

22 Dresden: design for House of Socialist Culture; architect: Rudolf Lasch (1959/60)

Dresden: air-view of Frauenkirche and Neumarkt before destruction

Dresden: city centre in 1947 with ruins of Royal Palace and Catholic Court Church

25 Dresden: House of the Socialist Culture

planning (*Neugestaltungsplanung*) for regional urban centres was to serve as a stage for the display of the power of the Third Reich. At the same time, planners of the state housing corporation (*Reichsheimstättenamt*) began to talk of 'total planning'.[4] This not only implied the reconsideration of each and every detail of human environment, but in particular a plan for the colonisation of the East, which meant a drastic and cruel expulsion and annihilation of the Polish and Jewish population. Thus the new town planning was based on death. The death of the supposedly inferior was made the precondition of the creation of future settlements for the racially superior.

This development was to culminate in the total destruction of Moscow. The city was to be literally drowned in a large lake. The drowning symbolised the overcoming of an urban tradition and the annihilation of the cultural and intellectual centre of the enemy.

With German troops in sight of Moscow the fate of war changed; insiders realised that the war was already lost. It was not Moscow that was wiped out but the urban centres of Germany. When Lübeck was bombed in March 1942 planners did not realise the whole impact of the coming air raids. But after Cologne was destroyed by one thousand bombers in May 1942, Karl Strölin, president of the International Housing Association and mayor of Stuttgart, invited the architect Paul Schmitthenner to join him, and they rushed to the site. Schmitthenner was shocked and, as he wrote a year later, could not imagine any 'reconstruction'. For him the traditional metropolis was the symbol of misery which was to be replaced by new towns reflecting contemporary needs.[5] The destruction of Hamburg followed in July, of Kassel and Hannover in October 1943, to name only the earliest heavy losses. Several statements from Hamburg tell us how severe the experience was felt by planners and politicians alike. The historic tradition seemed to be gone and the city dead, while still alive were only the topographic traits of the landscape, which were considered the immortal soul, the *genius loci*, which would never die. Planning of the future city would have to reinterpret these 'valid' conditions before a kind of reincarnation was considered possible; the period of a generation seemed necessary to prepare the landscape to house a settlement again. In Hannover Karl Elkart had difficulties in fighting his opponents like Gerhard Graubner, who only weeks after the destruction of the town proposed in November 1943 to abandon the historic town altogether and rebuild a new one nearby.[6] High-rise air raid shelters would form the centre, with the main traffic arteries located underground. Dispersed settlements would be developed in a circle around the centre, invulnerable to air raids.

Let me draw the evidence together: planners' thoughts were strongly directed towards a new city starting from scratch either on the site of a city that had been obliterated or on virgin ground. The past was not considered at all revivable; the historic urban tradition was considered despicable. This did not imply a change of society or of the political system. No planner questioned the 'Inal victory' or a continuity of Fascist Germany in autumn 1943. The fate of the cities seemed to be death, and resurrection was considered a 'natural' follow-up for a eugenic society.

A new discourse on Fascist town planning in Germany will have to face this image of the death of the urban tradition as the precondition for planning for the future. Moreover, I do not want to minimalise the activities of planners by simply seeing them as members of a specialised caste who will serve any political system. We shall also have to drop the merry tale of the 'zero-hour' (*Stunde Null*) of May 1945, the supposed new beginning which has been used to shield the activities of the new democracy from critical scrutiny and to obfuscate the continuities with the past. A new discourse must acknowledge a continuity of persons and ideas and the all-pervading feeling of power which planners enjoyed 'after Compiègne'. Town planning suffered under this hubris for a generation. Indeed, planning in postwar Germany was considered to have a 'total' quality which would encompass all aspects of environment. 'Order' was always considered a special virtue and a quality of the built-up environment. Germans feel uncomfortable in an environment which is not neat and clean, and planning was considered essentially a tool to produce an ordered space. The economic crises of the 1970s have revealed the vulnerability of these planning ideals. A society without growth seems unable to adapt in terms of planning; time is needed to develop new procedures and define new qualities. Thus it may be said that the time 'after Compiègne' has come to an end. The power of planners has faded away; the city of the future is the present one!

A new discourse on Fascist planning should aim at revealing details which otherwise tend to fall into oblivion with the active wartime generation slowly dying out. More knowledge enables us to see planning and not just planners in an all-pervading continuity – a fact which would eventually lead towards an identification of authoritarian traits of postwar planning. In that way, Fascist planning becomes an aspect of our present practice. A neutralisation of the practises of an expert culture can only be avoided if we clearly point at the inherent inclination of planners to missionise the world in order to create a eugenic environment, be it in the name of the power of the Third Reich or of the commitment to soil. The following account of Hamburg tells about the destruction of a metropolis, which for a moment was felt like the extinction of an urban tradition. The dreams for a future world reveal that this extinction was a kind of presupposition of Fascist planning. The different reactions are summarised in brief.[7]

## THE 'CATASTROPHE': THE BOMBARDMENT OF HAMBURG, 24–9 JULY 1943

The office for the new planning (*Neugestaltung*) of Hamburg stopped working on the master plan in summer 1941. New tasks had to be taken over, dictated by an increasing aerial warfare. Since May of that year the planners had been put in charge of the 'Office of important warfare operations' (Amt für kriegswichtigen Einsatz). Commissioned operations included building shelter for those who lost their homes through air raids, replacing damaged space for industrial production and administration, repairing partly destroyed buildings and building air raid shelters according to the decree of 10 October 1940.

The most important task for the coming two years was the organisation of self-help and the repair programme for damaged buildings. Rudolf Hillebrecht was in charge of this programme, and in April 1943 he tried to mobilise the last available resources with the menacing motto 'better dead than slave'.[8] He already realised that eventually the race between the builders and the 'Tommy' would become threatening if not hopeless.[9] By the summer of 1943, a total of 7000 homes and flats were destroyed, but for the period from December 1942 until July 1943, more new flats were built and damaged ones repaired than were destroyed. But what the town had suffered before was nothing compared to what happened in July 1943. The experience of Cologne had already shown what the Allied forces could do once they won superiority in the air, but the destruction of Hamburg was unprecedented.

Within six days, between 24 and 29 July, 18 000 tons of bombs were dropped over Hamburg by 3000 airplanes: 40 383 houses were destroyed, 263 000 homes and flats were lost – 48 per cent of the whole stock (see Plate 7). By 3 March 1944, 36 662 casualties had been accounted for but 3072 persons were still missing.

There are numerous accounts of the destruction of Hamburg.[10] Besides the statistics, there are reports of artists and planners like the City Architect of Lübeck, Hans Pieper, who wrote about his visit to Hamburg on 10 August 1943:

> With a car we followed only the main streets through totally destroyed quarters of the town. As far as we could look into the side streets, we could only see destroyed houses, not small or mediaeval houses like in our town, but metropolitan houses, 6–7 storeys high! We had the feeling, that no building whatsoever had remained undestroyed. . . . The quarters of Hamm, Hammerbrook, Horn, and Borgfelde are blocked off; nobody is allowed to enter. It is planned to isolate these quarters altogether and not to start any activity of salvaging.[11]

Hamburg was hit in many areas. The mediaeval centre along the canals was wiped out, as were the western working-class quarters like Altona and Eimsbüttel, but the heaviest losses were suffered in the east of the city. The quarters between Barmbek and Hammerbrook became an urban desert, an area of blight. They were called the 'empty' or 'dead zones' in the literal sense of the word: it seemed the city had lost these areas forever. The impact of the air raids was felt in such a way that people no longer spoke of the 'terror attacks' of the enemy. Instead, everybody spoke of the 'catastrophe' as if it had been a natural calamity. The fire had, in fact, caused a hurricane which had consumed the oxygen over large areas. Even in open spaces where people had been seeking refuge, everybody died of suffocation. Neither the bombs nor the fire killed the people but the hurricane, whose force was experienced as a force of nature. The planners, who until July 1943 felt able to master every possible obstacle, were shocked and busy with organising shelter for the homeless. No thought was devoted to 'planning' a future city.

## LANDSCAPING THE URBAN ENVIRONMENT: THE PROPOSAL OF MAX KARL SCHWARZ, 31 AUGUST 1943

The first and most fundamental reaction to the disaster came from a landscape planner. Max Karl Schwarz from Worpswede, a well-known protagonist of biological-dynamic agriculture, sent a statement to the office for the *Neugestaltung* dated 31 August 1943, which was a follow-up on an earlier letter dated 23 August.[12] He wrote:

> In the beginning of any reconstruction work stands the demand to transform the destroyed areas into landscape. It develops through an afforestation, which provides the 'forest' as raw material. It is a widely known fact that the inherent quality of forest is animation. Only after the destroyed areas are animated through forest will they become a true urban landscape (*Stadtlandschaft*), that is, with houses and gardens.

Schwarz proposed to blast the foundations of all buildings, level the debris and cover it with mud from the nearby watercourses. More fill material and vegetable mould would be gained if all natural watercourses were widened. Schwarz obviously considered the metropolis dead and the animation of the soil a precondition for a future characterised by landscape in order to overcome the traditional urban environment. A year later, when the planning of the future city had already started, the first shock was overcome, the blighted areas were no longer considered polluted by the traces of death. Instead, Robert Heuson, who was in charge of planting techniques at the Office of Water and Energy in Berlin (*Der Beauftragte für PLanzungstechnik beim Generalinspektor für Wasser und Energie*) demanded a transformation of the destroyed areas into landscape for aesthetic and hygienic reasons. Until the final plans for reconstruction were ready, the ugly sight should be veiled by trees and bushes.[13]

In 1944 Schwarz gave up his idea that the blighted areas would have to be animated by means of afforestation and only thus be available for settlement after a lapse of a generation. He considered the metropolitan environment with high-rise buildings the true expression of 'Jewish thought': 'In such an environment only masses in the sense of Americanism and Bolshevism could be bred.' True reconstruction should instead be a process of settlement with a new rootedness. Schwarz did not want to be misunderstood as a romanticist, but he wanted to propagate the new settlements as the basis for the 'vital fight of life against the eastern races'. He understood Germanic character as being fed through unity with nature. Thus, settling and reconstruction were to be understood as returning to the sources, as re-establishing a unity which had gradually been lost in the 'evil metropolis'.

Planning would have to establish a more rural environment

with neighbourhoods of low population densities. The disaster was understood as the liberating opportunity for mankind. Freed of the bonds of history, freed of the urban world, the future was considered as something like a rebirth. The 'catastrophe' as the end of the world had already been experienced. Now the conditions of a new life had to be envisaged.[14]

EVACUATION PROGRAMMES IN SEPTEMBER%OCTOBER 1943: ANOTHER APPROACH TO OVERCOMING THE MODERN METROPOLIS

In early September 1943 the regional planning office planned to bring those people back who had fled the town in July and were now scattered all over the country. Emergency shelter was to be provided in an extended area (*erweitertes Heimatgebiet*) around Hamburg, which finally included a larger part of North Germany (*Unterbringungs-Gaugemeinschaft Nord*), extending to Hannover in the south and Berlin in the east. Within the distance of a two-hour train ride, approximately 140 000 people were to be housed, with another 152 000 to be housed still further out in the countryside. Only two-thirds of the original 1939 population of 1 544 000 would remain in still-existing homes in Hamburg. It was taken for granted that by the end of the war 75 per cent of the densely populated areas and 37 per cent of the less dense quarters would be destroyed. These figures implied the destruction of altogether 300 000 homes and flats, leaving 927 000 people without shelter.

It was said explicitly that an extensive evacuation would slowly lead towards a new form of existence for the metropolis of the future. This new form was to be a dispersed one.[15] Somehow the evacuation was considered an opportunity to test the planned environment of the future metropolis. Living conditions were hard, but people were brought back nearer to the soil as the animating force. War had forced people to experience the ideal environment.

BUILDING PROGRAMMES FOR EMERGENCY HOMES, 1943–4[16]

The above mentioned evacuation and resettlement programme implied the building of 200 000 new emergency homes within the next two years. Although the *Amt für kriegswichtigen Einsatz* strongly favoured repair over resettlement programmes, the town planning office (since February 1941 under the leadership of Konstanty Gutschow, who in January 1943 became the head of the building department of the city administration) was forced to co-operate with the programme to build emergency housing. This programme was directed by a competing agency, the Deutsche Arbeitsfront (which had taken over the property and functions of the old trade unions abolished in 1933). In November 1943 there were seventeen projects under construction, more projects planned, and many more under consideration (see Plate 8). Although it was proved that five flats could be repaired for the cost of building one emergency home, the Gauwohnungskommissar (as the official of the Deutsche Arbeitsfront) insisted on building prefabricated homes as designed by Ernst Neufert. Larger groups of these houses were to be located in the periphery of the town as model communities, with all the amenities necessary for a neighbourhood (*Siedlungszelle*) that reflected the local party organisation (see Plate 9). The example of Wilhelmsburg (König-Georgsdeich) shows the town planning office's design for 210 homes around a central square with shops and a youth house (*Hitler-Jugend-Heim*). For every ten homes there was a small air-raid shelter located at street widenings, and green spaces designed by Heinz Paulus, the official landscape architect.

The design for the small community provides an early idea of what the future metropolis would look like as a dispersed settlement with the population tied to the soil. The low density was a direct answer to the threats posed by air raids, an answer to the disaster. The spatial qualities of the neighbourhood certainly reflected the design practice of the 1920s which gained a sudden revival in 1932 when emergency programmes were devised to settle the jobless in self-supporting units. Now such designs were more than a temporary answer. Although the product of an emergency situation, they were understood as a part of an all-pervading educational programme which would create a better future and eventually lead to an everlasting superiority of the Germanic race.

Very few of these resettlement programmes were realised. In early 1944 the scene was in such confusion that, in addition to the Deutsche Arbeitsfront, some departments of the city administration planned their own housing programmes. The architectural bureau of the public works department designed so-called war homes for civil servants of the sanitary board in November 1943. These two-storey terraced houses were to be located near hospitals and built exclusively with bricks and iron salvaged from the ruins. Everything was carefully designed to allow construction by way of self-help. Each house had two flats which later were supposed to be converted into a single home. The design was unostentatious, resembling in its austerity military barracks. We can point to the *Heimstättenbewegung* (building trusts) of the early 1920s and to the reconstruction programmes of East Prussia in 1917–18 to find the roots of this particular architecture. The architect, Karl Friedrich Fischer, was well trained in this style under his teacher Heinrich Tessenow in Berlin. There is nothing 'national socialistic' in particular in this design, but instead there is an unpretentiousness which we tend to appreciate in anonymous vernacular architecture. The new vernacular style was supposed to express the future rootedness, the tie to the soil.

The various resettlement programmes had only little success to announce in 1944. Nevertheless, their leaders were celebrated in pompous meetings. When the Reichswohnungskommissar Robert Ley spoke in January 1944 to the representatives of the emergency home programme of the whole country in Hamburg, he demanded – contrary to all futile efforts – the construction of one million emergency homes a year in order to produce an adequate supply rapidly.[17] Every victim of an air raid, Ley declared, had the 'right and the certainty of obtaining a new home the following day'. Ley called the emergency home programme a true weapon with which to fight the 'housing blockade' imposed on Germany by the enemy.[18]

## COMMENTS BY THE ASSOCIATION OF LOW GERMAN HAMBURG (VEREINIGUNG NIEDERDEUTSCHES HAMBURG), *c.* DECEMBER 1943

In contrast to the planners, to whom the disaster was an opportunity, the Association of Low German Hamburg considered the extinction of the urban tradition a loss. Its reaction to the destruction was, however, unique. In no other town has a comparable document been found. The Association accepted the loss of the Cremon island which as recently as 1941 had attained the status of a designated historic preservation zone, but now it demanded the creation of a new preservation zone in the neighbourhood of one of the old churches, St Katharinen. There a street should convey to later generations the qualities of space in old Hamburg.[19] Ruins from other streets and undestroyed fragments should be brought together to create a historic zone.

The demands of the Association, uttered only a few months after the destruction of the historic core, are indeed remarkable: the memory of the past was to be saved in a tiny little urban niche, a kind of proof that something else had existed. But even that seemed to have been too much for planners, and incompatible with the urban pattern envisaged for the future. The demands were reviewed by concerned authorities and were totally discarded. It was said that 'the will of our generation to create art (*Kunstwille*) will have to comply with the past experiences in air raid protection: new houses, new street dimensions and new street-patterns will create something completely new'.[20] Memory seemed to be treasonous to the ideals of a better future.

## FIRST PLANS FOR RECONSTRUCTION: DECEMBER 1943

It took the planners nearly five months to overcome the first shock aroused by the 'catastrophe'. Then hectic activity started to prepare a master plan, ready to be presented to the Führer in December 1944. Planning started with designs for the totally destroyed quarter of Eilbeck as an ideal neighbourhood community. Further plans were assigned to several planners so that terms of reference could be developed for the density of population, types of houses, and the spatial pattern of the ideal community. The party centre (*Gauforum*) was still discussed, but no work was devoted to further articulation of architectural dreams. All activity was directed towards the systematic development of model communities which would tie people to the soil, cause the birth-rate to rise, and be safe from menacing air raids. The envisaged destruction of 75 per cent of the densely populated areas made the planners free of any possible tie to the urban traditions of the past and individual ownership of land. Many commentators stressed that planning (at least in early 1944) had to take into account only the natural topographic conditions, because only these would remain undestroyed.[21] They were considered as something which would condition spatial development in quite a natural way, once it revealed its potential to a planner educated in the art of townscape. In contrast to the creations of mankind, these conditions were considered eternal. As the war had caused the destruction of the 'casual artefacts of man', the future would be built on the eternal foundations of a blessed topography.

Revealing the potential creativity of topography mainly meant stressing the importance of the natural watercourses in the Hamburg townscape of the future (see Figure 9, p. 227). In the summer of 1944, Gert Stalmann revived the proposal of Max Karl Schwarz by designing a 'state forest' in the Uhlenhorst section of town, east of the Alster. Thus a large continuum of water and forest would be created in the heart of the former metropolis. The design and commentary of Werner Kallmorgen[22] in March 1944 had similar intentions but was less radical. He proposed the extension of green spaces all around the Alster lake in order to regain the quality of a true rural lake.

## OUTLOOK: LANDSCAPING BLIGHTED AREAS (*TRÜMMERBEGRÜNUNG*) AS AN INTENTION OF PLANNING, 1945–9

No systematic landscaping of blighted areas was achieved in Hamburg. Max Karl Schwarz was commissioned to plan the landscaping of the reconstruction of Wilhelmshaven in November 1944, but it took five years, until June 1949, before he could – and then under completely different political conditions – propose the landscaping of demolished air raid shelters.[23]

In the meantime Oberbürgermeister Andreas Gayk of Kiel had revived the idea in his famous speech of 24 March 1947.[24] He asked men, women and children to come together once a year to celebrate a festival of reconstruction. On that occasion the planting of trees would symbolise the process of reconstruction. Conditions had changed; the country was about to overcome the agony of reconstruction. The plans for Kiel as designed by Herbert Jensen (who remained in office in 1945) were well ahead of those in other towns. The planting of trees in designated green spaces along the green belts was understood as a beginning in times of poverty. Collective planting of trees expressed the will to survive.

## CONCLUSION: DESTRUCTION AND PLANNING, DEATH AND REBIRTH

The destruction of Hamburg and the subsequent reactions by planners and agencies concerned with construction show a negation of all historic traditions. The death of the urban tradition was felt as the end of a millennium of continuity. A future rebirth would have to start from the beginning, with planning based on the eternal traits of topography.

Planners did not necessarily equate the end of the war with an end to the sort of planning to be found during the Third Reich. Their loyalty made them, in fact, blind to any consequences or any change of the political system. Instead, planners considered their dealings as 'timeless' and the results of planning as 'valid' under whatever political system; they believed their planning followed the 'laws of urban life' (*lebensgesetzlicher Städtebau*). Planners acted as specialists who order space for the future needs of man. It was taken for granted that the pattern of the future settlement was a dispersed one (*aufgelockert*) and that it was organised into neighbourhoods (*gegliedert in Siedlungszellen*). The change in urban patterns was felt to be so dramatic and incisive that the death of traditions was a welcome opportunity, if not a precondition, for new work. The war had led to the extinction of the urban tradition just as if the disaster had been planned by the Third Reich.

The emergency home programme with its neighbourhood designs, the evacuation programme, and the proposal to landscape and reforest the blighted areas in Hamburg were all efforts to overcome the traditional metropolis, the evil 'cancer of society'. Sorrow and grief over the losses could not well up, because the future life was supposed to be a better life. The disaster was considered the result of human hubris that nevertheless had a welcome cathartic effect. The metropolis had, according to planners, deserved this fate. Naming the destruction of the town a 'catastrophe' may be seen in this direction too. It seemed to be a natural death, to be followed only by the total extinction of the Germanic race and of Germany, as demanded by Adolf Hitler until the last minute in April 1945.

In Germany, hardly anybody knew in autumn 1943 that the 'catastrophe' was the retaliation for the destruction of Europe in the name of the 'ordering power of the Third Reich'. How else are we to understand the patient loyalty of the majority of the population and of the soldiers? With the end of the war the political order changed. The vocabulary of planning was denazified, but the basic implications remained unchanged. The neighbourhood ideology swept through all European planning offices, regardless of political systems. Abercrombie came to the same results in Plymouth and London in 1942–3, and the secret planning offices in Warsaw arrived at the same conclusions.

What remained characteristic for planning in Germany was how it discarded historic traditions. Urban planning somehow completed the destruction of the urban centres. The experience of the aerial warfare and of the Third Reich created an invincible faith in a better future, as if a look back into history would allow only a look into an unfathomable pit.

**Notes**
1.  A scholarly account of this period must remain subjective for me because it deals with my own past and that of my father, Konstanty Gutschow, who from March 1939 until December 1945 was the Architekt des Elbufers and then Architekt der Neugestaltung der Hansestadt Hamburg. For nearly two years in 1942 and 1943 he headed Hamburg's planning office, and from November 1943 he was chief planner of the reconstruction planning staff under Albert Speer. He was thus in power during the years discussed in this essay. Quotations from 'Papers of K. Gutschow' are from the private archive of K. Gutschow which *in toto* was handed over to the Staatsarchiv Hamburg in January 1987. When quoted, file numbers are contemporary, 1943–4. The whole corpus of documents at present is in the process of inventarisation.
2.  Saul Friedländer, *Reflets du nazisme* (Paris, 1982; New York, 1983; Munich, 1984).
3.  'In the shortest possible time through its new construction programme (*Neugestaltung*) Berlin must be made to represent its position, made possible by the size of its conquests, as the capital of a strong new empire. In the realisation of these many important building projects I see a major contribution to the ultimate securing of our triumph' (*source*: Brief des Reichsstatthalters an Baurat Gutschow vom 17.7.1940 mit Abschrift des Erlasses 'Adolf Hitler, Hauptquartier, den 25.6.1940', papers of K. Gutschow, Staatsarchiv Hamburg).
4.  *Siedlungsgestaltung aus Volk, Raum und Landschaft*, vol. 1: *Totale Planung und Gestaltung – eine politische Forderung* (Berlin, 1940). See also Karl Neupert, 'Totale Planung und Gestaltung', in *Bauen, Siedeln, Wohnen*, vol. 5 (Berlin, 1940).
5.  Paul Schmitthenner, *c.* September 1943: 'The deficient intelligence in the shaping of human life can be seen most clearly in the development of the metropolis, which is the most palpable manifestation of the

way technology shapes life. . . . The problem of the masses arose
in the metropolis, and with it today's social problem generally, the
problem of our period and the world. . . . A city is a firmly formed
manifestation of the community of humans. The city serves to house
people; everything else derives from the needs of the people and the
rights of the inhabitants. In the form of the community, however, one
finds also the greatness of civilisation and culture. . . . An old idea for
reducing the density of the metropolis is that of satellite cities, which
means simultaneously decentralisation in spatial terms but centralisation of the administration. A new and more sensible way appears to
be the building of entirely new, independent cities with rational living
conditions in all respects for the inhabitants, the human beings. The
necessity for this is general. It is to be expected that the world war
will bring with it huge political and economic dislocations, which will
lead to the creation of such new cities!'

    The destruction of Cologne was described as follows: 'over
three-fourths of the old city is entirely destroyed and the rest
so badly damaged that it must be demolished and cleared away.
Even those few buildings that are still usable probably must be torn
down, so that a clear new urban design can be formed. A completely
new plan is needed, so that a Cologne that is able to respond to new
needs will be a living representation of our age' (*source*: papers of Paul
Schmitthenner, in possession of Elisabeth Schmitthenner, Munich).

6.   Gerhard Graubner, 'Der Wehrgedanke als Grundlage der Stadt-
    gestaltung und Stadtplanung' [no date (*c.* December 1943], from
    the papers of K. Gutschow, Staatsarchiv Hamburg.
7.   See Jeffry M. Diefendorf, 'Konstanty Gutschow and the reconstruction
    of Hamburg', *Central European History*, 17 (1985).
8.   Rudolf Hillebrecht cites Liliencron's poem, 'Lewwer duad üs Slaav!'
    and says, 'If we are clear about things and don't lose our will, then we
    need not be too anxious, since our reserves are enormously large' (from
    *Nachrichten unserer Kameraden im Felde*, no. 16 (April 1943) p. 7).
9.   Rudolf Hillebrecht: 'There can be no doubt that one cannot keep
    up with the growing destruction of housing and that this competition
    between the Tommies and us builders will end to our disadvantage if
    one just puts one's hands in one's lap and does not take the needed
    organisational countermeasures at the right time and with sufficient
    intensity' (ibid., p. 4).
10.   For example, Martin Middlebrook, *The Battle of Hamburg: Allied
    Bomber Forces Against a German City in 1943* (London, 1980); Hans
    Erich Nossack, *Der Untergang* (Hamburg, 1943, reissued with photos
    by Erich Andres and an introduction by Erich Lüth, Hamburg, 1981);
    F. Werner, *Das Gesicht der Hansestadt Hamburg im Wandel der
    Jahre 1939–1945: Bilder aus Nachkriegs– und Kriegszeit* (Hamburg,
    1951); Rolf Stephan, *Hamburg – ehemals, gestern, heute* (Stuttgart,
    1981). Of special importance is the account of Alexander Friedrich,
    'Versuch über die Zerstörung Hamburgs' (12.8.1943). An artist and
    copperplate engraver, Friedrich did the 'official' engravings of Hitler's
    Reichskanzlei. His report was published privately in Hamburg in 1963

by Schacht & Westrich; it was partly published in *Nachrichten für unsere Kameraden im Felde*, no. 23 (April 1944) pp. 4–5.

11.   Hans Pieper, 'Hamburg – Bericht über die Angriffe vom 25./26. Juli 1943', Lübeck 16 August 1943. From the private archive of Klaus Pieper, Braunschweig.

12.   Max Karl Scharz, 'Gedanken zur Neuplanung der Hansestadt Hamburg unter besonderer Berücksichtigüng der Umwandlung zerstörter Wohngebiete in Auforstungen. 31.8.1943'. He wrote: 'In the beginning of rebuilding there was the need first to make a natural landscape out of the destroyed area. This evolved initially in the direction of afforestation, from which the raw material "forest" would come. It is a generally recognized fact that the forest conceals within it the element of strongest revitalisation. Only after these destroyed areas have been revived by the forest will it be possible to make a genuine urban landscape (*Stadtlandschaft*) there, that is, houses with gardens' (*source*: papers of K. Gutschow, Staatsarchiv Hamburg).

13.   Rudolf Heuson, 'Vorschläge zur Unterbringung von Bauschuttmassen der Stadt Hamburg', 11 March 1944: 'In the interest of public health and in order to conceal the ugly vistas until the ultimate completing of urban plans for these areas, the total destruction of entire quarters of cities requires among other things an intermediate solution through the planting of the masses of rubble' (*source*: papers of K. Gutschow, Staatsarchiv Hamburg, file E6).

14.   Letter of Max Karl Schwarz, Worpswede, to K. Gutschow, 31 July 1944: 'The desire for a house with a garden, even within the urban area, is only secondarily desirable for reasons of health and productivity; it is primarily desirable because the garden is the source of life. . . . It is the German fashion to derive spiritual abilities and physical strength from the connections with nature. However this source of vitality for the Germans has more and more been cut off by a pervasive alienation from nature. . . . It is clear to me that multistorey buildings are an expression of the Jewish spirit, and with such buildings we have recently been spreading the speculative and paralysing idea that everything can be built only on the basis of mass, number, and weight. . . . The planned reconstruction is a genuine resettlement, a new rootedness, rooted in the land. That is no romantic idea, but rather it is truly the only basis for the future life struggles that the now aged Europe has to carry out against the people of the east' (*source*: papers of K. Gutschow, Staatsarchiv Hamburg, file: Akte Hamburger Wiederaufbauplanung 1944/45, Bd. 4: Auftragsbearbeitungen 1–13).

15.   Landesplanungsgemeinschaft Hamburg (Konstanty Gutschow), Hamburg, 5 September 1943, Unterbringung der hamburgischen Bevölkerung: 'These conditions will have to be improved constantly and will thereby lead to a new form of existence for the metropolis of the future, a decongested metropolis that reaches far into the country, such as was already sketched out as an idea in the general plan of 1940–1' (*source*: papers of K. Gutschow, Staatsarchiv Hamburg).

16.   This section is based on the papers of K. Gutschow, Staatsarchiv Hamburg (Ile: Schnellbau-Wohnungen Hamburg).

17. 'This year one million temporary housing units must be built. In a few years we must have a surplus of temporary housing units. Everyone who is bombed out must be able to have a new place to live on the following day. Some speak of "Leyist" dog houses. These units must [if need be] be built of mud and manure, even if the architects refuse to see that. What happens after the war doesn't concern us now; I must forbid [thinking about] that' (*source*: Niederschrift über die Tagung der Gauwohnungskommissare in Hamburg am 27. und 28. Januar 1944; from papers of K. Gutschow, Staatsarchiv Hamburg, file 'Schnellbauwohnungen des Gauwohnungskommissar, 1944').

18. 'The programme to build temporary housing is a weapon in this war, used in order to combat the housing blockade which our opponents have forced on us' (*source*: Ansprache des Reichswohnungskommissars Reichsleiter Dr Ley auf der Gauleitertagung am 23. und 24. Februar 1944 in München; from papers of K. Gutschow, Staatsarchiv Hamburg, file 'Schnellbauwohnungen des Gauwohnungskommissar, 1944').

19. 'Vorschlag der Vereinigung Niederdeutsches Hamburg über die Einrichtung einer Denkmalszone in der Umgebung der Katharinenkirche' (no date or place), from papers of K. Gutschow, Staatsarchiv Hamburg.

20. Letter of Friedrich Dryssen to Landeskulturwalter Hans Rodde (no date). Appendix to a letter to K. Gutschow, 14 February 1944: 'The artistic will of our generation will have to be shaped by knowledge won in building air defenses. New forms of housing, new street widths and new street layouts will allow something new to be created' (*source*: papers of K. Gutschow, Staatsarchiv Hamburg).

21. Hermann Valett: 'We must proceed radically from the thought that only certain praiseworthy features which are not destroyed will remain: natural features – the Elbe, the Alster valley, the depressions of the marshes, the sandy uplands – all curiosities, oddities, and things of beauty, many geological and economic preconditions and relationships' (*source*: papers of K. Gutschow, Staatsarchiv Hamburg).

22. Werner Kallmorgen: 'The outer Alster must be restored to the character of a Holstein lake with meadows and parks on the east and with a beech forest from the steep western slope to the middle. In the narrow areas it will be widened to the edge of the marsh at the Harvesterhuderweg. This way a concentration of greenery can be obtained that now is randomly divided according to urban coincidences. The greenery of the Alster is to be valued as a representative green area in contrast to the hygienic green of the city parks' (comment on his design, dated 14 March 1944; from papers of K. Gutschow, Staatsarchiv Hamburg).

23. Niedersächsisches Amt für Landesplanung und Statistik (Hrsg.), 'Gutachten über die Grundlagen für den Neuaufbau der Stadt Wilhelmshaven', Reihe G. Heft 1 (Hannover, 1950), with articles by Wilhelm Wortmann and Max Karl Schwarz. In the papers of Max Karl Schwarz there are numerous manuscripts dealing with landscaping blighted areas: 'Die Bedeutung der Trümmerbegrünung

beim Wiederaufbau zerstörter Städte', 8 August 1949, and 'Praktische Vorschläge für die Begrünung und Bepflanzung insbesondere der Trümmerflächen zerstörter Städte als erste und vordringliche Wieder-aufbaumassnahme' (no date).

24.    'Kiels Friedensarbeit beginnt!', Rede des Oberbürgermeisters Gayk zur Haushaltssitzung der Stadt Kiel, 24, 25 and 26 (März, 1947) Schriftenreihe der Stadt Kiel.

# 9 German Reconstruction as an International Activity

## FRIEDHELM FISCHER

In the attempt to facilitate communication about complex states of affairs, people tend to use catchy, often metaphorical slogans. Typical phrases which were used to characterise the period after the Second World War in Germany included images such as the Zero Hour, the feeling of a new departure and the economic miracle (*Stunde Null, Aufbruchstimmung, Wirtschaftswunder*).

These images seemed to contain a measure of truth which appeared self-evident and almost physically palpable to everyone who had experienced this period. Who, for instance, could deny the emergency situation of the homeless, for whom nothing was more urgent than 'Inding a roof over their heads', or the problems of the building authorities, facing a shortage of building materials that made it so difficult to carry out even the most pressing repair work, not to mention long-term planning.

Because such phrases seem to make sense, they become common property and are taken up by historians. Later, in the light of changing research interests, it becomes obvious that such phrases are clichés, legends created and used with a particular interest in mind. The image of the economic miracle is losing its magic, with increasing knowledge about the impetus towards modernisation given to the German economy by the enforced growth of the war industries and the relatively low degree of war damage they suffered in relation to, say, workers' residential districts and infrastructure. From the perspective of the 1980s, it has become generally recognised that the Zero Hour cliché is basically a legend; some would say a lie. There was, of course, a Zero Hour. The war was over, the cities were destroyed, it was a time of new beginnings. Nevertheless, it was an illusion that the old structures had simply vanished all of a sudden. A whole country does not change its population and its ideologies overnight. The old structures lived on both in people's minds and in the institutions. So where the term Zero Hour has been utilised in order to suggest there was a complete, 'radically' new start from new roots, it has become at least partly a lie.

131

One of the effects of a whole range of clichés associated with the Zero Hour image has been that traditional urban historiography has treated its object of study, postwar Germany, as an isolated phenomenon. Typical is the stylisation of the Nazi past as something unique and entirely different from what went before and after, for example: the stereotype that Nazi architecture consisted of little more than the design of megalomaniac monumental buildings, which has, of course, found such widespread acceptance because these were the most spectacular and best publicised building projects of the Third Reich; the cliché of the German architects' complete isolation from foreign influences during the twelve years of the 'thousand-year Reich'; and, finally, the notion that postwar architecture simply connected back to the traditions of the 'good' 1920s swiftly while skipping over the 'evil' 1930s.

Gaining a balanced picture entails looking beyond the artificial boundaries which these clichés have helped to create. It requires re-evaluating the links to the periods before 1945 and putting the German reconstruction endeavour into perspective by looking at international developments of the period. For thinking about reconstruction was an international activity. One of the striking things about urban planning, whether in London, Hamburg, Warsaw or anywhere else, is the similarity of the problems and issues, of the questions posed, and many of the solutions. The housing crisis was, and had long been world-wide, and 'decent modern housing for all' was a universal plea. As to the question of the preferred urban pattern, the common denominators were decentralisation and new infrastructures, including networks of traffic arteries, open space and neighbourhoods.

In view of the common problems and the planning approaches developed in the 1920s and 1930s, a high measure of common features between the various reconstruction plans is not surprising. In the light of recent research, it has become an acknowledged fact that planning for postwar urban reconstruction began long before 1945. But interestingly, the phenomenon labelled reconstruction was not limited to cities or even countries affected by destruction through war. Throughout the 1940s, postwar reconstruction – be it that of cities or that of the economy in general – was an important theme everywhere, whether in the United States, Europe or Australia.

In Germany reconstruction planning flourished from the 1940s on, when the invasion of France was interpreted as a proof of the manifest destiny of German imperialism. To those in power it seemed obvious that now was the time to reshape the cities which would soon become the new centres of imperial power. The plans for the 'remodelling of German cities' (*Neugestaltung*), work for which had been initiated as early as October 1937, were pure, imperial architecture of dominance (*Herrschafts-Architektur*) at their core. But since imperialism is a way of life, not something that simply stops outside a country's borders, its spirit also determined the approaches towards solving the old problems associated with the city of the nineteenth century and with the various segments of its population. Sober, technocratic and inexorable, this was the other, less-well-known face of Nazi planning: not architectural at its core but technical, not an architecture of façades but technocratic, modern town planning.[1] And this is what remained as Germany's cities turned to rubble and as the megalomaniac splendour of *Neugestaltung* gave way to the more sober technical spirit of reconstruction proper.

The importance of the term reconstruction throughout the 1940s in all industrialised nations, whether affected by wartime destruction or not, might suggest that the term focused on the refurbishing of an economy disrupted by economic crises and war. However, it was often used in an even broader sense to encompass a complete restructuring and rejuvenation of society.[2] One moved from building directly to politics and morality: a wholesale clearance on a nationwide scale as a means of rejuvenating social conduct and the national economy.

Two of the most prominent German architectural emigrants, Walter Gropius and Martin Wagner, had this in mind when they developed their 'Program for City Reconstruction'[3] for Boston. The object of reconstruction was the same as for the bombed cities of Europe: urban settlements in a state of destruction. Whether destruction was rapid, due to bombs and blockbusters, or slow, due to urban blight, was not important from this point of view. What was important was the magnitude of the task and the common features resulting from this state of destruction. Shared world-wide by planners, administrators and the building industry, this attitude was captured perfectly in publications such as those by the US National Real Estate Boards. 'This is a blockbuster', explained one of their brochures.[4]

This is what it does to a city. . . . This is blight. This is what blight does. . . . The blockbusters going off in our cities . . . disintegrate slowly in the space of years, and generate decay and rot around them. . . . But every disintegrating building . . . is just as truly a blockbuster as a four thousand pound bomb that tumbles from a four-engined bomber. The effect is exactly the same.

Therefore it is not surprising that the basic remedy proposed was similar: large-scale clearance and wholesale reconstruction according to 'The New City Pattern for the People and by the People', to use the title of another of Gropius's and Wagner's articles.[5] An enormous task was awaiting planners as well as the building industry throughout the industrialised world. For the US itself, Gropius projected a 'demand of new residential family housing units alone of more than 1.2 million houses yearly for a full decade', corresponding to 'a total expenditure of over ten billion dollars per year for new building, employing not less than 5 000 000 men'.[6] The building industry's own estimates even ranged around 45 and 60 billion dollars of total expenditure.[7] As Gropius recognised, the 'task ahead . . . [was] so staggering that it should be appropriate to investigate into the state of our preparedness to meet it'.[8]

The key to solving this material problem lay in the conversion of war industries to peaceful production. But the tremendous boost which the war had given to industries in many countries was also seen as a problem. Gropius warned that 'as soon as the war [was] over, industry [would] have to switch back again to peace production', and 'preparations could not be made early enough for so involved a problem of industrial adaptability'.[9]

The building and real estate industries naturally focused on immediate programming and the implementation of recipes that were already at hand. Taking up the old Daniel Burnham slogan (and in accord with planners generally) they urged: 'Make no little plans. . . . A clean sweep must be made. New programs need new concepts . . . boldness and vision. New plans need new ideas.'[10]

For people like Gropius there could be 'hardly any doubt that . . . considering the recent evidence of our capability to gear the country's industry for war production in a very short time, we shall be technically fit to reorganize the huge machinery at hand for an equally tremendous volume of peace production'. The more doubtful question to him and to planners in the US as well as in Europe was: 'Are we mentally as well prepared for this task as technically?'[11]

It seemed obvious that reconstruction on a world-wide scale was not merely a financial and material affair. It offered an opportunity to change the life-patterns of the urban masses 'on both sides of the ocean' and thus also to influence their political culture, to exert an educational influence for the benefit of democracy – a task in which 'America could take the lead', as Europe would be 'most likely drained of most of its resources after the war'.[12]

As if this assumption had been heard in high places, it was only a couple of years after the war that Gropius was sent to Germany as a cultural ambassador and advisory expert in order to revive the processes of democratisation through advice on town planning. Gropius's prognosis of the exhaustion of resources had, of course, particular relevance for Germany, which was not only among the most heavily destroyed countries but also one whose population had been cut off from foreign influences for many years.

Twelve years of isolation, or so it seemed. But if we examine carefully contemporary patterns of communication, this judgement, though oft-stated, has to be taken with a grain of salt. It is true that currency restrictions and the tightening grip of the authorities in the 1930s reduced the number of journeys abroad and the influx of printed material. It was only with the outbreak of war, however, that the majority of the German population was entirely cut off from the outside.

After 1933, Karl Ströhlin had become the head of the International Federation for Housing and Town Planning, and its headquarters was moved to Stuttgart, proclaimed by Hitler to be 'die Stadt der Auslandsdeutschen'. This resulted not only in the added recognition desired by Hitler's regime but also, as the lists of participants indicate, in massive German attendance at the international congresses of the Federation, such as those in London (1935), Paris (1937) and even, only a few months before the outbreak of war, Stockholm (1939).[13] By that time, people like Gropius had already left Germany for good. Nevertheless, in the last couple of years before the war, planners such as Speer and Schelkes were still picking up important ideas for reconstruction planning on their journeys from Berlin to London, Paris and the US. Travelling to America, the architect for the *Neugestaltung* of Hamburg, Konstanty Gutschow, did not just bring back studies for the New York and Chicago type of skyscrapers for which the trip had been undertaken.[14] Preparations for a competition for the new German embassy also took him to Washington. There he assimilated impressions of the green-belt towns, which were relevant not only for his town planning work but also for that of his Hamburg colleagues throughout the period of reconstruction. His head of staff,

Rudolf Hillebrecht, later surmised that the small group of planners around Gutschow were probably the only ones in Germany who had any knowledge of American green-belt planning practices at the time.[15]

After the outbreak of war, planners were only allowed to visit the other Fascist countries, mainly Italy, and thus for most German architects and planners, 1 September 1939 meant the beginning of six years of isolation – but again, for most, not for everyone and not everywhere. Hamburg happened to be a place where some of the sources of information never completely dried up, The Hamburg World Economic Archives received information via obscure channels about British press reactions to many events relating to Germany (for instance, the air raids on Hamburg) but also to matters of planning (Abercrombie's plans for London) and planning legislation under the Churchill government. From England via Lisbon to Berlin, the *Informationsdienst Ausland* managed to supply the translated versions of English articles and papers, complete with maps and pictures, with no more than three days delay.[16]

Individual publishers also still had their antennae up for receiving information from the outside. Among them was Herbert Hoffmann, editor of the journal *Moderne Bauformen*. Private contacts with this publishing house were the second major source supplying copies of the current foreign planning periodicals to planners on the Gutschow staff throughout most of the war.

This flow of information is central in understanding how the Germans could quickly catch up with the international debate on planning concepts and legislation in the postwar years. While many of the ideas of decentralisation, neighbourhood planning and the like were simply 'in the air' at the time, it was also possible for at least a select group of German town planners to profit from what was being discussed abroad, certainly more than has been commonly assumed.

Even where exclusive connections enjoyed by the top planners such as those in Hamburg did not exist, important bits of information were gathered during the war years by officers of the German Occupation army or by prisoners of war, and turned into subjects for postwar planning discussion – subjects that would otherwise not have been debated in Germany until much later. Take, for example, Hans Kampffmeyer, son of the major promoter of the Garden City idea in Germany. While in Paris, as an officer of the German Occupation troops in 1943, he came across a printed copy of Le Corbusier's phrasing of the Charter of Athens, which was not, of course, available to planners in Germany.[17] Soon after the war he translated it for publication in German town planning journals,[18] thereby initiating a lively dispute in planning circles.

For the majority of the population, however, including architects and planners, isolation was complete during the six years of war, and so it is not surprising that they were greedy for information on what had been happening in the outside world. Great efforts were made to re-establish contacts with friends and colleagues abroad, first through letters and much later through overseas travelling. Requests for printed material were sent to the institutions of the allied forces; energies and information were pooled in associations, local and nationwide, for the promotion of international contacts. Some remained informal and shortlived, unimportant in matters of practical planning decisions, but still they helped to reactivate the flow of information to a broader range of people specifically interested in matters of reconstruction. The largest of these, in sheer numbers, was an 'association to collect material relating to reconstruction',[19] formed by 3000 students at the University of Berlin in 1947.

The most active among the shortlived ones was the Hamburg INTERPLAN (Internationale Studiengesellschaft für Planung), founded in 1946, and consisting of local architects, planners, statisticians and members of the department of building and construction. Their basic philosophy and planning aims were formulated at their initial meeting on 24 November 1946. Since it was clear that the structure of the population and the means of production and transportation had changed fundamentally after the war, the first aim of the association was to collect materials and to start broad-based research into these matters. Since these structural changes were common to most Western countries, INTERPLAN called for what they termed *Kontinental-Planung*. The 'basic problem of our time' was felt to be that 'the natural order of the environment, in which all forces are in balance, has been disturbed – by man. Whether he was simply acting according to his fate is not a matter of immediate concern. But the task is to re-establish an organic and therefore natural order.' While striving to be apolitical itself, the association's aim was to find a method of planning 'midway between total liberalism and total socialism'.[20]

In addition to pooling journals, literature and bibliographies, to reactivating contacts, mainly with British and American colleagues, to organising workshops and lectures by international experts, INTERPLAN also produced a small range of much-read publications, such as a study of the Greater Hamburg region, an international comparative study of city regions and an early annotated translation of the Greater London Plan.[21] INTERPLAN began to fade out of existence in spring 1950, with a call to members to attend the 20th International Congress of the Federation for Housing and Town Planning (IFHTP) in Amsterdam.[22] With the growth of the German branch of the Federation, the tasks of INTERPLAN had gradually been subsumed by the larger and more established organisation.

In 1946 the German branch of the IFHTP had been refounded in the small town of Gailsdorf (in Württemberg) to which files, library and archives had been evacuated during the war. The initiative for this new start had come from Mrs Paula Schäfer, who had been the Secretary of the Federation since 1928. Among the founders were also Hans Kampffmeyer, son of the Federation's previous Secretary General, whose name was familiar to a large planning public in connection with the Garden City movement, and Gottlieb Binder, the Minister for Reconstruction of Hessen, who was elected President of the new association.

Numerous applications for membership began to come in from professional circles and others interested in the pressing problems of German reconstruction. There was a growing demand for a series of conferences to serve as a common platform from which it would be possible to discuss the methods and technique of rebuilding the war-damaged cities and towns. Soliciting the membership of planners and architects, politicians, civic administrators, managers and bankers, representatives of the building industry as well as other interest groups, the aim of the Federation was not only to present a forum for discussions on planning for reconstruction within Germany but also to re-establish connections with planners abroad, perhaps one day even to regain the mediating function Germany had once had in the field of housing and town planning. In this respect, of course, the Federation had a long way to go. It was not until 1950 that it was readmitted to the International Federation, and only in 1954 was German recognised again as one of the Federation's registered languages. Its most valuable activity during the second half of the 1940s was the organisation of exhibitions and lectures by foreign experts on architecture and town planning, most of them from

Britain. It also made foreign journals and books available to a wider public of planners and set up a substantial international bibliography available on a subscription basis.

Among the first planners to give lectures in Germany were the representatives of the International Federation, Sir George and Lady Elizabeth Pepler, as well as Jacqueline Tyrwhitt, Gordon Stephenson and Max Lock, all lecturing on various aspects of reconstruction. The route usually covered the cities of Berlin, Hamburg, Kiel, Frankfurt and Hannover, where they often lectured in connection with an RIBA/British Council Exhibition shown for the first time in June 1948 in the town hall of Frankfurt, on the occasion of a Federation convention. The lectures were well-attended, but they did not meet with unanimous agreement. One of the reasons was that after the experience of the planned economy of the Third Reich, there was some suspicion about the British centralist approach, particularly their ideas of land reform. One of the practical results of the British 'crusades'[23] was that Hillebrecht, one of the most influential planners of the postwar period, took up the idea of organising town planning exhibitions similar to that of the British Council in order to gain the support of the public.

The same year the German Federation was founded anew (1946), the International Federation (IFHTP) held its first postwar convention at Hastings. The regional focus of the convention was on the reconstruction plans for Rotterdam, Liège and Warsaw, as well as on the County of London Plan and the approaches to regional planning as displayed in the plan for Exeter. Thematically it focused on decentralisation and housing. In contrast to previous conventions, no definite conclusions or resolutions were formulated, since it was felt that 'the problem of securing a decent home for the ill-housed . . . does not lend itself to easy solution, and . . . that no one pattern of action [was] going to be the perfect panacea'.[24] It was concluded that 'the fruitful contacts established and the starting of common experience across international lines made the delegates aware that particular local problems are in effect world-wide'.

The year 1947 brought major progress for Germany in terms of renewed access to international information – although the activity patterns were still rather one-sided. Germans still had little opportunity of leaving the country and so international conventions still took place without them. It was therefore an event of great appeal to a broad public when it was announced that the former director of the famous Bauhaus, Walter Gropius, would be coming to Germany

in August 1947. He was the first of the 'visiting consultants' sent
by the US Military Government in order to advise on matters of
town planning and reconstruction. Gropius, once one of Germany's
leading figures in architecture, and now a representative of victorious
and economically prospering 'Amerika', enjoyed the confidence of
many individuals holding divergent opinions. Little wonder that many
wanted to enlist him for their cause, from Hillebrecht via his former
Bauhaus colleagues and members of the Congrès Internationaux
d'Architecture Moderne (CIAM), both groups wishing to rejuvenate
the spirit in which they had worked before the Nazi disruption, to the
standardisation expert Neufert.

However, after the long absence of Gropius and everything
he stood for, planners in Germany were understandably rather
uncertain as to what to expect of the architect in exile. Would
his brilliant career in the US have alienated him to such an extent
that he would be unable to make a contribution to the problems of
reconstruction in Germany? Looking back in 1948,[25] Hillebrecht did
not conceal that he had expected Gropius to be a rather one-sided
doctrinaire defender of high-rise housing – pretty much in line with
the anti-Gropius propaganda of the Third Reich, one might add. But
even where Gropius was not able to correct prejudice, he left a deep
impression on many German planners.

It was a further sensation when the news leaked that the
US Military Government had commissioned Gropius to draw
up reconstruction plans for Frankfurt as the future capital of a
West Germany. The response in Germany ranged from enthusiasm
to moderate scepticism about the possibilities of 'planning from
overseas'.[26] That this news was political dynamite – a separate
West German capital was being planned while negotiations about
the political future of one or two German states were still in
progress – was not recognised for quite some time. It was only
when the Foreign Ministers' Conference in London[27] collapsed on
15 December 1947 that some journalists put the facts together and
wormed the secret political background out of Gropius by ringing
him up in the middle of the night.[28] Only forty-eight hours after
the conference, the international press was trumpeting that Gropius
had been told as early as August 1947 that 'American officials had
been working on the assumption of the Big Four Failure' and 'that
the most urgent thing in Germany was planning the new Frankfort
because there seemed little, if any, hope of reaching an agreement
with the Russians on the question of a united Germany'.[29]

The ensuing press stir[30] prompted Gropius to issue an immediate denial and to decide 'to ask United Press to stop any further publications about the interview as it has been distorted by them and given a political slant against which I have specifically warned them'.[31] But it is exactly this 'political slant' which was never refuted by Gropius. All he ever denied was that he intended to carry out the physical planning himself or with his students.[32] He repeatedly declared that he had 'definitely taken the stand that the physical planning and building of Frankfort as a capital for Germany should be done by Germans. No physical plan of Frankfort has been designed by me nor any model built'.[33] His tactics, if indeed that is what they were, paid off. What remains on record, whether in letters or in Reginald Isaacs' biography of Gropius, is the impression that all 'the sensational news about new plans for Frankfurt were just an invention of the press'.[34] As if to give a last proof of how silly the whole affair was, Isaacs concluded the relevant chapter of his book with the words: 'The tempest in the teapot would soon quiet down. . . . Bonn would be the eventual capital of Germany.'

Today we know, of course, that the capital city project came to nothing, but we also know that the United Press journalists were on the right track as far as the political background of Gropius's mission was concerned. By the time the London conference started, even the bank notes for the West German currency reform had long been printed in the US and shipped to Germany. Compared to this early and very massive kind of commitment for a separate West German state, Gropius's mission was almost a minor undertaking. It was, however, highly political, as was the entire concept of his visit. In Germany, more than anywhere else, reconstruction could not remain a merely technical affair but had to be understood in the broadest political sense of the term. Here, the task of 'Rebuilding Our Communities' was that of reconstructing the very foundations of life and culture. In his 'City Planning Report' on Germany, therefore, Gropius advocated 'organic neighborhood planning' as a means of 'social rehabilitation' and of 'promoting democracy . . . through a physical setting properly scaled to the individual'.[35] As he told the press some time after his return to the US, the first step would be for 'international planners [to] start working toward reforming the Germans by giving them "democratic" homes, factories and office buildings'.[36] Because of the high degree of destruction, Germany would be 'the best place to start breaking up cities into home towns and to establish the small-scale communities, in which the essential importance of the individual can be realized'.[37]

The beliefs that urban planning could exert a calculated influence upon the people's political behaviour and that political and urban structures could thus be made to correspond was internationally widespread at the time. But nowhere did it fall on more fertile ground than in Germany. Here it met with a prevalent attitude of anti-urban hostility, which, though an international phenomenon, had been nurtured in a particular way in the preceding decades, and which persisted as an important *leitmotif* through the period of German reconstruction. To some, the determinist interrelationship between built form and political content did not appear new, and it suggested approaches to planning in the Third Reich. For others, environmental determinism represented a simple bit of hope for a civilisation that had culturally come to a loose end.

For Gropius it was more than that, and it was not limited to Germany. Using Germany as a model, reconstruction as an international enterprise could grow into a scheme which could change the world physically, economically and politically. Thus his plea was 'that Germany be used as his architectural guinea pig. And when the planners get through with Germany, they can start working on the rest of Europe – and then the whole world'.[38]

As we know today, Gropius's assumption that 'America could take the lead' in town planning internationally has come true, though not quite in the way Gropius had predicted during the war. As for Gropius himself, his private practice in America flourished and grew. He no longer acted as an 'advisory expert to Germany', and his direct impact on reconstruction there remained negligible.[39] Nevertheless, he remained an exponent of international currents in planning thought during the reconstruction era. While it is true that his publications turned more and more into general statements 'directed at a universal audience',[40] the image of Gropius as a non-political architect-designer in an era that had turned its back on politics[41] is one of the clichés still to be revised.

**Notes**

1.   For this 'swing to technical planning' see Jeffry M. Diefendorf, 'Artery: Urban Reconstruction and Traffic Planning', *Journal of Urban History*, 15, no. 2 (1989); and Werner Durth, *Deutsche*

*Architekten. Biographische Verflechtungen 1900–1970* (Braunschweig, 1986) p. 206.

2.  For example, Walter Gropius's book, *Rebuilding Our Communities* (Chicago, 1945).

3.  Walter Gropius and Martin Wagner, 'A Program for City Reconstruction', *Archetectural Forum* (July 1943).

4.  National Association of Real Estate Boards, *Post-War Cities* (New York, 1944).

5.  Walter Gropius and Martin Wagner, 'The New City Pattern for the People and by the People', in *The Problem of the Cities and the Towns* (Cambridge, Ma., 1942).

6.  Walter Gropius, 'The Consequences for Housing of the Rapid Wartime Industrialisation in the U.S.', typescript, 1941(?), Gropius Archive, Houghton Library, Harvard University, pp. 1–2.

7.  See note 2.

8.  See note 5.

9.  Walter Gropius, 'Postwar Production – Capacity for Housing', typescript, May 1941, Gropius Archive, Houghton Library, Harvard University.

10. See note 2.

11. Walter Gropius, 'Modern Architecture and Tradition', typescript, 18 February 1943, Gropius Archive, Houghton Library, Harvard University, p. 3.

12. Ibid.

13. See the Lists of participants, Archive of the International Federation for Housing and Town Planning, The Hague.

14. See Gutschow's file on 'Amerika-Reise 1937', Papers of Konstanty Gutschow, Staatsarchiv Hamburg.

15. Interviews with Rudolf Hillebrecht, February and May 1987.

16. Gutschow Papers and interviews with Hillebrecht (see notes 14 and 15).

17. Interview with Hans Martin Kampffmeyer, April 1986.

18. Hans Martin Kampffmeyer, 'Die Charta von Athen', in *Die Neue Stadt*, no. 2 (1948) pp. 66–80.

19. US War Department, Press information for release, 17 August 1947.

20. Minutes of the INTERPLAN foundation meeting, 24 November 1946.

21. Karl Schneider (ed.), *London. Planungen für die Umgestaltung der britischen Hauptstadt* (Hamburg, 1947); and Ludwig Mecking, *Die Entwicklung der Gross-Städte in Hauptländern der Industrie* (Hamburg, 1949), both in the Schriftenreihe für Landesplanung und Städtebau.

22. INTERPLAN circular, Spring 1950.

23. Letter, Rudolf Hillebrecht to Walter Gropius, 7 September 1948.

24. International Federation for Housing and Town Planning, report on the conference at Hastings, p. 7.

25. Rudolf Hillebrecht, 'Gespräch mit Gropius', in *Baurundschau*, no. 8/9 (1948).

26. Report in *Die Neue Stadt*, no. 1 (1947) p. 129: 'We harbour some doubts as to whether someone on the outside can understand the

extraordinally complicated problem of rebuilding a city like Frankfurt' (my translation).

27. The conference had begun on 25 November 1947 and was called off prematurely on 15 December 1947.

28. Reginald Isaacs, *Walter Gropius* (Berlin, 1983/84) vol. 2.

29. Numerous papers, from the *New York Times, Herald Tribune* and the *Washington Post* to the *Clifton Forge (Virginia) Review*, carried this news on 17 December 1947. United Press went on to quote Gropius: 'I turned the plans over to Dr Litchfield, chief of the civil administration of the American zone. . . . Litchfield took them to London, where they were studied by American and British officials while the Big Four conference was in session.' It took two days before it made the headlines in the German Press: *Tribüne* and *Neues Deutschland*, Berlin on 18 December, *Frankfurter Neue Presse* 19 December 1947. *Neues Deutschland* protested under the headline of '48 Hours after London': 'Someday someone will have to answer for having speculated from the beginning on the failure of the London Conference' (my translation).

30. This press stir clearly followed the breakdown of the London Conference on 15 December 1947, not the conference in February/March 1948, as suggested by Isaacs (see note 28).

31. Walter Gropius, letter to Professor C. J. Friedrich, 17 December 1947.

32. To Hebebrand, then 'Städtischer Baudirektor' in Frankfurt, who was informed about such plans by Wagner (letter, Hebebrand to Gropius, 30 August 1947) he wrote: 'We once thought about the possibilities of tackling Frankfurt as a study project, but the plan has subsequently been abandoned' (letter, Gropius to Hebebrand, 19 December 1947).

33. Walter Gropius, letter to G. Gp. van Nostrand, War Department, 7 May 1948.

34. See note 28, pp. 961–2.

35. Walter Gropius, report to General Lucius D. Clay, typescript, p. 20.

36. Interview with Walter Gropius, quoted in numerous American papers on 1 January 1947; for example, the *Boston Globe, Star Ledger* (Newark, N.J.) and *Columbia City Post*.

37. Walter Gropius, 'Will Europe Build Cities or Shanty Towns?', in *Weekend* (the weekend magazine of *Stars and Stripes*) (3 January 1948) p. 15.

38. See note 11.

39. Jeffry Diefendorf comes to a similar conclusion in his 'Berlin on the Charles, Cambridge on the Spree: Walter Gropius, Martin Wagner and the Rebuilding of Germany', in Helmut Pfanner (ed.), *Kulturelle Wechselbeziehungen im Exil – Exile Across Cultures* (Bonn, 1986) pp. 343–58.

40. Ibid., p. 349.

41. As a recent example for this view, see Winfried Nerdinger, *Walter Gropius* (exhibition catalogue), (Berlin, 1985) p. 24: 'In the post-World War II era, his apolitical, general concept of architecture was quite suitable to the taste of times.'

# 10 The Lijnbaan (Rotterdam): a Prototype of a Postwar Urban Shopping Centre

## E. R. M. TAVERNE

### INTRODUCTION

Two structures attract particular attention in postwar Rotterdam. They are the Groothandelsgebouw (Wholesale Building), by the architect H. A. Maaskant, and the Lijnbaan shopping centre. The idea for the Groothandelsgebouw originated during the war when a large number of businesses lost their premises through bombing. The model was the Merchandise Market in Chicago, which was at that time the largest commercial building in the world. The idea of allowing lorries to drive into the building was, incidentally, also adopted from there. By Dutch standards the Groothandelsgebouw is built on a mammoth scale. Elevations 200 metres long and seven storeys high were unusual at that time in The Netherlands. The typology and architectural appearance of the building betray something of the intentions of the rebuilding plan for the city centre of Rotterdam, which was still being worked on in 1947 when Maaskant designed the Groothandelsgebouw. The building is based on the assumption that the new centre would be filled with large, free-standing building blocks. There is even a hint of a kind of nostalgia for an almost nineteenth-century closed townscape.

This approach was completely abandoned as the reconstruction progressed. The Lijnbaan shopping centre, which was built close by at the same time (1949–53), is based on a completely different town planning idea: an open concept of low, open streets alongside tall slab-like buildings (see Plate 10). The transplantation of a provincial and suburban shopping centre, developed on the American model (that of Victor Gruen), into the centre of the new Rotterdam was not a coincidence but symptomatic of the generally conflicting economic and socio-cultural concepts of the city that underlay the rebuilding plans for Rotterdam.[1]

## INDUSTRY AND COMMERCE

The Lijnbaan is a clear a piece of architecture as it is a complex one and its design and structure express as no other building in Rotterdam the radical new urban concept underlying the *Basisplan* (the Basic Plan) of 1946. Even during the war years it occurred to many people that the fire of 14 May 1940 had achieved what would otherwise inevitably have happened in the course of time. Mr Lichtenauer, General Secretary of the Chamber of Commerce in Rotterdam, was already able to write of Rotterdam that we 'are now going to renew and modernise the city, whereas we otherwise would have had to make do for a long time with obsolete premises, generally dating from a period that was not particularly renowned for its town planning achievements'.[2]

From industry and commerce in particular, voices were heard which were remarkably in accord with the opinions of the well-known American cultural sociologist, Lewis Mumford, whose 1943 pamphlet about the reconstruction of postwar society had already been translated and published in *De Rotterdamse Gemeenschap* (*The Rotterdam Community*) in 1946.[3] The wartime destruction had not been great enough, and he seemed to be saying to the Rotterdam entrepreneurs that 'we must therefore continue to do in a more deliberate and rational fashion what the bombs have done by brutal hit-or-miss'.[4]

These ideas about the city are also reflected in the new city plan, the 1946 Basic Plan, which provided for far more additional demolition than its predecessor, the reconstruction plan of 1941, and laid claim to scarcely any known urban form. The city of the future was not to be sacrificed to the cravings of nostalgia and the memories of a deprived generation. The plans for the empty area to the west of the Coolsingel and, particularly, its filling in with the Lijnbaan shopping centre were strikingly influenced by such ideas.

While the plans did not go so far as to require the demolition of the City Hall, the Post Office and the Stock Exchange – had not Mumford already referred in 1946 to a weak-kneed approach? – the Hofplein was ruthlessly scaled up into a traffic roundabout. This meant that the bold dreams of a bustling night-life, which were set down on paper for the Hofplein during the war, would have to be realised in the future on spacious boulevards, such as the widened Coolsingel, the principle axis of Rotterdam's business quarter. With the new Coolsingel as the surprising variant of Fifth

Avenue, the area as far as the Westersingel could at last be drawn into the centre, thereby formally confirming the *de facto* westward shift of central area activities.

After the leap over the Coolsingel, the plan provided here, by way of exception from the rule of functional zoning, for collective buildings. These were closed blocks for offices and businesses, but also with space for dwellings and shops on the ground floor.

## ENLARGEMENT OF SCALE

Although the arrangement of these collective buildings into city centre courts provided new standards of urban residential amenity with its green spaces and delivery roads and parking garages to separate pedestrian and motor traffic, it still adhered to the model of the conventional shopping street. Despite the fact that these relatively narrow shopping streets were attractive by the standards of the time, very few shopkeepers showed any enthusiasm to build. This was due not so much to the proposed urban form as to uncertainty about whether the location of shops west of the Coolsingel would be successful. Large department stores, such as C & A and the Bijenkorf, had not yet decided in favour of particular sites in 1947, and the retailers with an obligation to rebuild were increasingly coming round to the view that they would do so only as part of a joint enterprise. In these circles, too, considerations of profitability, cost savings and risk cover were pointing to the solution of collective buildings, of which the Groothandelsgebouw and the flat-roofed factories on the Oostzeedijk and Goudsesingel are examples for wholesaling and light industry.[5]

The type of collective building envisaged by the retailers did not in the least resemble the city centre courts proposed by the municipality for the Lijnbaan area. They were thinking much more of a kind of retailing emporium, a commercial building in which large and small stores could rent shop accommodation of varying sizes.

The proposal to put up collective buildings in the form of city centre courts (blocks 50 by 80 metres, with inner areas accessible to traffic, with shops on the ground floor on the outside, and offices and dwellings on the floor above) had a paralysing effect on the initiative of the retailers, because few of them had either the money or the wish to build substantial premises of which only a part would be needed for shops.

The idea of an independent shopping promenade was born at the moment when, under pressure from the retailers, the shops were removed from the city centre courts and linked together as independent shop units in a linear zone, the shopping avenue. The loss of dwellings above the shops was compensated by building additional storeys on the city centre courts, which were increasingly simplified during the evolution of the plan (1947–53) into tall slabs of residential flats (8 to 13 storeys) on largely open squares flanking the shopping centre (see Plate 11).[6]

## EMERGENCY SHOPS

As a result of this financial-economic operation conducted through the medium of a flexible urban plan, a number of important architectural features of the future Lijnbaan were presented, as it were, on a plate. Once a choice had been made for a broad, sunny promenade instead of a narrow asphalted shopping street, which meant a choice of something new, the image of the emergency shopping complexes, those wartime oases of relaxation, sociability and public entertainment, inevitably came to mind. This image was further strengthened by the proposed arrangement of the shopping centre. Now that the shops were no longer linked to the dwellings it became possible to build the whole shopping street as a single skeleton from beginning to end, thus economising on construction costs. Within the skeleton, built according to a defined module, the retailers were free in their choice of arrangement and finish.

The architecture of the design produce by Van den Broek and Bakema made no effort in principle to add anything to the chosen formula. In this respect it is as new and anonymous as the town plan to which it owes its existence. The choice of a concrete skeleton and a system of elevations with prefabricated slabs and stanchions closely met the requirements of dismantling, movement and change with which the Lijnbaan hoped to be successful as a new system of buying and selling. The fact that the image of the emergency wartime shops also emerged from the concept means very little to us in 1989, although, from the purely business point of view, it must have been appreciated at the time as a means of attracting the hesitant, acquisitive shopper over the threshold of the new age.[7]

## PROMENADE

In its anonymity, the architecture of the Lijnbaan shopping
promenade bears the signs not only of its complex town planning
origins – a low element contained between what are regarded as
distinctly urban forms – but the 'staging of movement' also makes
it very much theatre architecture. The transparent manner in which
the unity between interior and exterior has been achieved, the use
of inconspicuous columns and cantilevered canopies as transitional
elements and, particularly, the strictly maintained unity of dimension in paving and façades, all create a new spatial arrangement, a
prototype of that – to quote Jean Baudrillard – 'perfect circulation
machine', the Beaubourg in Paris.

In this the design is in complete harmony with the marketing
philosophy developed by the municipality and the developers, which
was based on the reciprocal reinforcement of the functions of looking
and buying. C. van Traa, the author of the Basic Plan, wrote in
1953: 'the profile must be: sunny, broad, traffic-free, furnished
with plant containers, seats, kiosks, a pleasant space where people
can devote themselves wholly to the activity of shopping. . . . It is
also a space for spectators, less hurried and less purposeful than
shoppers (spectators become shoppers), but initially more sensitive
to appearance and convenience.'[8] The new idea of a promenade, a
space for illusions, dreams and fantasy, is not so much given shape
by the architecture, as intensified and heightened by a treatment
of the shopping and street space derived directly from America.
Essential elements are the application of the open glass wall and a
refined lighting technique.

## REPORT OF AN AMERICAN JOURNEY

Is it a coincidence that the architect Van den Broek, in the
same year that his office became involved in the planning of
the Lijnbaan (1948), reacted enthusiastically in the report on his
American journey to the spectacular use of the shop window in
new shops and department stores? Coming from a country where
the war had only strengthened the existing reserve towards large
areas of shop window and illuminated signs, he was immediately
fascinated by the commercial and, particularly, the architectural
advantages of shop windows disposed freely in space:

The shop window is often intended to be inspected not only from the outside, but also from within. The absence of rear walls to the windows of clothes shops is a drawback, but the display has the form of an open stage decor, for which the highly developed, refined lighting techniques, employing mainly spotlights and projectors, either visible or concealed and with coloured or white light, afford new possibilities. The glass front is often so arbitrarily disposed in the plan that one can scarcely speak of a separation between interior and exterior. And this is precisely the intention of the shopkeeper, who in fact wants to lure the public without their being aware of it from outside to inside.[9]

## ESCALATORS

Van den Broek, with his great interest in technology and technique, discovered something else. Besides the striving for openness, there was in American department store structures the opposite tendency towards complete closure of the façade, with the exception, however, of the ground floor. Because of the highly developed lighting and ventilation techniques, it was possible to build department stores, for example, with closed elevations and without light wells. To balance the loss of the visual cohesion of floors in the interior, a 'remarkable new' means had been created of giving expression to that cohesion, namely the escalator. 'It might be said', according to Van den Broek, 'that static cohesion has been replaced by a dynamic one.'[10] In the case of the Lijnbaan, movement, not in the vertical but in the horizontal sense, is the true theme of this new architecture, and this makes the Lijnbaan 'modern' in the sense of being American.

As a mobile, changing, exterior space the Lijnbaan is just as American as the new Bijenkorf of the American architect, Marcel Breuer. It has the same sophisticated organisation, standardisation of counters and showcases, streamlining of inward movement of goods and people. But the Bijenkorf is situated on 'Fifth Avenue' and must have been experienced by many people in Rotterdam in 1957 even more intensely as 'made in the USA' than the Lijnbaan, if only because Dudok's Bijenkorf – one of Europe's most modern department stores before the war – apparently had been senselessly demolished a short time before. Even during the war, Dudok had himself produced a design for a closed façade, but the location of 'his' Bijenkorf stood in the way of the new urban design. The new Bijenkorf is not just a reinforcement and a 'considerable stimulus for lively shopping activity in the Lijnbaan'. Through the unknown enticement mechanisms of advertising, the glamour of its façades and, not least, the use of modern monumental sculpture (Gabo) in the service of town planning, it gives the Lijnbaan an 'indelible American stamp'.[11]

## CITY HALL

It was precisely that to which another American, Lewis Mumford, quoted earlier, was by nature least sensitive. In the same year that the public set the revolving doors in motion, Mumford published in the *New Yorker* 'The Skyline of the City, a Walk through Rotterdam', in which he tested his earlier ideas about postwar reconstruction against the example of Rotterdam. The Lijnbaan was central in his argument.[12]

Mumford had little eye for the more or less ostentatious interrelationship between the Lijnbaan and the neighbouring 'metropolitan' flats and the Bijenkorf. He pointed instead to the importance of the visual proximity of the City Hall, which brought the Lijnbaan into a quite different cycle of meaning. With his reference to the partial orientation of the Lijnbaan towards the City Hall, Mumford touched upon a theme which had held the interest of many circles in Rotterdam since the bombing. On all the plans which have left the drawing board since then we see an attempt to integrate the City Hall more closely into the cultural and administrative centre by means of the prolongation of a square. That this is not purely a technical correction suggested by the disaster is confirmed by the increasing popularity at the same time of the sociological theories of the neighbourbood concept.

This social scientific therapy for the sick city, which was developed in Chicago long before the war, aimed at a regional reordering of the urban fabric. Thanks to the disaster of May 1940 the theory was also in vogue in Rotterdam, because the bombing had left the way clear for a diagnosis which had been made much earlier to be succeeded by planned treatment. In 1946 there was published in Rotterdam a socio-cultural study of the city of the future, which declared that the city must no longer be 'a confused and structureless conglomerate' of constant additions of arbitrary rows of houses, but should be built up in a series of neighbourhoods into a 'structural unity'.[13] It was hoped that by dividing the city into communities on a human scale, a meaningful relationship could be created within all spheres of urban life – living, working and playing – between the individual and the community.

These ideas partly underlie the rebuilding plan for Rotterdam, which was approved in 1946 and had as its aim not only the radical renewal of the city as a built structure through the planned bundling of economic and cultural activities, but also, for convenience sake, the restoration of the 'community feeling of the citizens' (Mumford).

The neighbourhood concept is based on an articulation of the city into coherent parts, with a systematic hierarchical decentralisation of services. However, the latter remain subordinate to the city as a whole with its main centre, on which the Basic Plan is concentrated. In the social scientific planning model, a high-quality shopping facility such as the Lijnbaan – which is the hierarchical culmination of the series of neighbourhood and sub-neighbourhood shopping centres planned at strategic points within the city – demands a careful approach since, as a vital element of the city, it is designed to serve the whole of the city, not only through the quality of its assortment of shops, but especially through its scale and finished form. The resultant enlargement of scale threatens to disrupt the possibilities of social contact, the meaningful relationship between the individual and the community.

The whole layout and architectural design of the Lijnbaan is aimed in part at the restoration of this relationship and these are precisely the qualities pointed out by Mumford in his article about the Lijnbaan. In his view, the careful attention devoted to the pedestrian area makes the Lijnbaan a balanced environment *par excellence*. In contrast to the 'wrongly planned' adjacent housing, the Lijnbaan is an oasis in the midst of a city full of noise, carbon monoxide and nervous tension. For Mumford the Lijnbaan owes its success not to the massiveness derived from America, ingenious technical discoveries or expensive materials, but to a 'sedulous respect for the human scale and for pedestrian movement'.[14] Through this pronouncement Mumford appears to couple the neighbourhood concept with the Basic Plan.

In this view, the Lijnbaan becomes as it were a metaphor for the harmonious city. The carefully-carried-through unity of dimension of paving and elevations, which is also applied to all the recreational facilities, has a therapeutic significance, because it creates a balanced environment. The link with the new Raadhuisplein (City Hall Square) and the bringing into view of the City Hall from the Lijnbaan has become part of the envisaged social planning of the city, a sign that has to win back the members of the public from their excessive spending habits and make them once more stable citizens of the great community. In the words of Mumford: 'As far as I know, the work of the London County Council alone is Rotterdam's rival in the quality of its thinking and the extent of its postwar reconstruction of a devastated area.'[15]

## Notes

1. For a recent survey of the main events of the rebuilding of Rotterdam after the war, see F. Kauffmann, 'Towards a "Modern" City Center', in *Het Nieuwe Bouwen in Rotterdam 1920–1960* (Delft, 1982) pp. 77–107. For useful information and pictorial analyses see R. Geurtsen and M. de Hoog, 'Stad in stolling', in *Stedebouw in Rotterdam: Plannen en opstellen 1940–1981* (Rotterdam, 1981) pp. 99–115. For a full study of the planning and postwar development of Rotterdam see R. Blijstra, *Rotterdam, stad in beweging* (Amsterdam, 1965).

2. C. van Traa, 'Rotterdams nieuwe binnenstad', *Bouw* (1948) pp. 206–9. See also C. van Traa (ed.), *Rotterdam. Der Neubau einer Stadt* (Rotterdam, n.d.).

3. L. Mumford, 'The Social Foundations of Post-War Building', in *City Development Studies in Disintegration and Renewal* (London, 1946) pp. 131–64. This paper was first printed in England, in the famous *Rebuilding Britain* series, no. 9.

4. Ibid. p.131.

5. By chance the Van Tijen & Maaskant office had already in 1939 worked out a plan for an industrial building with numerous provisions that were advanced for that time. 130 workplaces could be made available at reasonable rents as an alternative for the small firms in the slum area scheduled for clearance between Goudsesingel and Kipstraat. See Kauffmann (note 1), p. 88: 'Many collective buildings of this kind had already appeared in Germany, England and the United States, but the direct model seems to have been the well thought out and functional "Workplace Building" that the architect/designer Koen Limperg had designed as a solution for the bad accommodation of the clothing industry in Amsterdam, but which he could not find anyone to take on.' After the war Limperg's ideas were adapted by the architects Van Tijen & Maaskant. See H. A. Masskant and A. G. van der Veen, 'Collectieve bedrijfsvestiging; de voordelen ener gemeenschappelijke exploitatie', *Bouw* (1947) pp. 253–4. See also J. Roding, 'Koen Limpberg's functionalisme. Bijdrage tot een plezieriger dagelijks leven', *Wonen-TABK*, 13 (1981) pp. 9–30.

6.   C. van Traa, 'Rotterdams nieuwe binnenstad', *Bouw* (1948) pp. 206-9.
7.   J. Joedicke, *Architektur and Städtebau. Das Werk von Van den Broek und Bakema*, Dokumente der Modernen Architektur, 3 (Stuttgart, 1963). See also J. Bakema, *Van stoel tot stad. Een verhaal over mensen en ruimte* (Zeist-Antwerpen, 1964).
8.   Van Traa, see note 6.
9.   J. H. van den Broek, 'Winkels in Amerika', *Bouw* (1948) pp. 259–60.
10.  Ibid.
11.  P. Johnson-Marshal, 'Rotterdam: How It Is Being Rebuilt', *Architects Journal* (27 October 1955) pp. 557–70.
12.  Lewis Mumford, 'The Skyline of the City, a Walk through Rotterdam', reprinted in L. Mumford, *The Highway and the City* (New York, 1963) pp. 31–40.
13.  For the Dutch concept of 'a harmonious life in a well-ordered city' and the different interpretations of the neighbourhood idea, see T. Idsinga, ' "Nieuwe Bouwen" in Rotterdam, 1940–1960: What is Urban Living in an Open City', in *Het Nieuwe Bouwen in Rotterdam 1920–1960* (Delft, 1982) pp. 108–38.
14.  Indirectly Mumford suggested that the idea of the Lijnbaan came from Victor Gruen's great achievements with respect to the planning of (suburban) shopping centres: 'In planning it [the Lijnbaan], the architects have made a dramatic contribution to the modern city, for they have shown that the advantages we associate in America with the suburban regional shopping center may also be made available in the heart of the city' (Mumford, see note 12, p. 36). See also V. Gruen and L. Smith, *Shopping Towns USA: The Planning of Shopping Centers* (New York, 1960).
15.  Mumford (see note 12) p. 40.

# 11 The Reconstruction of the Buda Castle Hill after 1945

## ERZSÉBET C. HARRACH

In the Second World War the entire territory of Hungary was the scene of heavy fighting, and Budapest was in the front line from late December 1944 to mid-February 1945. Twenty-six per cent of all buildings in the city and 94 per cent of the industrial buildings were reduced to ruins, and all the bridges over the Danube were destroyed. The Castle Hill of Buda – which preserved something of its strategic importance even in the twentieth-century warfare and thus was the Germans' final stronghold – suffered greatly during the fighting. The group of buildings of the Royal Palace occupies the southern one-third of the Castle Hill – the longish elevation lying on the western bank of the Danube – and the civil, or residential, quarter is situated on the northern two-thirds. Both are surrounded by a continuous rampart system, most of which still exists. Its rebuilding is the subject of this essay (see Figure 10, p. 228).[1]

The royal residence of the Hungarians, who had settled in the Carpathian basin in the tenth century, became Buda after 1241. According to the engravings and descriptions of the period, Buda was one of the most beautiful Gothic cities of Central Europe. Its golden age of the fourteenth and fifteenth centuries, during the reigns of King Sigismund and King Matthias, was ended by the Turkish occupation, which lasted for 150 years. The retaking of Buda from the Turks in 1686 destroyed those parts of the mediaeval city which had been left untouched during the Turkish occupation. In the eighteenth and nineteenth centuries, the palace and the residential quarter were rebuilt in a baroque style on the mediaeval ruins, and this style characterised the area until 1945. The building boom of the Austro-Hungarian monarch at the end of the nineteenth century hardly played a role in the residential area; rather, it was restricted to an impressive expansion of the royal palace.

Prior to the Second World War, the civil quarter contained some two hundred buildings one or two storeys high, with the exteriors dating from the eighteenth and nineteenth centuries but with mediaeval interiors. Of these, forty-two buildings were completely destroyed in 1945; sixty-two required considerable inner and outer renovation; and thirty-two required fundamental repairs. Fifty-two buildings suffered only slight damage; only one remained entirely undamaged, apart from broken windows (see Plate 12).[2]

Both the authorities and the population agreed on the pre-eminent importance of this part of the city, and consequently the very first measures dealing with rubble clearance and reconstruction which started immediately after the war ended, focused on the Castle Hill. The great value of the architectural ensemble in this area lay in its unique adaptation of the new to the old. The area had its own special atmosphere and constituted an enclosed unit within the surrounding metropolis unlike anything else in Hungary. In addition, the Castle Hill could be viewed as an architectural diary of Hungarian history.

The first actions were the removal of ruins and the securing of buildings that threatened to collapse. A special rail line facilitated the transport of the vast amount of debris to the depression of the Vérmező, which was almost completely filled up with rubble.[3] Once these measures had been taken the city had to deal with basic problems. Scientific research at excavation sites had already been started in 1945 by the Budapest Museum of Cultural History, which also took care that the sites were documented by surveys and photographs. The authorities had to determine the guiding principles for reconstruction. Here the question of how to fill in now-vacant lots in the residential area was especially important. New uses had to be found for buildings which had lost their previous functions in the new postwar economic and political conditions but which were still valuable as monuments. Most important was the fate of the Royal Palace, but uses for other palaces of aristocrats and for some ecclesiastical buildings also had to be found.

During the removal of ruins, immediate decisions had to be made about the protection of crumbling walls considered important either as monuments or as essential parts of the townscape, and about the demolition of valueless masonry. From 1946 to 1948 in addition to the renovations carried out by private persons, the state engaged in its own substantial projects, such as the reconstruction in the Matthias Church of the arch of the collapsed southern transept and the roof structure of the chapel of the Virgin Mary, and the reconstruction of the roof structures of the one-time Ministry of Finance, the Castle Theatre, the National Archives, the War History Museum and the Evangelical Church. By autumn 1949, since suitable conduits were available while electric power lines were not, gas street-lighting was introduced. This enhanced the atmosphere of the Castle District, which pleased both the architects and the public.[4]

Reconstruction work followed two main directions. The renovation of the large Palace was slower than the revival of the residential district, but the entire hill area was treated as a historical ensemble, with the principles of reconstruction determined accordingly. The protection of historical ensembles sought to preserve existing buildings of value and, when possible, enrich them with new elements. In the case of the reconstruction of the historic core of a destroyed city, careful consideration is always required to determine what can be demolished for new buildings and what should be preserved, even if only in fragments. In this case, there was another noteworthy factor. In the ruined buildings and beneath the fallen plaster, previously unknown mediaeval carvings came to light which confirmed the existence of a rich Gothic city; display of these fragments could enrich the postwar townscape. Thus the principles guiding the reconstruction of individual monuments were developed during actual work and crystallised in Buda prior to the drafting of the 1964 Venetian Charter of the International Council on Monuments and Sites.

Viewing the area as a whole, it was also considered essential to examine all of the elements which determine the character of the city: the road network, building lines, the divisions of lots, the planes of roofs, and the relations of the façades to one another. Filling in gaps between buildings that were part of a harmonious townscape formed over centuries was a difficult task even for the best architects. The guidelines for rebuilding major monuments were established very quickly, but guidelines for rebuilding lesser structures developed piecemeal. For example, buildings put up between 1945 and 1955 were affected by the questionable architectural tendency of that era, and buildings with 'neutral' façades were erected on the vacant lots. The façades were so characterless that they had nothing to do either with the historical environment or with contemporary progressive architecture.

By the 1960s, the filling in of the vacant sites in the residential district on Castle Hill came to a standstill. This was mainly due to economic reasons, but a series of unsettled questions of principle also played a role. In 1961 the Budapest Institute for the Preservation of Historic Monuments put the question on a conference agenda, resulting in a unanimous decision of all the authorities concerned that the missing buildings and empty sites in the Castle Hill district must be filled up with modern buildings within the shortest time.[5] The decision-makers accepted the fact that flats would be more expensive in this area than the city average. Naturally, beside economic questions, aesthetic ones were stressed most. Architects – in my opinion – finally found here a common denominator, whereby architects should still seek to design façades expressing contemporary forms but, even more important, they should adapt their creations to the historic surroundings.

In Hungary the buildings located in designated historic ensembles are protected as a group. This means that the individual buildings are protected independently of their own historic value, and construction on them is allowed only with the approval of the historic preservation office under the Historic Preservation Act of 1949, a law still in force.[6] During the early work in 1945 and 1946, however, the concept of ensemble preservation was seldom applied, but nevertheless much was achieved. It is enough to mention the preservation of numerous Gothic sedilias (seating niches in doorways), which came to light in clearing away the rubble of individual houses.

From the very start, reconstruction was centrally directed by the building authorities, but only in 1957 were supervisory mechanisms created for the special direction of work on historic monuments.[7] In the beginning, the majority of the buildings were still privately owned, but between 1946 and 1949 all property in this area became state-owned, which simplified proprietary relationships and removed obstacles to centrally directed rebuilding. Over time the scientific research and preparatory work by official organisations became more uniform and much more accurate, especially since the excavations were performed by members of the same research team, while in the beginning this had been done by the architects or possibly by the art historians of the Budapest History Museum, using only the available literature. Reconstruction combined with complete interior modernisation became a rule only in 1962. Since that date architectural design has been preceded by the preparation of scientific documentation based on the sources found in the archives, published literature and excavations on the site. The design must consider historical characteristics.

The plan of the residential area in the Castle Hill district was formed in the Middle Ages, and it has been maintained until today without much change. Only two large squares, Szentháromság Square and Kapisztrán Square, date from later periods. The majority of the buildings have mediaeval cores but received their present exteriors in the baroque age after the liberation from Turkish occupation. Rarely were the façades of this era redone in more recent styles.

The block surrounded by Uri Street, Szentháromság Street, Tóth Arpád Promenade and Nóegylet Street, which is situated in the centre of the civil town, provides a good illustration of the problems encountered in filling in vacant sites, as well as their usual solution (see Plate 14).[8] In the Middle Ages a series of Gothic palaces may have stood in this area; many ground-floor elements survived the sieges and even the battles of 1686 which liberated the city from Turkish rule. Baroque reconstruction incorporated every usable wall of the Gothic buildings in the new houses, as was the case in numerous other buildings. The existence of numerous mediaeval details – the rich sedilias which have been preserved in such a large number only in Hungary, the door-frames, the rooms with Gothic ribbed arches, the doorways – are due to this fact. In the nineteenth century only modest alterations were made to this block: rebuilding some individual façades in neo-classical and romantic style. On the corner of Bástya Promenade and Szentháromság Street there is a one-storey building of neo-baroque style dating from the 1930s.

During the Second World War, house nos 30 and 32 of Uri Street, as well as the part of no. 38 on the side of Bástya Promenade were ruined, but on the ground floor of no. 32, one of the richest Gothic doorways of the Castle Hill district came to light, and in the yard of no. 38 a large early-Gothic pillared and arched front and several minor details were revealed.[9] In rebuilding, the architect treated the preserved details not as fragments but as integral parts of the new building. He recognised that in the Castle Hill district, these ancient walls and vaults could constitute important elements of the centuries-old continuity of city life and the adherence to surviving cultural traditions. The outward appearance of the building, its vertical and horizontal proportions, harmonise with historic façades, and its general impression adapts to the atmosphere of the streets of the Castle Hill district.

The eclectic façade of no. 34 Uri Street was destroyed, and the architect[10] used the mediaeval structural elements which came to light from beneath the plaster, as well as the arches and the window bays, to form the new façade.[11] The new elements do not impinge on the historic ensemble but link together the remaining elements. The next building, no. 36 Uri Street, received its neo-classical façade in 1870. This building is also of mediaeval origin, but here the uniform elements of the last neo-classical architectural age – window, doors, staircases and railings – remained quite intact, and they were preserved carefully by the architect.[12] No. 38 Uri Street is the final building of the block. That part of the site on the side of Tóth Arpád Promenade now has a completely new building.[13] The reconstruction of the side towards Uri Street, however, utilised the mediaeval doorway and yard. It is noteworthy that the architect restored the rich romantic elevation on the Uri Street side together with all its ornaments.[14]

At the southern end of the Castle Hill district on Dísz Square, one lot is still vacant, since its foreign owner is unwilling either to build on it or to sell the lot, but this deficiency is hardly noticeable. Opposite this lot, the emptiness of lot no. 1 on Várszínház Street is more conspicuous, although it is made tolerable with its present horticultural arrangement. On the northern side of the square, the large, six-storey house which was built in place of the one-time 'Marcibányi palace' at the beginning of the twentieth century, was seriously damaged in 1945, and it had to be demolished, improving the streetscape of the Castle Hill district. An apartment house, built in a contemporary style with proportions reasonably fitted to the neighbouring buildings in spite of its modern details, now occupies the site, which marks the beginning of Uri and Tárnok Streets. Only the markedly horizontal solution of the façade is debatable in this environment.[15]

The other site where construction caused problems was at the corner of Szentháromság Square. Several projects were submitted, but the long delay in building was only partly due to architectural problems. The greatest difficulty was that several plots had to be built up jointly. Although the scale of the other buildings of the square had long since departed from the traditional scale of the façades of the Castle Hill district, in this case the architect wanted to suggest the old proportions. The completed buildings successfully fulfilled this desire.[16]

The apartment house built at the corner of Uri Street and Szentháromság Street was much debated. On the ground floor and in the cellar the White Dove restaurant was restored. With the application of up-to-date materials and structures, vertical and horizontal elements were combined successfully on the façade, and the high roof on the street side adapts to the roof planes of the adjacent houses (see Plate 13).[17]

The reconstruction of façades presented interesting problems.

For example, the so-called Bécsi kapu (Vienna Gate) and its surrounding at the northern part of the Castle Hill were first destroyed during the siege of 1686 and then seriously damaged in 1945. The owners of the buildings on Bécsi kapu Square restored the buildings before they became state property, though fortunately following the same guidelines as the authorities would have followed. An extremely valuable building on the square is no. 8, the one-time Esterházy palace. In this building many small flats were constructed after nationalisation. Scientific research on the building took place only at the beginning of the 1960s. On the basis of newly-found paint traces, the painted neo-classical façade decoration, unique in the Castle Hill district, came to light and could be completed. On the ground floor and on the Kard Street side, mediaeval fragments and paint traces were found. The two periods could be treated separately in the successful restoration.[18]

Some of the buildings in the area of the Castle Hill, since they are also visible from other points of the city, are important not only because they shape the internal cityscape of the Castle Hill district but also because they influence the external cityscape considerably. This is the case with the buildings situated on the two longitudinal streets of the residential city, Uri and Tárnok Streets. Building lots extend to the ramparts on the eastern and western sides of the Castle Hill, so the buildings located here also determine the outer appearance of the Castle Hill. On the sides of these plots facing the slope many of the buildings were totally destroyed. This meant that on the inner part of the lots damaged buildings could be reconstructed, but on the external sides entirely new buildings had to be erected.

One such building on the Danube side is the residence at no. 7 Tárnok Street. On the side facing Hunyadi János Street, at an important point on Castle Hill and visible from a distance, a tall new building was erected. The designer reconstructed the staircase using remnants of the eighteenth-century one-storey building on the Tárnok Street side and rebuilt the external front using walls which could be preserved. Modern flats were constructed in the building. On the part of the plot facing the rampart, a new building was erected whose façade was formed with vertical elements, and it fits in well with its surroundings.[19]

As was mentioned earlier, an important question in reconstruction was the utilisation of buildings protected as monuments. Sometimes the former uses of buildings were no longer suitable. For example, the former palaces of the aristocrats were not suitable for conversion to apartments. The situation was even more difficult in the case of buildings in the residential district of Castle Hill, where there were numerous large, old apartments with vaulted ceilings whose historic and aesthetic value were to be made public property. Such buildings could no longer be enjoyed by only a single family. Attempts were made to find the new uses right at the beginning, since numerous buildings were then vacant, but in many instances solutions to this problem were slow in coming. Even today, final determination of how best to use the former prime minister's office in the Sándor Palace and the partly ruined building of the former Ministry of War remains unsettled.

In general, however, many historic buildings received new tenants. In no. 13 Országház Street there is a library in the part of the house with a Gothic groined vault. The mediaeval synagogue at no. 26 Táncsics Mihály Street houses a museum.[20] Most frequently, restaurants have been installed in such buildings: in the rooms of no. 4 Hess András Square, with rich Gothic details, there is an elegant nightclub and bar;[21] in the original vaulted spaces of the single-storey, originally baroque building at no. 17 Országház Street, a restaurant was established by restoring the destroyed parts in an up-to-date manner; behind the Gothic arcades of the yard of the apartment house at no. 2 Országház Street there is another elegant restaurant;[22] on the ground floor of the baroque no. 7 Szentháromság Street is the so-called Ruszwurm confectionery with its restored Empire-Biedermeier furniture; there is a coffee bar on the ground floor of the mediaeval no. 14 Tárnok Street.[23] The one-storey baroque building at no. 15 Dísz Square has also become a public institution. On the ground floor there is a post office, while the rooms decorated with baroque frescoes on the next floor house the Preservation Office of the Housing Department. Frescoes are very rare in Hungary, and it was decided that they should not be hidden in private apartments which could not be visited.[24]

The most prominent example of a public building put to new uses is the former parliament of Buda at no. 28 Országház Street. After its rich, late baroque architectonical unity had been restored, the former assembly room on the first floor was turned over to the Hungarian Academy of Sciences, and even the vaulted spaces on the ground floor are suitably used.[25]

The simple baroque monument at no. 21 Országház Street is also utilised as a public institution.[26] Its peculiar charm is determined by the small square in which there is the earliest piece of statuary in Budapest whose subject is not religious. It is noteworthy here that in the reconstruction of the façade, the architect retained the original structural units, hardly breaking the original spaces by new dividing walls. On this site there had been two houses in the Middle Ages, both badly damaged in 1686. Using the remnants of these two houses, a baroque residence had been built with a series of stuccoed rooms and a chapel. Moreover, during the research prior to rebuilding, several mediaeval details and secondarily-used Roman stones came to light. In the Second World War, the building suffered only minor damage and thus remained habitable. However, because of the housing shortage after the war, almost every hallway had become a separate dwelling, and when reconstruction began there were twelve substandard apartments in the building. The characteristics of the floor plan made possible the creation here of a guest-house for the Hungarian Academy of Sciences.

The construction of the new Hotel Hilton looms large in any discussion of the reconstruction of the residential quarter and the very difficult task of finding new uses for historic monuments.[27] In the place of the present hotel there had been two very valuable buildings: on the northern side, the mediaeval church, cloister and college of the Dominicans, and on the southern side, a baroque Jesuit boarding school. These two buildings had not existed simultaneously; the cloister ensemble existed until the Turkish occupation, while the school was erected in the place of mediaeval residences after the occupation. The church and cloister might have existed already in 1254, because in that year the capitular meeting of the order, which had been held previously in Bologna or Paris, met in Buda.

The remains of these building ensembles were excavated through careful archaeological research. The significance of the remnants presented architects planning to build there with a difficult task. The official plan called for the erection of a public building on the site. The first concept suggested an elementary school, since there had been a school in the area north of the church before the war. However, this idea did not take into account the disorderliness of Szentháromság Square and Hess András Square. Another proposal, submitted by an architect who had prepared a design for the Hilton Hotel chain, called for a tall, slab-like hotel (to be named 'Hotel Mathias Rex') to occupy the entire site. While the first proposal best reflected the historic characteristics of the site, the second proposal was absolutely foreign to the Castle Hill district. After a fierce dispute both suggestions were rejected by the competent authorities. Considering the special importance of the place, six new proposals were solicited that would harmonise better with the existing monuments and townscape.

The chosen design was constructed without any substantial changes. A high-quality new hotel was to be built, but remnants of historic monuments had to be preserved and integrated into the new ensemble. Furthermore, the unity of the townscape of Buda had to be preserved and harmoniously completed. Another function of this design was a new arrangement of the area around the Matthias Church and the Fishermen's Bastion. By keeping the height of the main hotel structure as low as possible and by building up the whole area, the architect could obtain the greatest visual unity. The final design also made possible the optimum display of the mediaeval building remains.

The bulk of the hotel when viewed from the Danube roughly follows the line of the buildings destroyed during the war. Thus, the southern part is higher than the northern block of buildings next to the open church square. With its façades and roofing, the smaller building clearly is part of the hotel, but it provides at the same time a gradual transition to the lower buildings of Táncsics Mihálly Street situated farther back. The architect consciously avoided competition with the serrated contours of the Fishermen's Bastion and Matthias Church, and he solved this problem by means of calm roof sections.[28]

Numerous fragments of the mediaeval remnants were integrated into the ensemble, while the formal reconstruction of other parts was also carried out. In the latter case, historic elements were fitted together – without changes in form – by using new materials according to accepted international practice.[29] With minor additions, the internal space of the ruined church (the chancel, the triumphal arch, and the Gothic choir-screen) is now perceptible. On the north wall of the nave, three late Roman windows and the choir-screen imprint are presented. The Gothic pillars were completed in full height with cast stone and have a load-bearing function. The southern side was completed at a lower height, thus forming a platform for a part of the front of the hotel. The resultant open space offers a realistic spatial experience to the observer. The main entrance of the hotel was built in the preserved and reconstructed baroque façade of the former Jesuit school. When reconstructing this façade, the goal was not only to achieve authenticity but also to ensure that the present building was not larger in bulk than its predecessor.

Reconstructing historic elements and adding to them was often difficult. The architects used the ancient forms as the standard. An example of this approach is the cloister, where the courtyard was built according to the original design, but using modern materials. An extremely delicate problem was how to fit the mediaeval 'Nicholas' church tower, which remained intact to a considerable height, organically into the building of the hotel. The tower, which also dominates the view from across the river, was raised even higher by adding a modern storey and spire, and thus it remained a vertical accent within the main body of the hotel. The modern methods used in the addition also served a practical purpose: the separate water tank of the hotel is located here.

Another important public institution on Castle Hill is the building ensemble of the Castle Theatre. It also stands on mediaeval bases: there had been a Franciscan cloister church in its place. On its plinths, which had remained after 1686, a baroque Carmelite church was built between 1725 and 1736. In 1784 a decree of King Joseph II suppressed the order, and the church was rebuilt and became a theatre from 1787 to 1924.

During the Second World War the cloister and the church-theatre were seriously damaged; nothing remained from the theatre's interior. Between 1948 and 1950 the roof structure was reconstructed and the walls shored up. In 1961 the cloister building was turned over to the institutes of the Hungarian Academy of Sciences, while the former church was again rebuilt as a theatre. After archaeological research, the exterior of the building was reconstructed in its baroque form. When rebuilding the theatre, the architect tried to make the remains of the internal baroque architecture of the church – its vaults and pillars – as visible as possible; in an interesting solution, he placed the auditorium in the space of the church by means of an independently reinforced concrete 'shell'. This solution represents a successful harmony between old and new structures.[30]

The southern one-third part of the Castle Hill is occupied by the building ensemble of the Royal Palace. When the Soviet troops blockaded Budapest at the end of December 1944, the German soldiers who were trapped here withdrew to the Royal Palace, and were besieged for almost two months. Naturally, this is where the war damage was greatest.

It is hard to imagine the extent of the destruction. The art treasures accumulated there, the architectural masterpieces, and the facilities of the Royal Palace had been produced by the foremost workshops. Everything was in ruins, including 1900 square metres of old and 2600 square metres of newer inlaid parquet flooring; 9400 square metres of decorated oak flooring; 6600 square metres of white, 3500 square metres of gilded and 1400 square metres of richly gilded stucco ceiling.[31] After rubble clearance the walls of the Palace towered towards the sky almost naked.

The guidelines for rebuilding the palace and the surrounding area were already determined by the Budapest Council for Public Works in 1945. Architects were 'not to copy what had existed, not to try to remake what had been destroyed, and still less to create "new old" things'. This led to the construction of a modern group of buildings that fulfilled new needs while respecting the history of the completely ruined Palace.[32] The reconstruction of the castle complex had two parts: the reconstruction of the royal palace of the Habsburgs, and the excavation and restoration of the remnants of the mediaeval royal palace which had become buried over time.

The historic core of the present building of the baroque Royal Palace is the southern wing (wing E), built about 1714–15 during the rule of King Charles II. The basic form, height and body of this building, during the reign of Maria Theresa, were the basis for the baroque Palace of the 1750s, created by a northern extension (the present wings C and D). Fulfilling the demands for a royal residence for the Austro-Hungarian Monarchy from 1890 to the turn of the century, architect Alajos Hauszmann practically doubled the mass of the baroque building of Maria Theresa by extending the front toward the Danube (wings A and B), thereby placing the present wing C in the centre and forming a new central axis with the cupola. In the first half of the twentieth century only minor alterations were made.

During reconstruction the two major problems were to determine the new function of the building and the appropriate architectural style. The final decision on the use of the complex was made in 1958 by a government decree which ordered the establishment of a cultural as opposed to a governmental centre. The rebuilding programme was then determined according to which institutions were to be located in the individual buildings. In view of its very valuable collections, the National Gallery was located in the most stately, centrally-situated section (wings B, C and D) facing the Danube. The section housing Hungarian works of art is properly framed by the buildings of the Museum of the Hungarian Workers' Movement (wing A) and the Budapest History Museum (wing E) located in the connecting wings, as well as by the building of the Hungarian National Library (wing F), which completes an enclosed courtyard.

Due to its important aesthetic role and its dominant position when viewed from the city below, the reconstruction of the baroque-eclectic Palace was accompanied by fierce debates, especially regarding the style of the façades and the cupola. Several study plans and proposals were prepared before the final solution was adopted. The wings of the National Gallery facing the Danube were constructed – with minor modifications – on the basis of the baroque façade-system of the Palace of Maria Theresa, and this was followed by the neo-baroque cupola. The seccessionist roof superstructures were retained, and the cupola, adapted to the new façade and constituting a harmonious unity with it, was given a different significance. The baroque front conceals a modern internal architecture. The façades and inner spaces, formed in different architectural styles, required a system of windows that would not have a disturbing effect either on the front or on the inner architecture. In the case of the palace, uniformly large, undivided windows were put into the baroque window frames. The unified system of windows and the colouring of the façade provided a calm, uniform picture, stressing the function of the building.[33] The western wing (F) on the side of Krisztinaváros, which offered a new and adequate home for the Hungarian National Library, was reconstructed with the eclectic baroque external architecture of Hauszmann.

The new cupola is somewhat higher than Hauszmann's cupola, and it is absolutely different in style and function. The reinforced concrete cladding of the cupola covered with copper plate, which was formed from different stylistic elements, and its supporting tambour with a covering of stone, overlay another internal space-forming cladding. The internal cladding enabled the architect to form a modern cupola space which is independent of the external architecture, and the double cladding enables visitors to walk through the cupola.

Since the war destroyed all the original palace interiors, and since approved guidelines on historic restoration prohibited a reconstruction based solely on photographs or archival plans, the interior architecture of the palace had to be absolutely modern. The architect applied costly materials: the entrance hall and main staircase below the cupola is especially beautiful, where the white and red marble, bronze and glass surfaces constitute a truly impressive place.

Even in such a brief outline, one of the most interesting aspects of reconstruction, namely the excavation and display of the remains of the mediaeval and Renaissance Royal Palace, should be mentioned. Before the war there was no visible trace of the mediaeval remnants which were hidden under the castle garden and in the cellar walls of the baroque palace, their existence suggested only by old illustrations and descriptions. Perhaps the only positive aspect of the great devastation was that during reconstruction, systematic excavation and research became possible. The remains of the big round southern bastion, gatehouse, Stephen-tower, knights' hall and Gothic castle chapel were brought to light through excavations. These fragments made authentic reconstruction possible, and this in turn makes the mediaeval face of the castle of Buda conceivable for today's viewers. Moreover, the locating of the Budapest History Museum on the south-eastern side of the palace near this rich archaeological material proved highly successful. The sculptures, carved building decorations, Gothic glazed tiles and other objects could be displayed almost *in situ*.

Naturally, this account of the reconstruction of the Castle Hill cannot aim at completeness. Many volumes could be written about the large tasks undertaken by the whole Hungarian nation after the destruction in 1945. Nevertheless, the rebuilding of Castle Hill serves to illustrate the basic concepts and principles that underlay our efforts. I believe that we may be proud of the results, and the fact that in 1987 UNESCO included the Castle Hill of Buda as part of the cultural world heritage of mankind proves that its reconstruction became more than just the local achievement of a small nation.

**Notes**

1. The author of this study took part, from the 1950s onward, in the restoration of the Castle Hill district, so many of her conclusions are based on her own notes and observations.
2. Laszlo Gerö, *The Restoration of the Castle in Buda* (Budapest, 1951) p. 54.
3. Ibid., p. 76.
4. Ibid., p. 78.
5. Mihály Zádor, 'Conference about the New Buildings of the Castle District in Buda', *Müemlékvédelem*, 7, no. 1 (1963) pp. 9–10.
6. The 1949 Resolution of the Government is the first law about protection of monuments after the war.
7. Government Resolution 1045/1957/IV.25.
8. Miklós Horler, 'A Block of Houses in the Castle District', in *Magyar Epitömuvészet*, no. 2 (1967) pp. 2–9.
9. Architect: Zoltán Farkasdy.
10. Architect: Tamás Dragonits.
11. Horler, see note 8.

12. Architect: Irén Lipták.
13. Architect: György Jánossy.
14. Architect: Ferenc Bognár.
15. Architect: Zoltán Farkasdy.
16. Architect: Csaba Virágh.
17. Architect: Csaba Virágh.
18. Architect: Lóránt Radnai.
19. Architect: János Sedlmayr.
20. Architect: Meldina T. Papp.
21. Architect: Gyula Riedlmayer.
22. Architects: József Csemegi, Aurél Budai, József Király.
23. Architects: József Csemegi, László Boros.
24. Károly Pereházi, 'New Functions of Historic Buildings', *Müemlékvédelem*, no. 3 (1967) pp. 166–72.
25. Architect: Lajos Meczner.
26. Architects: Lajos Meczner, Irén Lipták.
27. János Sedlmayr, 'Restoration on the Site of Hilton Hotel Budapest', *Müemlékvédelem*, no. 1 (1979) pp. 1–23.
28. Architect of the new parts: Béla Pinter.
29. Architect of the historic parts: János Sedlmayr.
30. Architect: László Kékesi.
31. Gerö, see note 2.
32. 'Buda Castle Palace', *Magyar Epitömüvészet*, no. 5 (1976) pp. 14–19. Team of architects.
33. 'Buda Castle Palace, Budapest History Museum', *Magyar Epitömüvészet* no. 6 (1968) pp. 16–21. Team of architects.

# 12 Reconstruction of the City Centre of Dresden: Planning and Building during the 1950s

## JÜRGEN PAUL

Dresden, as it was before its destruction at the end of the Second World War, has become somewhat of a legend. Its fame lingers on as a city of the arts and one of the most beautiful among the large cities in Europe, although neither Dresden's present appearance nor its cultural life today measure up to their prewar standing.[1]

The city was founded by the Margraves of Meissen in the thirteenth century and laid out behind the castle guarding the bridge over the Elbe. It was based on a systematic plan typical of newly founded towns in the eastern part of Central Europe, with a rectilinear street system and the large, roughly square market place in the middle. This plan was preserved until the city's destruction in 1945, although the architectural appearance of the small mediaeval centre of the city and its surrounding area was no longer mediaeval. It was actually largely dominated by baroque façades and houses built during Dresden's Golden Age from the end of the seventeenth century until the end of the eighteenth.[2]

The city's image was characterised by several major elements. There were such well-known monumental buildings as the Zwinger, the Hofkirche (Catholic Court Church), the Frauenkirche with its elegant bell-shaped dome, and the Kreuzkirche, rebuilt in the late eighteenth century on the site of the Gothic main parish church which had been destroyed by Frederick the Great's canon shells. Then there were the other buildings that composed the famous view from across the Elbe river, and finally there were the artistocratic palaces and citizens' houses with their baroque façades lining the streets on both sides of the river (see Plate 15).

Dresden before its destruction was, however, in no sense primarily a baroque city. In fact it was predominantly a city of the nineteenth century. Although the art and architecture of its Golden Age under the reign of August the Strong and his successors now constitute the posthumous fame of 'the splendours of Dresden', its tradition as a European-wide centre of the arts actually originated in the Romantic period, and it was during the nineteenth century that

170

the cityscape of Dresden largely received the shape it had before its destruction. After 1800 Dresden had been a very prosperous city, but politically and socially a rather quiet and idyllic place. The 'Florence on the Elbe', as Johann Gottfried Herder dubbed it, became the centre of the Romantic movement in Germany, a favourite place to live and a meeting point for writers, musicians and painters. Yet, in the second half of the century, Dresden grew rapidly into a large city, the fifth largest in Germany, although it acquired a special character among Germany's great cities. As the capital and royal residence of the Kingdom of Saxony, particularly as a centre of cultural life, and as a favourite settlement of aristocratic families and other wealthy people of culture from Germany and abroad, Dresden was a sophisticated and rich city, a city of administration rather than industry, for retirement rather than a place of working life. Although it was the capital of rapidly industrialising Saxony, public planning and construction policies for decades decidedly opposed large scale industrialisation of Dresden. Although it eventually became something of an industrial centre, restrictive measures provided that the city be protected as much as possible from extreme building concentration and speculation, and that Dresden, even though a large city, should retain what was called its 'rural character' with the gardens and parks it had acquired in the baroque and Romantic periods.

Consequently, the nineteenth century left its mark on the city not only through the monumental public buildings by Gottfried Semper and his school, or through the opulent neo-baroque commercial architecture of the end of the century, but also through the extensive residential districts consisting of detached villas set in large private gardens on wide, tree-lined avenues, extending immediately from the edge of the city's commercial centre and the main railway station way out into the surrounding hills on the outskirts. There was very little of coherently built-up residential blocks and no densely built-in courtyards of the kind seen in nineteenth-century Berlin or Vienna. Even the workers' districts consisted largely of apartment buildings that were free-standing and surrounded by gardens.[3] No wonder, then, that it was in Dresden that the English-influenced German Garden City Society was founded and its first housing project, the Gartenstadt Hellerau, realised.

At the end of the Second World War, during the night of the 13–14 February 1945, Dresden was bombed and 85 per cent of the city destroyed – the centre and the residential areas east and south of the centre almost totally, the industrial quarters west of the centre and in the Neustadt across the river to a lesser extent (see Plate 24).[4]

The present, reconstructed Dresden is quite a different city, where only a few architectural monuments – restored or surviving as ruins – and some districts at the far outskirts still remind one of prewar Dresden. The new Dresden was rebuilt with the programmatic claim of creating a new city shaped by the 'socialist society' on the site of its old 'feudalistic' and 'bourgeois' predecessor. Considering the destroyed city's cultural importance, this programme of a new socialist city was postulated here with a particular cultural claim.

The contradictions that are apparent in the incomplete, present cityscape reflect, however, the insecurities and political shifts about what a socialist city actually is, what form its urban planning and architecture should take, what its cultural expression – its own as well as in relation to the cultural heritage of the past – should be like. Thus, the reconstruction of Dresden was also a struggle against, and for, the beautiful that was. Although the socialist state had given itself complete control and freedom of planning, thus creating the prerequisites to let the 'ideal city' become reality, the inconsistent, fragmentary urban structure and architectural form of the new Dresden is the result of an infinitely complicated story of planning, a history of ever-changing urban concepts that were always conceived with comprehensive total claims, yet one that always remained mere patchwork, not only because of the constant gap between the planning visions and the reality of economic means in the socialistic political system. This chapter can only summarise the planning history for the former historic centre of Dresden.

In the official terminology of the history of the German Democratic Republic, the first few years after the war before the GDR was founded in 1949 were called the phase of the 'Antifascist, Democratic Revolution' (or rather 'alteration' – *Umwälzung*). At this time, vehement cultural, political and ideological debates on the question of reconstruction arose in the Russian zone just as in the Western zones of occupied Germany. In this context, the problem concerning the rebuilding of historical urban centres formed the focus of the discussions, with sharply opposed propositions for either complete restoration of all historic buildings that had been destroyed or totally new plans for radically modern cities, even at new locations. Within a short time, however, altered political and economic conditions were created in the Russian zone of occupation. One of these was the nationalisation of the building material industry and large construction firms following the guidelines for economic policy set up by the German Communist Party in 1946. The second was the much more radical removal of ruins and debris. The authorities disposed of numerous burned-out and partially destroyed, artistically valuable historic buildings in the town centres, which, had they been in Western cities, would have been restored and considered as essential elements for urban reconstruction on the basis of a compromise between old and new, between the restoration of the historically developed urban and architectural structure and the principles and aims of modern town planning. But in Dresden from 1946 to 1953, the year when the actual reconstruction began here, complete streets lined with houses gutted by the fire of the bombs were cleared. In one large project in 1950, for instance, Dresden's new mayor Walter Weidauer ordered the demolition of scores of remaining ruins of baroque façades, which hitherto had been preserved for eventual restoration, as well as of numerous nineteenth-century buildings. Among the latter were such important works of architecture as Gottfried Semper's Oppenheim Palace and Villa Rosa. Because of their unpopular character, these activities were often carried out during the night. Also around the ruin of the collapsed Frauenkirche, many cut stones, which had already been ordered and numbered for eventual reconstruction, were removed. Even during the late 1960s, numerous burnt-out nineteenth-century public buildings, villas and residential blocks as well as churches were demolished. Large parts of the destroyed city remained an empty desert.[5]

The first initiative for the reconstruction of the destroyed city was an exhibition entitled 'The New Dresden' which the city government organised in 1946. Its main objective was the programmatic rejection of any individualistic rebuilding on the old foundations by private property owners, and instead the proclamation of a systematic reconstruction on the basis of a consistent urban and building plan.[6] This was similar to the state of the debate in West Germany, although there such plans serving as a basis for reconstruction were established between 1946 and 1947, whereas a concrete plan in Dresden was many more years in coming. Abundant plans and propositions were conceived and submitted on barely official and even private initiative, however, by designers and architects; for example, by Paul Wolf, who had served as Dresden's urban planning commissioner in the 1920s and who now proposed rebuilding the city in the sober, flat-roofed forms of modern architecture.[7] The obvious obstacles resulted only secondarily from the lack of economic prerequisites. The primary barrier was formed by the insecure political and social circumstances in these first postwar years.

The political and subsequent legal and organisational conditions were not provided until 1949, when the German Democratic Republic was founded in the Russian zone as a reaction to the proclamation of the Western zones of occupation as the new Federal Republic of Germany. In the same year, a Ministry for Reconstruction was established (renamed in 1958 as Ministry for Building), and in 1950 the Law Regulating the Reconstruction of Cities in the German Democratic Republic (Gesetz über den Aufbau der Städte in der DDR) was proclaimed. The decisive consequence of this law was the socialist state's legal right of disposition over land. In terms of reconstruction, this meant the expropriation (more or less without compensation) of private property in the war-destroyed urban districts.[8] This law also provided for the planned organisation of all building work. A governmental decree of 27 July 1950 formulated '16 Principles of Urban Planning', giving political, social, economic and cultural guidance for reconstruction of the cities in the GDR.

These principles rejected, first, the demands of socialist circles, repeated since the nineteenth century, for the dissolution of the large cities as a prerequisite for a socialist society, and instead stressed that further urbanisation is fundamental for the build-up of socialism on the basis of scientific, technical progress. Yet for the basic social orientation, 'the goal of urban planning is the harmonious satisfaction of the human right for work, housing, culture and recreation'. Many fundamental points articulated in the Charter of Athens are echoed in these sixteen principles and claimed as basic preconditions to 'supersede step by step outdated economic, social and cultural disproportions'. The ultimate principle should be the primacy of the new society's needs, of the social community as opposed to materialistic and idealistic demands of the individual. Consequently, a cultural programme for the new cities was prescribed that would adequately represent the new political life and new system of power, and renew and transform the national identity in terms of socialism, while at the same time respecting the historically developed urban character and artistic singularity. The sixteen principles set out the functional, architectural forms for these objectives: the most important political, administrative and cultural facilities are to be located in the city's centre; in the squares of the city's centre, political demonstrations, parades and popular festivities are to be held; the inner city is to be distinguished by the most important and most monumental buildings that will dominate the ground plan and the architectural silhouette of the city. This is in contrast to the Charter of Athens which defined the 'functional city' of modern civilisation independently from ideological aspects. Here, however, the city was destined to become the image of socialist society and its public life.

In his commentary on the sixteen principles, Edmund Collein, the Head of the Advisory Council for Architecture in the Council of Ministers (that is, the government), stressed the antithesis to the rebuilding of the city centres in West Germany, where the situation was determined purely by interest in private profits, where no priority was given to humanistic ideals and the chaos of the capitalist city reiterated. In the same year, 1951, the German Academy of Architecture, the revered institution founded in 1799 and associated with the name of Karl Friedrich Schinkel, was founded anew in Berlin as a branch of the Ministry of Construction; it was to be the scientific institution to direct architectural planning. At the inauguration of the Academy, Walter Ulbricht, head of the United Socialist Party, explained: 'The innovation offered by the German Democratic Republic is that architecture, as well as all the other cultural areas, serves the whole of the people. The buildings should satisfy the needs of the society and lend expression to progressive ideas of a struggle for a life of happiness for the people in a unified, peace-loving and democratic Germany.' Architecture should be rooted in popular feelings and be of emotionally irradiating quality. The historically developed, individual character of a city should initiate a homogeneous architectural and aesthetic form of the city which, as a whole, would exemplify and symbolise the new quality of social life. Yet new monumental buildings should be created as manifestations of the new society, the state, the party and mass organisations of society, thereby representing the power of the socialist people.[9]

This, in sum, was a political and cultural programme for adapting urban planning and architectural theories and models from the Soviet Union in the Stalinist period, with its ideologically determined opposition to the functional formalism of modern architecture in the capitalist West. The Deutsche Bauakademie initiated an official architectural periodical entitled *Deutsche Architektur*. (In 1974, after the party had changed her political objective from reunification of Germany to the theory of the development of two separate and antagonistic states on the territory of the former German Reich, its name was changed to *Architektur der DDR*.) Its first volume was filled with programmatic statements invoking the cultural tasks of architecture and city building under socialism, praising the Soviet example[10] and condemning the 'formalism' of capitalist architecture. The opening phrase of Walter Ulbricht's introduction predicted that 'the buildings which our German architects are now designing and executing will be buildings for centuries to come'. This was followed by an article by Kurt Liebknecht, the president of the Bauakademie, saying that the new architecture had to be founded on the national tradition of German architecture and on the example of Soviet architecture and urbanism.[11]

The National Programme of Reconstruction within the first Five Year Plan initiated in 1951 foresaw the rebuilding of fifty-three destroyed cities, emphasising the monumental development of city centres.[12] The centre of every major city was to have a vast square for political parades, a wide 'Magistrale' (main avenue), and a tower house according to the prototypes of Moscow's development under Stalin. The intention was to build political manifestos. In the same year, construction of the Stalinallee in East Berlin as the prototype of a socialist 'Magistrale' in the GDR was begun.

In planning practice, however, there was a great uncertainty as to what functional and structural form should be assumed by the general guidelines of the sixteen principles. Furthermore, there was strong and more or less open opposition on the part of local forces against the party directives from Berlin. This resulted for several years in an almost total lack of comprehensive urban development plans, including Dresden. Given the party decision for a forced development of the inner city, the controversial unsolved problem was how and how far the historical character of a city should be respected and could be reconciled with the planning and architectural manifestations of the new society. In Dresden that meant the question of preservation or disintegration of the historical city centre street plan, adjusting to the proportional dimensions of the surviving historic monuments or creating a new urbanistic structure with a new order, new spatial and architectural dimensions, preserving the famous historical silhouette of the old towers, or allowing it to be dominated by a new vertical accent formed by a skyscraper as prescribed by the sixteen principles. These years abound with publications written by art historians and others in which the unique beauty of prewar Dresden was conjured up and reconstruction principles postulated which should at least respect and follow the former spatial and dimensional structure.[13] The most crucial controversy was over the plans for a new tower. This included the question of what kind of use such a building should have, whether it was to be a palace of the party or a palace of culture, or, in other words, whether it was the party or the 'socialist culture' that would claim for itself the right to join, or even dominate, the famous silhouette of Dresden. In the many plans which were made over the years, this project was ambiguously referred to as 'Haus der

SED' (House of the United Socialist Party), 'Kulturhaus' (House of Culture) or, most frequently, just as 'Turmhaus' (Tower House).

In 1950, an initial conceptual competition for a building plan of the city centre was held. It was based on a very vaguely defined programme, the future of Dresden seeming too uncertain at the time.[14] The results of the competition were unsatisfactory and were not followed up. Then, in 1952, a 'Magistrale' leading north–south and cutting through the former historic city centre was demanded, and a new planning competition was held – again without any comprehensive plan. These plans, too, ended up filed away. Under pressure of a date to start construction set by the Ministry in Berlin, yet another, limited competition for a building plan for the city centre was held later in the same year. Although this second competition was supposed to establish decisively the guidelines for the rebuilding of the city centre, it was open for merely seven weeks. Only four architects' collectives, not individual private architects, were invited to participate. At last, the new political and ideological urban planning programme found its expression here. Once again, however, great uncertainty was apparent, demonstrated by the fact that no first prize was awarded.[15] The second and third prizes went to the Herbert Schneider and Johannes Rascher collectives, which had given priority to the new elements of urban planning demanded by the sixteen principles: the vast, cental square for mass parades, the 'Magistrale'. The Schneider collective proposed a tower house as 'Socialist Dominant' on the north side of the Altmarkt and a new, second large square for ceremonies between the tower house and the former Royal Palace, that is, on the site of the former narrow streets of the historic core of old Dresden (see Plate 16).

Nevertheless, the local reluctance to accept the guiding principles set in Berlin was demonstrated by the fact that the fourth prize was awarded to the Wolfgang Rauda collective from the Technical University of Dresden. Rauda was an architect of conservative orientation. He had written a dissertation on the urban development of Dresden in the Middle Ages, worked as Hugo Ermisch's assistant on the restorations of the Zwinger during the 1930s and served as head of the city department of planning, housing and preservation from 1935 to 1945; during the first postwar years, he received numerous commissions for reconstruction and repair of public buildings and churches. Rauda had already taken part in the 1950 competition. In both competitions, he largely disregarded the guidelines set by the party. He did not include a project for a tower house in his project, and he proposed the reconstruction of the city centre in agreement with restorative concepts of reconstruction as realised in a number of historic cities in West Germany (for example, in Nuremburg, Munich, Freiburg and Münster). Rauda's plan was based in principle on the historical street plan with only minor enlargements and corrections to accommodate modern traffic and to gain open space inside the formerly densely built-up blocks of the centre. But the primary aim of his plan was to retain the historical proportions between the lot size and building height in relation to the architectural monuments which had survived or were to be restored. In an extensive study on the 'problems of space and form in old and new Dresden', Rauda claimed some kind of innate structural law for Dresden which was to be taken up and continued; it was published only in 1956 when the case for it had already been lost.[16]

With the 1952 competition, once again a bitter controversy arose on the question of priorities: restoration of the city's historical, architectural structure or reconstruction to reshape the city to the new socialist society. The opinion was that, in only seven weeks and with only four participants, the competition had been badly organised and its results were not mature enough for setting the decisive directions for a reconstruction of Dresden's central area. The main points of dispute were over the spatial and proportional structure; that is, the question of preservation or abandonment of the historical street plan, but especially about the tower house project, how such a new 'dominant' of socialist society in the city centre would relate to the historic silhouette of towers. The Department for Preservation of Historic Monuments attempted to prevent the latter by referring to the fact that even in Moscow the new skyscrapers were so placed that they would not overlap with the historic silhouette of the Kremlin. In fact, hardly anybody in Dresden wanted the new tower, but the party in Berlin demanded it.

In 1953, although nothing had been decided on the question of a comprehensive scheme for the city centre, the government in Berlin suddenly decreed that building of the new 'Central Square' must be started immediately. The intention was to create a urbanistic and political *fait accompli* for the reconstruction of a city as important as Dresden. The urbanistic scheme was based on the Schneider plan because it included the tower demanded by the party. The Altmarkt, the old market square of the city's mediaeval plan, was expanded – even beyond the proposition made by the plans of both Schneider and Rascher – to three times its original size, resulting in a square of 140 by 240 metres (459 by 787 feet), to be framed by continuous architectural walls with an average height of 27 metres on both sides of the square, thus eliminating the breaks afforded by the narrow streets which formerly entered the square. Only the corners of the square were to be left open, making contact with the 'Magistrale' running west–east along the north side and leaving an outlet for the north–south axis taking up the historic line of the old main street extending from the bridge. This type of a closed-in square with wide-ranged, composed, palatial façades reached back to the prototypes of Renaissance and baroque squares such as the Capitol at Rome, the Plaza Mayor in Madrid or the royal squares of Paris. In order to avoid any controversy on the question of a comprehensive building scheme for the entire city centre, merely the square itself with its surrounding architectural walls were to be build. A construction plan for the adjoining districts was not included. The touchy question of the height and form of the tower project which was to be erected on the north side of the square was also avoided for the moment. On 31 May 1953 party leader Walter Ulbricht himself laid the foundation stone for construction of the Central Square. Because Schneider's architectural schemes were considered unsatisfactory, the first buildings on the west side were shaped after Rascher's design.

Eventually the architectural form followed the designs of Herbert Schneider for the eastern side of the square, and those of Johannes Rascher for the western side.[17] For the stylistic forms, decorative details and building materials (local amber-coloured sandstone) of the façades, both designs were meant to take up – with only slight divergence – the specific tradition of Dresden's baroque architecture (see Plates 17 and 18). The patchwork composition of monumental architectonic elements with badly designed and rather clumsily executed decorative details stretched out on these façades – which in height as well as length are completely different from their baroque prototypes – is only distantly reminiscent of Dresden baroque. The function of these new buildings was after all primarily to produce monumental façades at any cost for a pretentious open public space. Their ambitious appearance is that of public buildings. But the situation urgently demanded other functions. Thus, the ground floors were filled with stores, the upper floors with apartments, most of them – reserved for honoured activists – of a two-room type which was only with difficulty accommodated behind the pseudo-baroque façades.

Nevertheless, the ambitious project for Dresden's socialist monumental square – devised in feudalistic forms – remained but a fragment. Only the east and west sides were completed by 1956, with the decoration gradually reduced to save costs. The north side was set aside as the site for the tower; the architectural solution for the south side remained an issue which has been debated for decades and is still open. At present, the giant square is an empty space; with its superhuman dimensions it neither appears aesthetically distinguished, nor can it be enlivened by its daily uses. It serves chiefly as a car park.

The beginning of construction of the large central square resulted in a definite decision against restoring the historical spatial organisation and architectonic proportions, however, in favour of a totally new urbanistic structure. It was typical of the reluctance in Dresden to accept the new ideological spirit that the new square retained its traditional name 'Altmarkt'.

In the autumn of 1953 a general building plan for the rest of the city centre was to be appended.[18] Therefore, a new competition was organised with the goal of laying out the great avenue.[19] The programme once again required a tower, with a large platform in front of it for the party officials at political parades. The crucial questions of the height and form of the tower, however, were once again left out of the competition. The outcome was a project for widening the old lateral street running east–west through the city centre; the western part of that thoroughfare had been put through the former mediaeval town only in the late nineteenth century. The street was to be widened to three and a half times its original width, that is 65–70 metres (214–30 feet), and it was to be lined with almost uninterrupted rows of buildings, a monumental façade architecture more or less closing off the areas behind it (see Plate 19). The decorative forms of the monumental façades provided by the original scheme were repeatedly simplified before it came to realisation in 1961–2 (the eastern section) and 1962–7 (the western section).[20]

Once again the result of this competition was not promoted as, or integrated into, an official and comprehensive zoning and construction plan, because the building administration of the city in Dresden was still reluctant to accept these demands of the party centre in Berlin as definite guidelines for the rebuilding of the rest of the former historic city centre. The partly-completed 'Magistrale' (Ernst-Thälmann-Strasse) remained a fragment, just as the large square did, but nevertheless it was a definite urbanistic fact. The disproportionately wide and, for its width, relatively short avenue tore apart the formerly compact form of the small, mediaeval centre, leaving it at both ends in an almost unlimited void.

The controversies continued concerning the plan for the tower which the party demanded but which Dresdeners tried to prevent. In

May 1953, Herbert Schneider submitted a new design for the tower in a form which followed much more closely the Soviet prototypes than had his competition design of the year before (see Plate 21). The Technical University's faculty of architecture submitted a study using persuasive photomontages to prove that the tower would destroy the silhouette of Dresden's historic towers as seen in the famous view from across the Elbe river. The purpose of the study was to have the building's size reduced and its effect at least toned down, if it could not be prevented altogether. With a sophisticated allusion to the sixteen principles, the question was raised: Is a new tower really the only adequate expression of the new, progressive social system? Could it not also be demonstrated in a building that respects – in Marxist terms – the 'historic-economic' epochs embodied in the old silhouette of Dresden, or at least 'plays along harmoniously in the existing, urban architectural orchestra'?[21] The suggestion was for a low building that made no impression whatsoever on the silhouette. If it had to be a tower, then it should be a modest one.

Due to the lack of a comprehensive zoning and construction plan, the question remained unanswered as to how the area between the new main avenue and the Elbe River should be reconstructed. Before the destruction, this area was the most valuable district of Dresden's historic centre with its compact groups of baroque houses and palaces, and its great architectural monuments, the Royal Palace, the Hofkirche and the Frauenkirche (see Plate 23).

In the programmes of both 1953 competitions, it had been generally anticipated that the area around the Frauenkirche would be rebuilt within the old building lines and the old proportions, and that the collapsed church itself would also be restored. In the second issue of *Deutsche Architektur*, Kurt W. Leucht, a member of the Deutsche Bauakademie, closed his article on George Bähr, the architect of the Frauenkirche, with the words: 'The restoration of the architectural monument of the Frauenkirche is an obligation not only to Dresden but to the whole of progressive mankind.'[22] In 1955, the emeritus professor of architecture at the Technical University, Oswin Hempel, presented a study of sketches for the rebuilding of the area around the Frauenkirche.[23] Hempel, who had earned great esteem in Dresden, accepted the fact that the new Altmarkt and the 'Magistrale' building form had been established and somehow had to be adapted for this sensitive area of the former historic city centre. The principles of Hempel's construction plan were very much in line with conservation concepts adopted in West German cities. These principles rejected the restoration of individual historic buildings and façades that were destroyed, except of the very great monuments, but advocated the reintegration of these important monuments into the historic structure of urban space, that is, the restoration of proportional relationship of volume and space. Under the title 'Can We Achieve the Old Style?', he opposed not only the copying of individual houses (noting that this would be absurd, after the ruins of original façades and decorative details had all been cleared away and destroyed), but also just as strongly the 'socialist' neo-baroque of the new buildings on the Altmarkt. Consequently, Hempel proposed the restoration of the baroque domed church, because it was an important monument of architectural history and was essential in reinstating the famous Dresden silhouette. The new construction in the vicinity would keep within the old building lines and continue the architecture of the new Altmarkt in much more modest dimensions and forms.

After even the Academy of Architecture in Berlin had criticised the fact that Dresden was not able to work up a comprehensive construction plan for the inner city, let alone for the whole of the city, in 1957 the Office of the Chief Architect of Dresden presented a reconstruction plan by Kurt Röthig for the area around the destroyed Frauenkirche.[24] This plan adopted the essential propositions of Oswin Hempel's plan. It foresaw the restoration of the church building and an architecture for the surrounding area that retained the old building lines, yet it also connected with and continued the uninterrupted architectural walls of the new buildings on the Altmarkt and the Ernst-Thälmann-Strasse.

Only one year later, however, this plan was abandoned, and the question of how to rebuild the area surrounding the Frauenkirche was postponed for an indefinite period. In 1959 the City Building Department developed within the framework of the new Seven-Year Plan of Economy a reconstruction scheme for the city centre.[25] It discarded almost completely all previous conceptions. The sole vestiges of former plans were a project for buildings to close up the south side of the Altmarkt, the completion of the 'Magistrale', and the building of the projected tower with the platform in front of it. In order to disarm the controversies and settle the unanswered question of the purpose and meaning for such a gigantic skyscraper, it was no longer referred to as 'Haus der SED' but now definitely entitled the 'House of Socialist Culture'. This designation was to suggest that the building's aim was not just that of a political demonstration of the power of the party but that it was actually to serve the people of the city (see Plate 20). Through its central location and its prominent height, it was to be an expression of the triumph and power of the working class. The remaining areas of the former old town were now designated as open spaces to be partially planted and partly left as car parks. Restoration of historical architectural monuments was no longer envisaged. Although the United Protestant Church of Germany offered financial support from West Germany, the Frauenkirche was no longer to be restored, but to be left in ruins as an antiwar memorial, as it still is. Furthermore, other architectural monuments that had earlier been considered for restoration were doomed, such as the late Gothic Sophienkirche, the former Franciscan church that was the only remaining mediaeval church building in Dresden. Despite the protests of the State Department for Preservation of Historic Monuments, the ruins of the church were finally blown up in 1962.

In the meantime, what official terminology called the 'great revolution in socialist architecture' reached its completion; that is, the reorientation of architectural planning based on the new political and cultural bearings that resulted from the politics of de-Stalinisation in the Soviet Union. In the Soviet Union, the shift took place at the Union Conference of Construction held in Moscow in December 1954. The East German party adopted the new direction in the following year.[26] The party convention of 1955 criticised the high construction costs of the monumental building projects, the excessive expense of planning and the slow course of reconstruction n the cities, and demanded a shift in priority from representational architecture to housing. The historicism of architectural style was condemned as 'dogmatisation in architecture'. To speed up construction on the road to 'complete victory of socialist methods of production', the party demanded increased productivity based on intensified industrial building techniques. Following the governmental decision of 1955, the first architectural conference 'on the most important tasks for construction' was held in 1956. It resolved fundamental questions on building cheaper and faster, on typification of buildings and the standardisation of construction elements. The 'principle of socialist housing complexes', of large, standardised projects produced of prefabricated concrete elements, was introduced. The organisation of construction in the entire GDR was now almost totally centralised in Berlin, and the Institute for Standardised Projects (within the Ministry for Reconstruction) and a permanent Commission for Architecture (in the Soviet bloc's Council for Mutual Economic Assistance) for the establishment of International Norms were founded.

At the fifth party congress in 1958, it was decided in the

Decree for the Reorganisation of the Urban Centres that the sixteen principles of 1950 were outdated and that the last traces of the war were to be cleared from the city centres by 1962. This again also applied to numerous historical architectural monuments, for example, the baroque Royal Palace in Potsdam, demolished in 1960. The reconstruction of the centre of the capital of the GDR (that is, East Berlin) and of the other large cities was to be completed by 1965. This was the start of new, ambitious planning schemes for the reconstruction of the city centres and of new large satellite towns for all cities in the GDR.

At first, however, the Academy of Architecture and the leading official architects had difficulties acknowledging the 'Great Revolution in Architecture'. For some time they were only reluctant participants. The volumes for 1958 and 1959 of *Deutsche Architektur* abound in fundamental and controversial articles on principles. They include discussions between Soviet and German architects on the culture of socialism and its artistic expression through the true architectural form of Socialist Realism according to the materialist principles of reflection of a society in its culture. There were also discussions on the relationship to the 'formalist' style (or rather, lack of style) in the architecture of capitalism. In 1960, the Academy of Architecture held its first conference on theory. The new doctrine declared that socialist architecture and urban planning could only develop adequately if they were realistically and consistently derived from the actual needs and demands of the socialist society, and that a true socialist architecture therefore had to display clear and simple forms. (The Western models were not mentioned.)

How this influenced the planning and reconstruction of Dresden can be briefly sketched. At first, the new building policies were employed only outside the city centre with housing projects consisting of freestanding blocks. The 1959 scheme for the city centre, already mentioned, was still based on a decision to continue the style of 'regional types'. In 1960, however, a new competition among architects' collectives was opened for the House of Socialist Culture, the old tower project.[27] In the programme for the competition it was prescribed that the building should 'express the greatness and superiority of socialism in form of an urbanistic dominant'. Again, the dispute over the project in general and its form in particular was reflected by the fact that no first or second prizes were awarded. The third prize was given to a scheme by the Lasch collective (see Plate 22). This and all other designs accorded special mention were no longer of the Soviet type but modelled on prototypes of modern architecture of the 1920s or modern architecture of Western style; all proposed towers of a slim, cubic form, with that of Lasch closest to the projects of the Dutch architect Dudok. The jury was, however, dissatisfied with these towers and suggested that the design of Lasch's tower would have to be improved in its relationship of height and volume. The design was not executed.

The first project of the new urbanistic direction was the Webergasse, a shopping mall with low-rise, flat-roofed buildings that were in a most inorganic way attached to the sober backs of the pseudo-baroque Altmarkt houses of the 1950s. The Webergasse clearly reflects the model of Rotterdam's Lijnbaan and its derivations in West Germany, England and other Western European countries.

In 1962 the planning boundaries of the city centre were redesigned and extended beyond the limits of the former historic centre to the main railway station on the south and across the river into the Neustadt on the north. A conceptional competition was opened in 1962 for the district between the main railway station and the former old town including the Prager Strasse, previously Dresden's elegant main shopping street.[28] The result was a project of a type ultimately based on the urbanistic scheme of Rotterdam. A pedestrian zone between 68 and 85 metres wide is lined with one very long building block on one side and a series of lateral blocks on the other side. The buildings are used as hotels, apartments and a department store; a cylinder-shaped cinema building was meant to provide a decorative accent. Construction started in 1970. The Prager Strasse development served as the basis for the comprehensive plan for the extended city centre area finally developed in 1967, the main elements of which are a vast traffic plan featuring multilane, inner-city highways, some of them elevated, and groups of high-rise buildings along the ring-road surrounding the former historic city centre.[29] This scheme, which totally disregarded the prewar street plan and made the former central area of Dresden into a vast open space punctuated by isolated, freestanding building blocks, was then carried out in the 1970s – at a time when this kind of urban development was considered in the West a mistaken destruction of environmental quality of urban space and had already been abandoned.

Projects for high-rise buildings were developed in competitions held in 1965 for the Postplatz and the Pirnaischer Platz, formerly the busiest squares and traffic crossroads directly adjacent to the historic centre.[30] Once again, these competitions ended with no first prizes. The second prizes proposed high-rise slab buildings to round off optically the new expanse of space. The western models for this urbanistic scheme of placing high-rises around the edges of the centre (for example, in Rudolf Hillebrecht's plan for Hannover) and for the architectural forms are obvious. But only one of these buildings was subsequently erected following the competition.

From 1967 to 1969 the open north side of the Altmarkt along the 'Magistrale', the site of the earlier, controversial tower house project, was finally built up with a 'cultural palace' that serves as a multipurpose convention hall, in the form of a low, flat building that clearly follows western prototypes of the late 1950s (see Plate 25). However, no thought was given to the difficult problem of how this isolated, freestanding building was to relate to an eventual reconstruction of the area towards the north, that is, what used to be the most important historic zone between the former Royal Palace (which was and is still in ruins) and the Frauenkirche. No plans existed then for this area, although it was in close vicinity to the ruins of the Frauenkirche, while the surviving nineteenth-century monumental police headquarters was expanded by adding a steel-and-glass box of the most banal kind.

Since then, however, another shift in urban planning and architecture has taken place in the GDR, albeit a rather tacit one so far. Whereas in the West the urbanistic schemes and buildings of the Stalin era are now considered rehabilitated – from an historical point of view – as an expression of a specific phase of postwar history, so in the GDR 'functionalist' principles and results in planning and building have come under fire, though again belatedly following the trends of theory and practice in the West. In 1982 the area of the former Neumarkt between the Royal Palace and the Frauenkirche, the 'Magistrale' and the Elbe river, was made the subject of an 'International Design Seminar' organised by the city following the model of the post-modernist international design seminars which had been held in West Berlin.[31] The programme for the projects provided for construction along the old street lines adapted to the historic proportions, and it included reconstruction of the baroque façades of some houses that had been standing there and an eventual rebuilding of the Frauenkirche. The aim now was to restore at least a section of Dresden's former historic centre to its previous structure and beauty. But these projects too have ended up in the filing cabinets, due to the shortage of construction capacity within the planned economy and the lack of building material and specially skilled craftsmen for such a task. For the same reasons, the rebuilding of the Royal Palace has also been postponed until after the year 2000. Instead, a luxury hotel, chiefly to attract tourists from western countries, will be built next to the ruins of the Frauenkirche. This large building will definitely make it impossible to restore the historic spatial and proportional context of this area. Because the construction industry in the GDR % almost totally concentrated on building methods using prefabricated elements – is unable to handle such a task, the hotel project has been contracted to a Swedish building firm. In the same way, the new Hotel Bellevue, designed and built ready-to-use by the Japanese general contractor Kajima, now occupies the place of the former baroque houses on the Grosse Meissner Gasse across the Elbe. These hotel projects were put up without any overall building plans of their area.

Except for its fragmentarily surviving famous river front, Dresden today is a banal, aesthetically boring, even downright ugly city. The large, still unbuilt areas, together with the wide open spaces of traffic lanes produce an appearance of windy emptiness. Its central areas are without any coherence in urban space, architectural structure and artistic physiognomy; instead, the cityscape is full of breaks, inconsistencies and contradictions. The new Dresden is quite the opposite of an 'homogeneous architectural and pictorial representation that is to exemplify and symbolise, as an intact entity, the new quality of social life', as the political and cultural programme of reconstruction had always claimed. Its new cityscape visibly reflects the gap between the revolutionary claim of socialist ideology and its cultural uncertainty and incompetence, or, in other terms, the erratic search for a unique cultural expression for a new society that pretended to be based on the working class, but that, in fact, has always been strongly dependent on the bourgeois cultural tradition which actually underlies it.

First, in the early 1950s, the new political system and its governing party had set out to build a monumental city in whose urban spaces and architecture socialism would prove its cultural strength and demonstrate its claim to the national cultural heritage. The reconstruction of Dresden, the formerly beautiful city with its great cultural tradition, was a particularly difficult test. The claims about Dresden's splendid past had been hovering the whole time over the controversies about how to rebuild it as a beautiful city. The result was the Altmarkt houses with their imitational and badly made *bourgeois-gentilhomme*-style façades, a borrowed cultural form whose representational pretension was in total contradiction to the social and economic reality in the GDR. Nevertheless, these buildings of the 1950s are the only ones which today lend the new city centre at least some sort of distinctive physiognomy.

In the second phase of reconstruction, Dresden was to become a modern city. The ruling system had more realistically determined

188 *Rebuilding Europe's Bombed Cities*

that socialism had to prove its superiority first on the basis of technical and social progress. The result, the rationalised city, was an imitation of urbanistic and architectonic models from the West, of models which had developed the specific interests, priorities and faults of capitalist civilisation. Dresden's urban development and architecture of the 1960s and 1970s is a combination of Brasilia and mass-produced social housing in France or West Germany, but worse in design and cheaper in realisation. The socialisation of planning and construction – that is, the complete freedom from private interests – did not bring about a consistent and coherent city, but resulted instead in an unrealistic tendency to Utopian, oversized planning that time and again had to capitulate to the hard reality of economic scarcity. The second phase of the 1960s reveals an evident contradiction in that the socialised planned economy was forced to employ the means of capitalist economic maximisation, but because of its economic weakness and dependence on the world markets conditioned by capitalism it could not achieve anything other than minimisation in making use of the socialist possibilities of planning uninhibited by private interests, economic and cultural. Evaluated culturally, the new Dresden demonstrates that there is no unique cultural expression of socialism.

## Notes

1. Wolfgang Paul, *Zum Beispiel Dresden* (Frankfurt/Main, 1964).
2. Fritz Löffler, *Das alte Dresden* (1955) rev. edn. (Liepzig, 1982).
3. Volker Helas, *Architektur in Dresden 1800–1900* (Braunschweig and Wiesbaden, 1985).
4. David Irving, *The Destruction of Dresden* (London, 1963).
5. Götz Eckardt, *Schicksale deutscher Baudenkmäler im zweiten Weltkrieg. Eine Dokumentation der Schäden und Totalverluste auf dem Gebiet der Deutschen Demokratischen Republik* (Berlin, 1978), vol. 2, pp. 372-442.
6. Otto Schubert, 'Brief aus Dresden', *Neue Bauwelt*, Heft 9 (1946) pp. 4–5; Walter Weidauer, *Die Verwirklichung des gro en Dresdner Aufbauplanes für das Jahr 1946* (1946).
7. Paul Wolf, 'Vorschlag für den Wiederaufbau der inneren Stadtgebiete von Dresden', *Die Neue Stadt*, 3 (1949) pp. 13–20; Heinz Hampe, 'Planungsgrundlagen und Planungsergebnisse für den Neuaufbau der Stadt Dresden', *Der Baumeister*, 47 (1950); Heinz Hampe, 'Dresden die Zukunft einer ausradierten Stadtmitte', *Der Baumeister*, 48 (1951).
8. Ullrich Kuhirt (ed.), *Kunst der DDR 1945–1959* (Leipzig, 1982) pp. 204–25; Frank Werner, *Stadt, Städtebau, Architektur in der DDR, Aspekte der Stadtgeographie, Stadtplanung und Forschungspolitik* (Erlangen, 1981); Klaus von Beyme, *Wiederaufbau. Architektur und Städtebaupolitik in den beiden deutschen Staaten* (Munich, 1987).

9.  Walter Ulbricht, 'Die Aufgaben der Deutschen Bauakademie im Kamp für eine deutsche Architektur. Ansprachen anlässlich der Eröffnung der Deutschen Bauakademie (Berlin, 1952)', in *Deutsche Architektur*, 2 (1953) pp. 146–55.
10. L. Bylinken, *Stalins städtebauliche Grundsätze*, Reihe Studienmaterial der Deutschen Bauakademie (Berlin, 1953).
11. Kurt Liebknecht, *Deutsche Architektur*, 1 (1952) pp. 3–12.
12. Heinz Prässler, 'Die Bedeutung des Nationalen Aufbauwerkes für die Architektur', *Deutsche Architektur*, 2 (1953) pp. 159–61.
13. Eberhard Hempel, 'Wiederaufbau von Dresden', in *Europa* (Salzburg, 1952) pp. 19–26.
14. Kurt Leucht, Johanes Bronder and Johannes Hunger, *Planungsgrundlagen, Planungsergebnisse für den Neuaufbau der Stadt Dresden* (Dresden, 1950).
15. Kurt Junghans and Hellmut Bräuer, 'Kritische Bemerkungen zur Neugestaltung Dresdens', *Deutsche Architektur*, 2 (1953) pp. 13–19.
16. Wolfgang Rauda, 'Raum- und Formprobleme im alten und neuen Dresden', *Jahrbuch zur PLege der Künste*, 4 (1956) pp. 49–84.
17. 'Dresden: Altmarkt, Ostseite, Westseite', *Deutsche Architektur*, 3 (1954) pp. 128–35.
18. Helmut Bräuer, 'Wo bleibt der Dresdener Plan?', *Deutsche Architektur*, 2 (1953) pp. 173–8.
19. Georg Funk, 'Wettbewerb für die städtebauliche und architektonische Gestaltung der Ost–West–Magistrale in Dresden', *Deutsche Architektur*, 3 (1954) pp. 240–70.
20. Hagen Bächler, 'Die Ernst Thälmann-Strasse – eine sozialistische Magistrale', *Deutsche Architektur*, 9 (1960) pp. 196–7.
21. Fritz Bergmann, 'Zentrales Haus als Turmhochaus oder Turm mit hohem Haus', *Deutsche Architektur*, 5 (1956) pp. 552–70.
22. Kurt W. Leucht, 'George Bähr', *Deutsche Architektur*, 2 (1953) p. 79.
23. Oswin Hempel, 'Die städtebauliche Gestaltung des Dresdener Neumarktes und seiner Umgebung', *Deutsche Architektur*, 6 (1957) pp. 718–19.
24. Kurt Röthig, 'Um die städtebauliche Gestaltung des Neumarktes in Dresden', *Deutsche Architektur*, 6 (1957) pp. 618–19.
25. Hans Hunger, 'Der Aufbau des Zentrums der Stadt Dresden im Siebenjahrplan', *Deutsche Architektur*, 8 (1959) pp. 596–7.
26. Kurt Liebknecht, 'Die Bedeutung der Unions-Baukonferenz in Moskau für die Aufgaben im Bauwesen der Deutschen Demokratischen Republik', *Deutsche Architektur*, 4 (1955) pp. 50–64.
27. Editorial, 'Ideenwettbewerb für das Haus der sozialistischen Kultur in Dresden', *Deutsche Architektur*, 9 (1960) pp. 670–3.
28. Georg Münter, 'Wettbewerb Prager Strasse in Dresden', *Deutsche Architektur*, 12 (1963).
29. Gerhard Krenz, Walter Stiebitz and Claus Weidner (eds), *Städte und Stadtzentren in der DDR* (Berlin, 1968).
30. *Deutsche Architektur*, 14 (1965) p. 18.
31. Werner Wachtel and Heinz Michalk, '3. Internationales Entwurfsseminar – Rekonstruktionsgebiet Neumarkt in Dresden', *Architektur der DDR*, 31 (1982) pp. 36–48.

# 13  Reconstruction in the German Democratic Republic

## KLAUS VON BEYME

### SOCIAL, ECONOMIC AND POLITICAL PRECONDITIONS

Reconstruction in the German Democratic Republic (GDR) had to overcome a number of problems, which put the country into a position marked by serious disadvantages in comparison with West Germany. First, though her towns were less heavily bombed than West Germany's, the average size of the apartments in the GDR was smaller, the age of the apartments was higher (see Appendix, Table 13.1) and the standard of equipment of the apartments tended to remain below the level of western nations (see Appendix, Table 13.3, row 6). In international comparison, the GDR was at the level of Italy. Only with regard to the number of persons per housing unit was the GDR in a better position than the Federal Republic of Germany (FRG). This is one of the reasons why she could afford to build fairly small apartments, even by East European standards (see Appendix, Table 13.2, column 1).

Secondly, the territory of prewar Germany was cut into six pieces, with the GDR suffering most from this dismemberment of the German Reich. At two borders and in the inner circle around its capital, towns such as Görlitz and Guben were cut in half. Stettin, Berlin's harbour, was lost. All this was decided against the initial intentions of the Western powers and the Polish government in exile.[1] Many towns originally located in the centre of Germany, like Eisenach or Halberstadt, lost their functions and were marginalised.

Thirdly, whereas the Western powers soon ceased to demand reparations, the administration of the Soviet occupation zone insisted on compensation from the GDR, including goods and industrial equipment which the Western zones of Germany failed to deliver.

Fourthly, there were enormous population changes. Eighty per cent of all refugees (about nine million from the territories east of the Oder–Neisse border and three million from the Sudentenland in

Czechoslovakia) migrated into the Federal Republic. Between 1950 and 1961 (when the Berlin Wall was built), 3 583 000 of the GDR's more active citizens fled to the West.[2]

Fifthly, West Germany received Marshall Plan aid, and this had some impact even on housing construction. Fifteen new suburbs were built in the Federal Republic with American support. Though these satellite towns were heavily criticised for their lack of social and architectural quality, this was an important experiment, even if it only taught the younger generation of German architects the mistakes which had to be avoided in the future.[3] These experiments provided an opportunity to catch up with international developments in architecture, just as did later foreign contributions to the Interbau in Berlin in 1957–9.

Sixthly, talented architects in the GDR became opportunists. Some, like Kurt Liebknecht, who was among those coming back from a Moscow exile, were ready to abandon their former dedication to modern building in the Bauhaus tradition. Even staunch modernists, like Hermann Henselmann, were ready to give up their modernist credo and to succumb to Walter Ulbricht's *petit bourgeois* ideas. (Ulbricht was a former joiner's apprentice, who unfortunately showed early in his life some interest in art and architecture.[4])

The GDR leadership tried to compensate for these disadvantages by demonstrating a fanatical will to create socialism. The essentials of this political orientation, which also dominated the rebuilding of bombed towns, can be reduced to two principles which had no importance for West Germany: promotion of socialist state-ownership of the land and central planning of reconstruction.

If one compares only the constitutions of the two German states of 1949, the differences on this matter appear slight. Both constitutions protect property and both guarantee compensation for the nationalisation of land, with the exception that the GDR excluded former Nazis, monopolists and 'speculators' from this protection of property rights (Art. 24). This opened the door for political pressure on many owners of land and buildings. Compensation procedures, moreover, were not regularised until 1960. In fact, the taxes and fees the state charged for the removal of ruins exceeded normal compensation, a policy which greatly contributed to the exodus of GDR citizens before 1961.[5] GDR lawyers have stressed that they did not imitate the Soviet example of nationalisation of the land, but the real differences in policy were small.[6] In most urban centres of the GDR all land was expropriated in the 1950s. Less effective was the creation of a central planning agency. Most of the architects were employed by the districts and the smaller territorial administrative units (*Kreise*). But this did not erase the existence of 13 000 private enterprises in the building sector. Together with the work of 1900 collective enterprises, their activities accounted for 35 per cent of the building effort and 50 per cent of all repair work.[7]

An integrated policy of land use was developed relatively late in the GDR.[8] Town planning and economic planning can hardly be said to have been intimately linked before the 1960s. At the seventh Socialist Unity Party (SED) party congress in 1967, Ulbricht came out in favour of more decentralisation in construction planning. But even then, over-ambitious central planning was not avoided. Prime Minister Willi Stoph declared in 1970 that new projects had to be stopped and priority given to industrial investment.[9] Regional planning was also introduced comparatively late.[10]

## THE IDEOLOGICAL *LEITBILD* OF RECONSTRUCTION AND ITS PHASES OF DEVELOPMENT

*Leitbild* was a term of compromise in West Germany; one looked upon ideologies with suspicion but could not avoid the need for some guidelines to provide orientation. *Leitbild* seemed to be an appropriate expression. It was less clear-cut than a consistent theory, smoother than a true ideology, but still full of a number of military connotations, as Theodor Adorno, the head of the Frankfurt School, remarked.[11] The GDR did not share the same aversion against ideologies, but from the outset it defined its policies in a non-ideological manner. The GDR stressed that there was no ideal of a socialist town, and its first minister of construction emphasised that not even the Soviet model could be imitated.[12] There was hardly any discussion about the old Soviet ideals of *Sotsgorod* (the socialist city) and the linear city. (These ideas had had a greater impact on Hans Scharoun's 'collective plan' of 1945 for Berlin than on the results of socialist planning in the GDR afterwards.) Architecture played an important role in the GDR's attempt to neutralise Western influences in West Germany. Reconstruction thus became integrated into a 'national mission'.[13] The Soviet fascination with new towns influenced the GDR even less dramatically. More than other Comecon countries, the GDR deliberately neglected housing construction in order to build up socialist industry. This policy had enormous human costs. In the long run, however, it paid off. The GDR is now economically stronger than other Comecon states, and it soon took over the lead with regard to housing construction within its bloc[14] (see Appendix, Table 13.2).

Unlike the Soviet Nowa Huta and other towns, which reflected socialist industrial megalomania, new towns in the GDR were more solid and more profitable enterprises. Here the construction of four new towns, Stalinstadt (later Eisenhüttenstadt, 1951ff, Hoyerswerda-Neustadt, 1957ff, Schwedt, 1957ff, and Halle-Neustadt, 1964ff) was accompanied by a lot of socialist propaganda. Later on, however, leading architects of the GDR admitted that even this programme 'was out of proportion'.[15] There was no clear-cut plan to relate these projects to the old small towns.[16] No literary paeans to the construction workers, like Fedor Gladkov's *Cement* of 1925, were created by East German writers. Even poets supporting the regime criticised what they called 'a miserable architectural solution: a centre, a heart surrounded by dead flesh, mere dormitory suburbs'.[17] The only really successful new town was Halle-Neustadt, attractive because it was near an old large town. It came closest, however, to those satellite towns which were explicitly condemned by the first Minister of Construction, Lothar Bolz.[18]

The GDR *Leitbild* for urban construction was formulated in the 'Sixteen Principles' decreed by the Council of Ministers in 1950. They were meant as a counterproposal to the Charter of Athens, though they contained some of its ideas. However, the West German ideology of 'organic town building' – a strange mixture of the old biological irrationalism, now justified by Anglo-Saxon variations from Frank Lloyd Wright to Saarinen – did not stop at Checkpoint Charlie. In the GDR it was used, as it was used by Western functionalists, mostly as a synonym for 'functional', and it was adopted because it seemed to avoid the 'formalism' of the Bauhaus and its followers.[19] Some of the 'Sixteen Principles' would have been acceptable to Western modernists. These included: limitations on the growth of towns (Principle 4), a strategy in which the GDR was extremely successful for demographic and other reasons; and emphasis on a monumental city centre (Principle 6); criticism of the garden city concept (Principle 12), which was considered to be the 'favourite ideal of American and British presidents of police forces, who would like to transform the workers into breeders of rabbits and cauliflower growers, in order to keep them away from political demonstrations;[20'] and propaganda for the construction of skyscrapers (Principle 13).

The *Leitbild* of GDR city planning was by no means static. As in the West, it underwent certain stages, of which one can differentiate three.


## THE ERA OF NATIONAL RECONSTRUCTION UNTIL 1955

The first of the sixteen principles declared that the city should be the 'expression of the national consciousness of the people'. In fact, there was a propaganda contest between the two German states over who best preserved national cultural traditions.[21] Walter Ulbricht thus condemned the 1954 Heidelberg railway station as 'American'. (Today we rather suspect that it was 'late Fascist' in many of its elements.) While Freudenstadt was hailed as the best example of the successful reconstruction of a West German town, the Americanisation of Frankfurt was condemned as national treason.[22] Before the war, the conservative architect Paul Bonatz had described Stuttgart's Weissenhofsiedlung – the Mecca of modern architecture since 1927 – as an 'Arab City', and Ulbricht produced a kind of echo, without knowing which tradition he followed, when complaining of houses 'which could as well have been built in South Africa'.[23] The Bauhaus at this time was referred to as the 'so-called Bauhaus', a strange terminology for a country which suffered from being dubbed 'the so-called GDR' in official documents in the West. Even Hannes Meyer and his 'Red Front Group' were not rediscovered as architectural pioneers until 1960. Only in 1976 was the Bauhaus in Dessau restored. The former *Baubolschewisten* (architectural Bolsheviks) who had supposedly turned into 'agents of rotting imperialism' were at only a relatively late point in time accepted as pioneers of industrial building, and then only after the Russians had rediscovered the progressive Bauhaus and the German architects who had worked in the Soviet Union, like Ernst May or the Taut brothers.[24] GDR modernists like Henselmann had to make concessions in this first period of rebuilding. When Ulbricht criticised his first draft for the Stalinallee, Henselmann submitted another draft five days later in the late Stalinist decorative style (*Zuckerbäckerstil*). Later on, this was excused in GDR literature by saying that Henselmann had had no other option. The state was still uncertain in its architectural judgement, and architects who did not want 'to cross over to the other side of the barricade' had to join the state in committing blunders.[25]

Looking beyond ideology, the first phase of town construction work presents a rather confused picture. Only a few areas of monumental architecture, which enjoyed high visibility throughout the Republic, were completed – for example, the historical reconstruction in Rostock (the Lange Strasse) and some projects in Dresden, Berlin and Leipzig. Elsewhere in larger cities, this first phase – in GDR military jargon *Etappe* – usually led to buildings four to five storeys high, just as in the West, though in Moscow buildings had six to eight storeys.[26] In the provincial towns only a few projects were completed in this period. Eilenburg has frequently been mentioned as a conservative type of reconstruction – a GDR version of Freudenstadt.[27] The reconstruction of Neubrandenburg was initiated in a historicist manner by Hans Hopp in 1954. Hopp was later severely criticised for neglecting industrial building.[28] But even in these early years, modernisation of small towns like Rathenow were planned without taking into account historical considerations.[29]

## PHASE TWO: INDUSTRIAL BUILDING (1955 TO ABOUT 1973)

What caused the first change in the guidelines for town planning and construction? Some authors emphasise Moscow's influence, others an independent attempt to define a uniquely national propaganda.[30] Probably both motives were closely linked. At this stage it was hardly feasible for the GDR to take steps in foreign affairs without Moscow's endorsement.

In December 1954 a Moscow conference issued the slogan: 'Build better, faster and cheaper'.[31] The GDR reacted promptly. After the upheavals of 1953, this reaction was combined, however, with a warning that no one should confound the changes decided upon in Moscow with modernist concepts which some have noted in 'Western architectural periodicals'.[32] 'Industrial building' was the new slogan, with the architect largely replaced by the engineer. Soviet colleagues, like Baranov, had to warn that 'one cannot construct each single house in an industrial way'.[33] In this phase the four categories of 'reconstruction towns', which had been defined in the reconstruction law of 1950 and which included almost every important town, became more realistic. The Fifth Party Congress of the SED now specified eleven towns. Priorities had also changed. Rostock was now ahead of Magdeburg, for example. The district capitals were given more importance.[34] The fewer towns mentioned, the more hierarchical became their treatment.

Berlin's planning under Henselmann showed inconsistencies. The construction of a huge axis with a length of 3.5 km, too long to create a true urban atmosphere, was begun at different points but interrupted time and again. It was not by chance that one frequently compared Henselmann with Albert Speer, although without great justification. Speer anticipated all the wishes of his Führer. Henselmann resisted up to a certain point and then had to be forced into the framework of a mediocre construction ideology.[35] Soviet proposals for the reconstruction of the centre were much more moderate, because they were in the spirit of the cultural palace in the Kremlin, which enjoys better proportions.[36] The first part of the Stalinallee has been criticised recently by authors in the GDR, while the second part has found greater acceptance because of its functional differentiation and its opportunities for communication. In West German literature, the second part of this street is seen as just another modern street, while the first part arouses a kind of nostalgia for the 'roaring fifties'.[37]

The centre of East Berlin was completed fairly late. Reconstruction of the historic buildings on Unter den Linden continued, but Marx-Engels square remained empty. Money was scarce and had to be spent 'according to the needs of the population', so the Alexanderplatz area was reconstructed first. On Marx-Engels square the buildings of the Council of State, the Ministry of Foreign Affairs and the Palace of the Republic – the latter not in place until the mid-1970s – remained optically cold and unsatisfactory. Even propaganda lyrics have difficulties in praising this ensemble: 'Its monumentality loses in part its political orientation but acquires the depth and penetration of philosophical poetry.'[38] As in Frankfurt on the other side of the wall, nostalgia affected the republic and encouraged the creation of more cosy ensembles. Hence the 'Nikolai quarter' is being rebuilt in a historicist style for the celebration of Berlin's 750th anniversary in order to create at least one area which reproduces the atmosphere of 'Old Berlin.'[39]

With regard to the other district capitals, it seems fair to say that Dresden was ruined by a rather dull socialist construction concept. Leipzig was comparatively better preserved, and many monuments were saved. In the second phase of reconstruction in the GDR,

Leipzig – home of the famous fair – did its best to ruin certain ensembles, such as the university quarter. In the first phase the old town hall had been rebuilt; a seven-storey cube of low quality built in the second phase competes in a very awkward way with the fine Renaissance building in front of it.[40]

Rostock and Potsdam preserved more of their old character. Well-preserved cities like Suhl – a sleeping beauty, which even in Thuringia, the country of Duodez princes, could not have dreamt of becoming an administrative capital – had to pay for their new prominence. Suhl's silhouette was ruined by huge buildings close to the town centre, but this happened in the West as well, from Wertheim to Tübingen. Towns lower down the hierarchy which had been badly destroyed, like Anklam, were ruined further by unattractive housing projects.[41] Halberstadt and Nordhausen boast of a 'protective reconstruction', but this is hard to believe when one is confronted with dreadful blocks right in the town centre, built without any regard for the old monuments and the old streets.[42] We should try, however, to be fair. Towns with predominantly half-timbered houses in the West, like Hildesheim or the old centres of Kassel and Frankfurt, were all ruined to the same extent. There was no honest way of rebuilding them, and where this was attempted, as in Hildesheim at the Market Square or in Frankfurt at the Roemer Square, the result is highly disputable.

The main problem for the GDR was the protection of those old towns which were not destroyed. Remarkable restorations have been accomplished around the Harz mountains in Stolberg, Blankenburg and Wernigerode, and in some tourist centres, like Quedlinburg or Meissen. In other towns work has now begun, for example, in Freiberg or Altenburg, but elsewhere history has stood still, and towns like Schleiz, Hildburghausen and Meiningen seem to have had to wait all too long for revival. The hierarchy in reconstruction efforts gave new industrial areas in the East (Frankfurt/Oder, Cottbus, Rostock) preference over the rest of the country.

Most of the planning done in the second phase of the reconstruction of towns produced results in many ways comparable to those in the West. Instead of rebuilding the city centres, satellite towns spread in both Germanies. In the West, for example, even Bremen lost its Anglo-Saxon tradition of low-rise, high-density building and experimented with the high-rise suburb of Neue Vahr. Rostock experienced an equivalent to the loss of Hanseatic moderation with its satellite Lütten Klein – the most misnamed town in Germany (in Low German it means 'Little little').

Still, the reconstruction of town centres was more neglected in the East than in the West. The old buildings, which existed here in higher proportions than in the West, were even more dramatically neglected.[43] Revitalisation with the help of bulldozers was progressing. The old Anglo-Saxon principle 'low-rise, high-density' was perverted into high-density and high-rise. The old ideas of an organic, orderly town were forgotten, though the GDR has always advocated the compact city and has never supported the Western idea of a 'loosely structured organic city'. Monumentalism modernised and brutalised. Thus little skyscrapers ruined the silhouette of towns like Magdeburg, Frankfurt/Oder and Bautzen, and even of smaller towns like Neubrandenburg which had been rebuilt in a more traditional way during the first period of reconstruction. This development was later harshly criticised as a futile attempt 'to win the class war in architecture *ex post facto* – against the wrong enemy with hardly convincing weapons, like skyscrapers or hotels against churches'.[44]

At the end of phase two, the zeal for monumental buildings declined. Important projects at the Altmarkt in Dresden, at the bank of the river Elbe in Magdeburg, or at the Kröpeliner Tor in Rostock were abandoned.[45] The technology used in building became more creative. Henselmann was able to finish his project of a TV tower in Berlin, and at a site for which permission was originally turned down. The scientific-technical revolution led to new forms of monumental university buildings in Jena or Leipzig. The perspective of art was admitted again. The merely additive types of prefabricated buildings were given a greater degree of variation. Colours were rediscovered. As in the West, flat roofs were used. The construction of apartments in rows became more imaginative, in spite of increasing complaints against regressive tendencies toward handicraft production and the waste of material.

A theory was needed. The first attempt was the concept of 'the socialist way of life' as a new architectural *Leitbild*.[46] It was conceded that planning did not sufficiently consider the wishes of the population, and 'emotional mistakes' were admitted. The 'subjective factor' was reintroduced into the debate after long periods of dogmatic discussion about objective laws in constructing socialism.[47] *Etappe II* ended with a prolonged discussion on monotony in the GDR architecture.

## THE PHASE OF QUALITATIVE TRANSFORMATION
## OF TOWNS

Class war had ended, and the so-called 'socialist human community' was in vogue.[48] Pedestrian malls were constructed, first in Leipzig in 1965 and in Rostock in 1968, and the town centres were revitalised.[49] The Soviet 'univermag' type of a department store was supplemented by individual shops. Urbanity was acknowledged as a value, though other terms were used for it.

Housing construction focused again on the town centres.[50] In many towns there were still large free spaces, which was the case only in West Berlin among West German towns. It was admitted that the development of satellite towns had been a mistake, because economic calculations proved that they were not cheaper. Article 9 of the new Land-use Act of 1965 stated that, in principle, new buildings had to be erected inside the towns.[51] Energy saving and the reduction of infrastructural costs became as important as the old considerations of economic profitability.

Old cities were now rediscovered. *Heimisch sein* became a positive value, which meant much the same as the more easily translatable terms 'identity' or 'belonging' in the West. Tearing down old houses was allowed only 'in case they [were] no longer acceptable to people looking for apartments' – a formula vague enough to allow further abuses.[52] The protection of historic monuments, however, had been declared undialectical in phase two, which had resulted in concentrating efforts on only selected monuments.[53] Now new buildings in an imagined baroque-classicist style were constructed to close existing lacunae. They were better than the former ways of building in the old towns, but still highly schematic, since the same type was used from Wismar to Weimar.

Postmodernism is still under ideological attack. Supposedly it is not needed in the GDR because there were 'no excesses of formalism' in the phase of modernism. Architectural quotations form the past are rejected, but 'production of memory-laden references' is allowed, which amounts to practically the same thing.[54] There is less possibility, however, for excesses in postmodernism. Less glaring use of light and colour in advertising still accounts for a great difference.

There are undoubtedly certain advantages for the GDR in comparison with its Western counterparts. The pedestrian malls are less likely to be gathering places for criminal elements. There is less of a tendency to transform these areas into purely consumer centres, which are dead at night or change in the evening into night club centres. A mixture of dwellings and shopping areas and less segregation of classes and strata of the population can be observed in the GDR compared with West German towns.

## RECONSTRUCTION IN COMPARATIVE PERSPECTIVE

Both German states are deeply convinced that they followed competing strategies in their architectural policies, and that no facile convergence theory can blur the differences. It is remarkable, however, that both states constantly reacted to and anticipated what the other did. The enormous successes of West German social housing can not be separated from the reaction to the GDR's attempt to build up socialism. The Federal Republic was able to rebuff plans for socialisation in industry by proclaiming its great success in increasing private home ownership. Nevertheless, both German states rank at the bottom in their respective political blocs in private ownership of houses (see Appendix, Table 13.3). Whereas the role of state-subsidised social housing in the West declined in the 1970s, private house-building has won importance in the GDR since 1971, after having withered from 61 per cent in 1950 to 5 per cent in 1969. Today it still remains at a level of about 10 per cent and below.[55] The 'datcha' movement is an equivalent to the Western escape from the towns to the countryside.

The peoples' democracy of the GDR defines itself quite differently from the parliamentary democracy of the West. In both parts of Germany, however, political city centres were architecturally impoverished. The SED, like the Federal Chancellor and the Federal President in Bonn, usually made do with old buildings transformed for new purposes. The monuments of the great corporations in the West, which built skyscrapers as symbols of their power in a democracy, had equivalents in the East, namely the administration buildings of the state-owned industries. Traffic played a smaller role in the GDR than in the West, but automobile dominance is progressing. One of the main problems of the system is that even the huge magisterial avenues do not suffice, and parking has been neglected.[56]

It has been argued that there is no such thing as a socialist town, which is true only if one looks for a unified *Leitbild*.[57] But there are undoubtedly common features, from Magdeburg to Vladivostock, in the structure of space, the distribution of shops and the way of building housing.[58] Both German states have imitated their respective superpower. The old controversies between *Heimatschutz* and *Werkbund* seemed to have been territorialised in 1945. But the GDR did not become the heir of the Bauhaus; and the FRG, as reluctant as many towns seemed to be in following the New Building movement, was convinced by American successes and the return to Germany of a softer variant of Bauhaus ideas. 'Reconstruction' in a literal sense, rebuilding the historic towns, as Poland did in Danzig or Warsaw, was not an attractive option for the GDR. Polish architects were motivated not by a contempt for modern architecture but by the fear that they would have been obliged to accept the Soviet style of building.[59]

The GDR never shared the ideal of frugality which had wide currency in West German discussions, and in fact, both German states quickly converted to a new kind of megalomania. In Düsseldorf the Thyssen skyscraper has reminded the Germans since the late 1950s of their successful comeback. The GDR tried to do the same with its dominant buildings like the Berlin TV tower, though the ideological discussion of the tower was rather ridiculous. Architectural theory was scarcely understood by the people, and the view that the tower in Berlin was a symbol of the 'spreading idea of socialism' was hardly convincing for a population which every night via western TV admits the class enemy into its living rooms.[60] Moreover, East Berlin lost its uniqueness, for even small towns in the West – like Wesel – could afford such a symbol right in the centre of their city.

The traditionalism of the Germans right after the war was heavily criticised from abroad. 'Impoverished Nazi architecture' was one of the verdicts.[61] A lack of talent was diagnosed by the *Journal of the American Institute of Architects*, talent which was also extremely biased towards the construction of housing.[62] Later on, certain pioneering achievements were discovered in West Germany, such as church building and the construction of certain theatres, concert halls, museums and social buildings.[63] Unfortunately, the GDR shared few of these achievements. In the second phase of reconstruction, the style of building was internationalised, but still the obsession with prefabrication resulted in great difference, even in the reconstruction of town centres. The latent German inclination for expressive forms and lack of order makes both German states more receptive to postmodernism than the Latin countries, and this again may lead to a *rapprochement* between the German states and to a new kind of architectural détente.

## APPENDIX

Table 13.1   Comparative indicators for housing conditions
in the two German states

|  | GDR | | FRG | |
|---|---|---|---|---|
| 1. Remaining pre-1918 apartments | | | | |
| in 1950 | 71% | | 65% | |
| in 1958 | 66% | | 45% | |
| 2. Private apartment ownership | 23% | (1971) | 45% | (1968) |
| 3. Persons per apartment | | | | |
| in 1939 | 3.2 | | 3.9 | |
| in 1946 | 3.9 | | 4.8 | |
| in 1970 | 2.8 | | 2.9 | |
| 4. Persons per room | 1.2 | | 0.7 | |
| 5. Persons per household | 2.6 | | 2.9 | |
| 6. Private WC | 56.6% | (1971) | 87.7% | (1968) |
| 7. Apartments constructed per 10 000 inhabitants | | (by private builders) | | |
| 1950 | 17 | 61% | 74 | |
| 1960 | 47 | 6% | 104 | |
| 1970 | 45 | | 78 | |
| 1980 | 100 | | 154 | |

SOURCES:   Statistical Yearbooks of the GDR and the FRG; W. Hoffman, *Wohnungspolitik in der DDR* (Düsseldorf, 1972) p. 197; H. G. Peters, 'Sorgen um den Wohungsbau in der DDR', in E. H. Isenberg (ed.), *Zwischen Rostock und Saarbrücken* (Düsseldorf, 1973) p. 124; H. K. Schneider and R. Kornemann, *Soziale Wohnungsmarktwirtschaft* (Bonn, 1977) pp. 27ff.; K. von Beyme, *Economics and Politics within Socialist Systems* (New York, 1982) pp. 339ff.

Table 13.2   Apartments constructed per 1000 inhabitants

|  | dwelling size (square meters) | 1955 | 1960 | 1970 | 1980 | 1985 |
|---|---|---|---|---|---|---|
| Bulgaria | 64.6 | n.d. | 6.3 | 5.7 | 8.4 | 7.2 |
| Czechoslovakia | 69.5 | 3.9 | 5.6 | 7.6 | 8.4 | 6.7 |
| GDR | 57.8 | 1.7 | 2.9 | 4.5 | 10.1 | 12.8 |
| Hungary | 62.7 | 3.2 | 4.2 | 7.3 | 8.3 | 6.8 |
| Poland | 56.7 | 3.4 | 4.2 | 5.8 | 8.9 | 5.1 |
| Rumania | 47.5 | n.d. | n.d. | 7.3 | 8.9 | 4.6 |
| USSR | 47.1 | 7.6 | 14.0 | 9.4 | 7.5 | 7.2 |

SOURCES:   Economic Commission for Europe, *European Housing Trends and Policies* (Geneva, 1957) p. 2, and (Geneva, 1961) p. 2. *Statisticheskii ezhegodnik stranchlenov SEV* (Moscow, 1986) p. 155.

Table 13.3   Housing conditions

| Country | Year | Owner-occupiers | % Tenants | Average no. of persons | | Amenities | | |
| | | | | Per room | Per house-hold | Running water | WC | Electric lighting |
|---|---|---|---|---|---|---|---|---|
| Bulgaria | 1965 | 71.0 | 17.1 | 1.2 | 3.2 | 28.2 | 11.8 | 94.8 |
| Cuba | 1953 | 37.2 | 36.5 | n.d. | n.d. | 38.9 | 40.4 | 55.6 |
| Czechoslovakia | 1961 | 50.4 | 42.0 | 1.3 | 3.1 | 49.1 | 39.5 | 97.3 |
| GDR | 1971 | 23.0 | 69.3 | 1.2* | 2.6 | 82.1 | 56.6 | 100.0 |
| Poland | 1970 | n.d. | n.d. | 1.4 | 3.4 | 47.3 | 33.4 | 96.2 |
| Rumania | 1966 | n.d. | n.d. | 1.4 | 3.2 | 12.3 | 12.2 | 48.6 |
| USSR | 1965 | n.d. | n.d. | 1.5 | 3.7 | n.d. | n.d. | n.d. |
| Yugoslavia | 1971 | 70.7 | 29.3 | 1.5 | 4.0** | 34.0 | 26.5 | 87.9 |
| For comparison: | | | | | | | | |
| FRG | 1968 | 34.3 | 65.7 | 0.7 | 2.9 | 99.7 | 87.7 | 99.9 |
| Greece | 1971 | 70.6 | 25.1 | 1.5 | 3.0 | 65.0 | 45.0 | 88.3 |
| Italy | 1961 | 45.8 | 46.8 | 1.1 | 3.6 | 62.3 | n.d. | 95.9 |
| Spain | 1960 | n.d. | n.d. | n.d. | 4.0 | 45.0 | n.d. | 89.3 |
| Sweden | 1970 | 35.2 | 51.6 | 0.7 | 2.6 | 96.5 | 90.1 | n.d. |
| USA | 1970 | 62.9 | 37.1 | 0.6 | 3.2 | 97.5 | 96.0 | n.d. |

NOTES
*Figure for 1960. For 1970 the figure 1.1 was given. See M. E. Ruban, 'Wohnungsbau und Wohnungswirtschaft in den RGW-Ländern', *Deutsche Architektur*, 22 (1973) p. 1313.
**1961.

SOURCE:   *UN Statistical Yearbook, 1973* (New York, 1974) pp. 728ff.

**Notes**

1.  G. Rohde and W. Warner, *Quellen sur Entstehung der Oder-Neisse-Linie*, 2nd edn (Stuttgart, 1959) pp. 166f.
2.  Detailed figures in S. Bethlehem, *Heimatvertreibung, DDR-FLucht, Gastarbeiterzuwanderung* (Stuttgart, 1962) pp. 26ff.
3.  The Economic Co-operation Administration (ECA) distributed Marshall plan funds. H. Wandersleb (ed.), *Neuer Wohnbau*, vol. 2 (Ravensburg, 1956) pp. 81ff., 127ff.; Ch. Hackelsberger, *Die aufgeschobene Moderne. Ein Versuch der Einordnung der Architektur der Fünfziger Jahre* (Berlin, 1985) p. 51.
4.  C. Stern, *W. Ulbricht* (Cologne, 1963) p. 24; K. Liebknecht, 'Jetzt schlie e ich mit den Architekten Freundschaft', *Deutsche Architektur*, 1 (1952) pp. 156ff.
5.  F. Schenk, *Im Vorzimmer der Diktatur: 12 Jahre Pankow* (Cologne, 1962) pp. 146ff.
6.  R. Arlt and G. Rohde, *Bodenrecht* (Berlin, 1967) pp. 18ff.; H. Heineberg, *Zentren in West- und Ost-Berlin* (Paderborn, 1977) p. 58.
7.  H. Zimmerman *et al.* (eds), *DDR-Handbuch*, vol. 2 (Cologne, 1965) p. 1305.
8.  D. S. Rugg, 'German Democratic Republic', in N. N. Patricios (ed.), *International Handbook on Land Use Planning* (New York, 1966) pp. 351–99, esp. p. 369.
9.  *Protokoll des VII. Parteitages der SED*, vol. 1 (Berlin, 1967) pp. 182ff.; *Neues Deutschland* (11 December 1970) p. 4.
10.  New planning vocabulary entered the German language in the GDR, such as '*Bezirksharmonogramm*'. See K. Wiedemann, 'Die sozialistische Umgestaltung des Dorfes – eine Sache der Bevölkerung', *Deutsche Architektur*, 8 (1959) p. 666ff.
11.  Th. W. Adorno, *Ohne Leitbild* (Frankfurt, 1967) p. 70.
12.  L. Bolz, *Von deutschem Bauen* (Berlin, 1951) p. 30.
13.  E. Collein, 'Nationales Erbe und Neuplanung im deutschen Städtebau', *Deutsche Architektur*, 15 (1966) pp. 160–71.
14.  K. von Beyme, 'Policy Output in the GDR in Comparative Perspective', in K. von Beyme and H. Zimmermann (eds), *Policy-Making in the GDR* (Aldershot and New York, 1964) pp. 301-14.
15.  R. Paulick, 'Diskussion um Schwedt', *Deutsche Architektur*, 12 (1963) p. 269.
16.  H. Schmidt, 'Städtebau unterwegs', *Deutsche Architektur*, 12 (1963) pp. 270–3.
17.  B. Reimann, *Franziska Linkerhand: Roman* (1974) 6th edn (Berlin, 1980) pp. 546ff.
18.  Bolz, see note 12 (p. 39).
19.  Ibid., p. 42.
20.  Ibid., p. 49. Only at a later stage was the garden city concept recognised as a necessary step in the development of architecture. K. Junghanns, 'Gartenstadt im deutschen Städtebau', *Deutsche Architektur*, 16 (1967) pp. 59–60.
21.  On the use of the terms *Wiederaufbau* and *Aufbau*, see K. von

Beyme, *Der Wiederaufbau: Architekturtheorie und Städtebaupolitik in beiden deutschen Staaten* (Munich, 1987) ch. 6.

22. E. Hoffmann, 'Ideologische Probleme der Architektur', *Deutsche Architektur*, 1 (1952) pp. 73–5; E. Collein, 'Die Amerikanisierung des Stadtbildes von Frankfurt am Main', ibid., pp. 150–5; W. Ulbricht, 'Ueber Fragen der Architektur des Städtebaus', ibid., pp. 146–50.

23. Ulbricht, see note 22 (p. 149).

24. Ibid., p. 150; Hoffmann, see note 22 (p. 73); L. Pazitnov, *Das schöpferische Erbe des Bauhauses 1919–1933* (Berlin, 1963) pp. 32ff.; H. Meyer, *Bauen und Gesellschaft. Schriften, Briefe, Projekte* (Dresden, 1980) pp. 93ff.; K.-J. Winkler, 'Hannes Meyer', *Architektur der DDR*, 28 (1979) H. Schmidt, 'Deutsche Architekten in der Sowjetunion', *Deutsche Architektur*, 16 (1967) pp. 625–9.

25. W. Heise, 'Ueberlegungen zu Werk und Gestalt Hermann Henselmanns', in H. Henselmann, *Gedanken, Ideen, Bauten, Projekte* (Berlin, 1976) p. 11.

26. F. Werner, *Stadt, Städtebau, Architektur in der DDR* (Erlangen, 1961) p. 33.

27. 'Wiederaufbau der Innenstadt Eilenburg', *Deutsche Architektur*, 15 (1966) p. 315.

28. H. Hopp, 'Der Wiederaufbau von Neubrandenburg', *Deutsche Architektur*, 6 (1955) pp. 293–9; Criticism by K. Junghanns in *Deutsche Architektur*, 6 (1955).

29. Fortunately were the proposals for Rathenow by the important pioneer Otto Haesler were not carried out, but neither were the more conservative projects planned for Prenzlau. O. Haesler, 'Rathenow', *Bauhelfer*, 4 (1949) pp. 204–6; von Tettau, 'Prenzlau', ibid., pp. 202ff.; F. Rupp and G. Gisder, 'Der Aufbau der Innenstadt von Prenzlau', *Deutsche Architektur*, 9 (1960) pp. 479–83.

30. F. Schöller, *Städtebaupolitik, Stadtumbau und Stadterhaltung in der DDR* (Wiesbaden, 1966) p. 20; Werner, see note 26 (p. 32).

31. V. M. Semenov (ed.), *Zastroika sovetskikh gorodov* (Moscow, 1957) p. 11.

32. K. Liebknecht, 'Die Bedeutung der Unions-Baukonferenz in Moskau für die Aufgaben im Bauwesen der DDR', *Deutsche Architektur*, 4 (1955) p. 61.

33. N. Baranov, 'Einige aktuelle Fragen der Architektur und des Städtebaus', *Deutsche Architektur*, 5 (1956) pp. 296ff.

34. *Protokoll des V. Parteitages der SED* (1958), vol. 1 (Berlin, 1959) p. 63; *Gesetzblatt*, II, (1961) pp. 179ff.

35. Speer was reminded of his planned 'Ostdurchbruch' when he became acquainted with Ulbricht's plans through the newspapers in his Spandau prison. See F. Werner, *Stadtplanung Berlin* (Berlin, 1976) p. 139.

36. Naumov and other Soviet architects were criticised for their low-level building in a 'garden city' style, whereas the Soviets criticised the East German proposals by saying that 'proportions' were sacrificed to 'dimensions'. B. Flierl, 'Wie wird das Zentrum von Berlin gestaltet?' *Deutsche Architektur*, 9 (1960) p. 134.

37. Thomas Topfstedt, *Abri der Städtebaugeschichte der DDR von der Mitte der 50er Jahre bis zum Beginn der 1970er Jahre*, diss. B at Karl Marx University (Leipzig, 1984) p. 53. U. Kultemann, *Zeitgenössische Architektur in Osteuropa* (Cologne, 1985) p. 125.

38. The chilly buildings seem to repent Ulbricht's decision to demolish the ruins of the imperial Hohenzollern palace in 1950, which was originally meant to be rebuilt. H. Letsch, *Plädoyer für eine schöne Umwelt* (Berlin, 1965) p. 175.

39. G. Stahn, *Das Nikolaiviertel am Marx–Engels–Forum* (Berlin, 1985) p. 65. The area is none the less full of post-modern architectural citations.

40. Topfstedt, see note 37 (p. 99).

41. J. Gerlach, 'Innerstädtischer Wohnungsbau im Stadtzentrum von Anklam', *Deutsche Architektur* 14 (1965) pp. 20–4.

42. K. Worf, 'Zum Wiederaufbau des Stadtzentrums von Nordhausen', *Deutsche Architektur*, (1960) p. 549; and H. Scholke, *Halberstadt* (Leipzig, 1977) p. 142.

43. P. Doehler, 'Die sozialistische Umgestaltung der alten Wohngebiete der Städte der DDR', *Deutsche Architektur*, 12 (1963) pp. 457ff.

44. B. Flierl, *Zur sozialistischen Architekturentwicklung in der DDR*, diss. B at Humboldt University (Berlin, 1979) p. 106. Similarly critical is Topfstedt, see note 37 (p. 162).

45. Topfstedt, see note 37 (p. 70); Flierl, see note 36 (pp. 92ff.).

46. G. Krenz, 'Architektur und Städtebau vor neuen Aufgaben', *Einheit*, 11 (1965) pp. 46–57.

47. B. Geyer, 'Städtebau und Unifizierung', *Deutsche Architektur*, 15 (1966) pp. 629ff.

48. K. Andrä, 'Zentren – Stätten der menschengemeinschaft', in *Deutsche Architektur*, 19 (1970) pp. 262–4.

49. K. Andrä *et al.*, *Fu gängerbereiche in Stadtzentren* (Berlin, 1961).

50. K. Lembcke, 'Standpunkte und Auffassungen zum inner-städtischen Wohnungsbau', *Deutsche Architektur*, 31 (1982) pp. 266–9.

51. *Gesetzblatt*, DDR I, no. 17 (1985).

52. K. Kuhn and B. Hunger, 'Wohnen in älteren Wohngebieten', *Deutsche Architektur*, 9 (1960) pp. 121–5.

53. H. von Tümpling, 'Was wird aus unseren alten Städten', *Deutsche Architektur*, 19 (1970) p. 197.

54. 'Die Herstellung memorialer Bezüge'. H. Wirth, 'Historische Werte im gegenwärtigen Architekturschaffen', *Architektur der DDR*, 31 (1982) pp. 347–52, and Ch. Schädlich, 'Der Postmodernismus – eine alternative Architektur?', *Architektur der DDR*, 31 (1982) pp. 340–6.

55. H. Hoffmann, *Wohnungspolitik der DDR* (Düsseldorf, 1972) p. 66.

56. O. Büttner, 'Wohin mit dem ruhenden Verkehr?', *Deutsche Architektur*, 19 (1970) pp. 432–5.

57. A. Karger and F. Werner, 'Architektur in der DDR', *Geographische Rundschau*, 34 (1982) pp. 519–29.

58. R. A. French and F. E. Hamilton (eds), *The Socialist City: Spatial Structure and Urban Policy* (New York, 1979) pp. 11ff.

59.  A. Tomaszewski, 'Polnische Denkmalpflege im europäischen Vergleich', in H. H. Rieseberg *et al.*, *Wiederaufbau und restaurierung historischer Stadtbilder in Polen* (Berlin, 1985) p. 91.
60.  Flierl, see note 36 (p. 174).
61.  H. Schoszberger, 'Blick über die Grenzen', *Neue Bauwelt*, 5 (1950) p. 197.
62.  Cited in Ph. Rappaport, 'Städtebau und ECA', in H. Wandersleb (ed.), *Neuer Wohnbau* (Ravensburg, 1952) vol. 1, p. 47.
63.  J. Burchard, *The Voice of the Phoenix: Postwar Architecture in Germany* (Cambridge, Mass., 1966) pp. 1–6.

# 14 Reconstruction: its Place in Planning History

## GORDON E. CHERRY

The course of postwar urban development in Europe, covering a period of unparalleled urbanisation during which cities have expanded territorially and transformed internally, has attracted considerable analysis. For the historian the period is simply one stage in a sequence of many, in almost a millenium of urban development;[1] for the social geographer it is a period when increasing public interventionism has shaped city environments.[2] Cities of particular cultural style have formed the subject of enquiry: in Mediterranean lands[3] or with regard to the socialist city.[4] Cities characterised simply by their bigness or complexity have been described: in world comparisons[5] or as separate case studies in which their present postwar characteristics are seen as part of a lengthier historical canvas: Paris[6] or British regional cities,[7] for example.

Urban history teaches us that change takes place in a series of discontinuous leaps. Particular dramatic events may or may not determine massive change; Christopher Wren's plan for London after the Great Fire of 1666 was not implemented, but Lisbon's central area was redesigned after the earthquake of 1755. Individuals, and the institutional settings in which they find themselves, may occasion certain developments of long standing significance; Napoleon III's energetic administrator for the Seine, Georges-Eugène Haussmann engineered his great boulevards for a reconstructed Paris, but by comparison the Metropolitan Board of Works for London at the same time was never given the power, money or authority for such radical urban surgery. Urban development is never ordained; there are always special reasons why change takes place in a particular form and at a particular time – and why it does not.

Natural calamities or the fortuitous presence of personalities are by definition highly localised. But war in Europe between 1939 and 1945 was not; its impact and consequences were international. It was the first period in world history when air strikes took place against cities in any real sense, and as a consequence, massive urban dislocation disrupted a large number of European urban centres during this time. This was the substance of the Bellagio Conference, which served to assemble a number of papers which dealt with the traumatic circumstances of more than forty years previous. Planning history often establishes certain bench marks on occasions of anniversaries or after conventional periods of time; forty years on, it was obviously a good opportunity to cast a sober, objective gaze on the period of the 1940s – the years of destruction and the first approach to rebuilding – when new material was brought to light and scholars from the warring nations could talk without (open) emotion about the damage inflicted on each other's cities. The selected case studies mirrored the recent interest shown in this period of twentieth-century urban history and suggested the abundant scholarship which could now be drawn upon to illumine a particularly difficult, but crucially significant, period in city building and city planning.

My own experience of the war years were privileged ones, at school and living in a small town which suffered no bomb damage, but I shall not forget from the safety of my South Yorkshire bedroom, the orange glow in the sky one December night as Sheffield, fourteen miles away, burned after its blitz. For many years afterwards the ravaged central area of that city provided a gaunt background to a resumption of the normalities of shopping. Some years on, I worked in the same city for a short while as a planner when reconstruction was still the most important term on the agenda for planners and politicians. Since then the passage of time has healed the scars and we can study more dispassionately this particular period in our contemporary history, and so make a new contribution to a comparative understanding of European developments at that time. Bellagio provided that opportunity.

## THE PRECURSOR

We should acknowledge at the outset that even before 1939 the notion of radical urban reconstruction was 'in the air'. This emanated from a number of sources: a dissatisfaction with the legacy of the nineteenth-century industrial city; from the realisation that social privation stemmed from the failure of the same international economic order that had given earlier prosperity; and, in certain intellectual quarters, from the impression of gloom which attended the prospects of the West as a cultural force. The literature of the interwar period is instructive.[8] The romanticism of the Georgian poets in Britain for example had gone: the predominant mood of rural England and escape to the English countryside for inspiration was replaced by a different view articulated by cosmopolitans like T. S. Eliot and Ezra Pound, and on the continent European experiments came face to face with social realism. James Joyce's description of Dublin was as a sordid city, and *Ulysses* (1922) stressed the futility of modern city life. In the 1930s George Orwell wrote both of the squalor of the northern English cities and the featurelessness of the new suburbs. A world view from Lewis Mumford at this time offered a pessimistic view of the history of urbanism: from village community (*eopolis*) to an association of villages (*polis*), to a city merged within its region (*metropolis*), to a stage of decline through the consequences of size (*megalopolis*), to a period of moral decadence and governmental failure (*tyrranopolis*) to a city racked by war, famine and disease (*nekropolis*).[9] This imagery was very powerful to an uncertain world.

Professionals suggested a variety of new responses, many of which were radical and required the sweeping away of the old, comprehensively: city reconstruction was not just a question of the physical redesign of space, it involved the renewal of political, economic and social structures, too. The Modern Movement in architecture suggested itself as an heroic adventure capable of improving man's condition. In Britain the *beaux-arts* tradition remained strong but in a number of continental European centres a revolutionary fervour was built up for the harnessing of science and technology for new city forms. Le Corbusier's novel ideas for the future city, the innovations of Germany's social housing programme of the Weimar Bauhaus, and the new functional town planning principles enshrined in the International Congress of Modern Architecture (CIAM) all suggested that city building was on the frontiers of change.

There were important precursors, then, to the urban reconstruction of the next decade. An era already conducive to creating the future, rather than reconstructing the past, was in the making. Significant psychological thresholds had been overstepped, and a positive groundswell of conviction in the need, at least, to experiment in new urban forms had become established. In America Clarence Perry was working on the 'neighbourhood unit', with its new design principles, and Frank Lloyd Wright's 'Broadacre City' was yet another urban solution, this time in an extreme form

212 of decentralised living

of decentralised living. Even in conservative England, wedded as
it was to its garden city and vernacular style of housing in low
density estates, the Modern Architectural Research Group produced
a radical master plan for London in 1939. When the bombs fell, it
was no wonder that reconstruction groups from Warsaw to Coventry
sprang up within days with practical schemes for the rebuilding of
their cities.

There had at least been a forewarning of air attack and the
likelihood of physical damage on an unprecedented scale. In the
Spanish Civil War the lesson of the destruction of the Basque city
of Guernica by German bombers was not lost on the observers of
the time. In Britain the much respected and (ultimately) the highly
influential Royal Commission on the Distribution of the Industrial
Population, set up in 1937, put great store in its report (the Barlow
Report[10]) on the need to decentralise metropolitan London and to
relocate particular industries to other parts of the country, in part
because of the threat of aerial bombardment. No previous armed
conflict between nations had threatened the destruction of cities
from the air; the new strike weapon was all too soon to be in
evidence.

The attack on Rotterdam in 1940 was the first major example
of what was in store. In Britain the German Luftwaffe began the
systematic bombing of London and industrial towns, and between
September 1940 and May 1941 centres including Belfast, Clydeside,
Merseyside and a range of industrial and port areas including
Sheffield, Coventry, Plymouth, Hull, Bristol and occasional cathedral
cities became particular targets; the east of London bore a major
brunt. In the last year of the war attacks by flying bombs were less
concentrated spatially but on occasions were even more destructive.
In the whole country around half a million dwellings were totally
destroyed. In Germany all cities of any size were bombed, many
heavily and repeatedly. In Berlin over a third of the housing stock
had been destroyed by the end of the war, but higher proportions
were lost in the Ruhr, particularly in Duisburg, Dortmund, Essen
and Bochum. Elsewhere Cologne and Würzburg suffered badly. But
air attacks were not the end of the matter: for certain cities there was
a conscious plan for destruction as in Warsaw, but happily schemes to
destroy Paris did not materialise. Elsewhere, land fighting as armies
wrested cities from occupying foes completed the record of destruction. For one reason or another a range of towns and cities suffered
considerable damage: Le Havre, Marseilles, Rotterdam and Turin

are simply illustrations of the geographical extent in the West.

The opportunity to rebuild came quicker and in different circumstances from what the radical visionaries of the 1930s had imagined. In Britain in particular, because it was the one country of the allied nations that did not have an occupying force on its soil, not only did plans for reconstruction proceed at a fast pace but progress was sustained. The State harnessed the drive for social and spiritual renewal and applied it to economic power, physical reconstruction and military might. 'Planning' was a popular word and the notion of town planning for the future cities had widespread support. It all seemed so simple; planning was winning the war and planning would win the peace. New cities would be built and old ones rebuilt to a standard as never before; the State would be a steersman to a nobler future.

It was in this context that the mechanics for postwar plan-making were established.[11] In Britain new arrangements were entered into at unprecedented speed. The Barlow Report of 1940, bold in its prescription for spatial redistribution, was yet cautious in how it was to be achieved: it merely suggested the setting up of a National Industrial Board, comprising a Chairman and three other members, with a range of general responsibilities. These were to collect and co-ordinate information relating to the location of industry, to undertake research, to advise Government and to submit annual reports to Parliament. It needed a Minority Report prepared by Patrick Abercrombie (Professor of Town Planning at the University of London and a foremost planning consultant of his day) and two other fellow Commissioners to suggest the setting up of a new government department, with full executive powers and an adequate staff. In 1940 that must have seemed remote, but by 1943 a separate Ministry of Town and Country Planning had been created. Planning control powers were extended to cover the whole country and an intense period of plan-making began. *The County of London Plan* (1943) prepared by the Chief Architect for the London County Council, J. H. Forshaw, in collaboration with Abercrombie was, in fact, a reconstruction plan. A plan for the much wider area of Greater London (1944) was prepared by Abercrombie and a small team; in establishing the basic philosophy and practical measures needed for the planned decentralisation of a major urban area it commanded national respect. The ground rules for reconstruction fell into place with an overall design for Greater London in the form of concentric rings according to population numbers and density, industrial location, and use of open land for agriculture and recreation. Further regional plans for other parts of Britain put forward similar proposals for the redevelopment of blitzed and blighted inner cores, the redistribution of an over-congested population and the building up of outer town settlements through town expansion or new towns.

Other plans prepared during this period of the middle 1940s attended to the detail of civic design, with specific proposals for town centres and residential areas. We can marvel today at the sheer fertility of ideas and confidence of expression shown in some of these plans, often prepared in the darkest days of war. Abercrombie's plans for Plymouth, Hull and Edinburgh, and Sharp's plans for Oxford and Exeter are all classics in their way. Not all came to fruition, but at Plymouth, with virtually no economic appraisal, a new central area layout, with a 40 per cent increase in shopping provision, was designed to replace the haphazard mediaeval street pattern: and so it has been. Elsewhere in this naval town the old environmental intimacy was retained, notably in the old port in the Barbican area from where the Pilgrim Fathers had sailed three centuries earlier.

But it was the plan for the City of London (1947) prepared by consultants Charles Holden and William Holford (Professor of Town Planning at Liverpool and wartime civil servant) which took the eye from the point of view of its design proposals. The City, the small financial and commercial core of the capital, had suffered heavy war damage, with one third of the prewar commercial and industrial floor space destroyed, though with St Paul's Cathedral in the centre miraculously unscathed. Holden and Holford sketched out a programme for reconstruction, governing height and site coverage of buildings, new street patterns, sensitive-use zoning and a design emphasis on precinct development, particularly around St Paul's and the city churches.

Meanwhile, the methodological tools for urban reconstruction were being fashioned. Holford, again, was a key figure through his leadership of a research team in the Ministry of Town and Country Planning during the wartime years and immediately after.[12] The Ministry's *Handbook on the Redevelopment of Central Areas* was published in 1947 to provide local authority guidance on how to handle problems of rebuilding, the preparation of surveys, advice on use-zoning and on layout, design and programming: a thorough package for comprehensive planning. One particular methodological advance centred on density control: the Floor Space Index, which expressed a flexible, statistically-based relationship between the curtilage of a site and the floor area of the building erected on it, proved a workable technique for almost twenty years.

Another issue for redevelopment concerned highways and road traffic, and during the war years a number of important threads were brought together as principles on which reconstruction should take place. Two were to have enduring impact. One was the advocacy for comprehensive road systems based on a hierarchy according to function, in which the circular ring road was of paramount circulatory importance. This pattern was endorsed in the 'ring and spoke' layout for Greater London, proposed by Abercrombie; it had been advocated earlier by an Assistant Commissioner of Police, Alker Tripp, and brought together the issues of highway engineering and urban design.[13] The other issue of significance for reconstruction was the design principle of precincts, from which through-traffic would be deflected. Tripp took his example from the Inns of Court in London, which formed an enclave where general traffic was excluded. Twenty years later Colin Buchanan was to advocate the same principle in 'environmental areas' as a major proposal in a government study, *Traffic in Towns*;[14] but in the meantime, commercial and residential traffic-free zones became popular features in most reconstructed areas. Government advice to local authorities on these matters came in a report from the Ministry of War Transport, *Design and Layout of Roads in Built-up Areas* (1946).

Local authority guidance on housing reconstruction completed the range of advice from central government. A Committee of the Central Housing Advisory Committee reported in 1944: the Dudley Report on *The Design of Dwellings* which dealt with densities and layouts. An official *Housing Manual 1944* dealt with the architectural detail of the forms of mixed development that were then advocated.

So the components for reconstruction were all in place between 1943 and 1947: design norms for central areas, functional road layouts, new standardised housing forms, the neighbourhood and, integrating the whole, a vision of a dispersed, decentralised city. It was a remarkable achievement of professional application, supported by political consensus. The promise was no less than the well housed, socially acceptable, environmentally attractive city, to replace the outmoded, unhealthy, over-congested city of the past.

THE AFTERMATH

In one country at least, Britain, all the essential ingredients had been prepared for the feast of reconstruction. Other countries were clearly less well advanced because of professional disruption and political dislocation. But the intellectual energy that had been in evidence before the war could not be denied, and the networks established in the 1930s, particularly among architects, were never totally broken. International journals were in circulation, and although Germany was especially isolated, Portugal and Sweden were points of contact for a significant information flow across Europe.

Inevitably, however, we look to events after 1945 to explain how common reconstruction ideas were diffused so rapidly across a ravaged continent. Britain had a head start: already in the process of establishing its own comprehensive planning system based on national arrangements for the control of all forms of development and the compulsory preparation of statutory plans, it had an evident plan-making capacity for reconstructed cities. This experience could readily be exported and planning expertise for the profession was boosted by short courses for those serving in, or recently demobilised from, the armed forces.

It helped enormously that design innovation in Sweden expressed similar ideas – brilliantly, as it transpired. As described by Barnett,[15] the Sergelgatan, the principal shopping street in the Hötorget district of Stockholm, became a pedestrian precinct running through a two-level shopping concourse, with foot bridges and office towers above. In suburban Stockholm, Vallingby was developed as a high-density satellite with courtyard groups of housing and office and shopping development in precinct settings. A significant trend was established, with the design forms implanted into reconstructed cities across Europe.

The role of the International Federation for Housing and Town Planning in the immediate postwar years was significant for both diffusion of knowledge and for boosting the morale of fragmented professions. The first postwar meeting was at Hastings in England (1946) when the reconstruction plans for Rotterdam, Liège, Warsaw, London and Exeter were considered. For some years German planners remained relatively isolated from European contact; they had difficulty in leaving the country; their country was readmitted to the International Federation only in 1950; and it took until 1954 for German to be recognised again as a registered language. However, British planners made lecture tours in German cities under the auspices of the British Council and in 1947 Walter Gropius revisited Germany by permission of the US Military Governor. The housing aspect of reconstruction was an early focus for conferences, including the particular issue of prefabrication as well as the general question of architecture in relation to state and society. These were represented at the International Federation's Conference at Zurich in 1948 and Amsterdam in 1950, but by the later 1950s more attention was being devoted to regional planning, as at Vienna in 1956 and at Liège in 1958.

By this time the reconstruction years were beginning to pass. The main postwar features of urban Europe had now been re-established. The basic programmes of rebuilding had settled the conditions for the remainder of the century and the urban map of the nation states proceeded to take on its new evolutionary form. As ever with the forces of urbanisation, the future had surprises in store.

In the first place, remarkable prosperity soon attended the European economy. Physical recovery was far faster than anyone had reason to expect and within a surprisingly short time the consequences of material prosperity, born of economic growth and (for some) American aid, contributed their own urban problems. Higher residential expectations fuelled sustained housing demand, consumerism in general created new pressures on living space and community facilities, while the insatiable drive for car ownership both demanded and created new urban forms and structures.

The capitalist economic motor was urban-oriented. An already urbanised Europe became even more urbanised. A massive resorting of displaced people came to rest in the growing cities. Here, refugees found new homes – a not unusual urban phenomenon, bearing in mind the forced displacement of Jews and Christian minorities over the centuries; urban Europe was running true to form. Reconstruction was soon a question not just of rebuilding the old, but of providing a springboard of infrastructure and basic provision from which the new, later twentieth century city would grow. The form became that of the dispersed metropolitan city, and this now characterises much of the urban heartland of Europe. In this context, immediate postwar reconstruction was a necessary phase of rebuilding, but the general principles of decentralisation, which at least the British plans explicitly endorsed, had a longer-term, seminal significance. The dominant feature of postwar Europe has been that of a generalised diffusion of urban living.

Hall and Hay have identified seventeen urban zones in Europe where megalopolitan growth characteristics are exhibited.[16] In total their population increased by 25 million between 1950 and 1970 (52.6 to 77.5 million), each zone having a population of at least one million and having achieved a growth rate of more than 30 per cent over the two decades. Fourteen of these were located within a Golden Triangle, the corners of which were North Holland, Madrid and Rome, as follows: Madrid; Basque Coast (Spain); Turin; Lorraine; Milan; Rome; Barcelona; Provence–Côte d'Azur; Lyon–Grenoble; East Randstad–North Rhine; Geneva–Lausanne–Annecy; Paris; Upper Rhine (East Bank)–Central Switzerland; and Munich. The other three were: the North London Fringe; Stockholm; and Valencia.

The geographical map to emerge suggests two broad categories of growth. First, there is a pronounced axial development along the Rhine, with lesser concentrations along its tributaries, the Rhone–Saône valleys and the Côte d'Azur. The second is in southern Europe with dramatic population increases being recorded in the big cities such as Madrid, Barcelona, Bilbao, Valencia, Rome, Turin and Milan. Intriguingly, the characteristics of the two areas are different in that in the first, growth has taken place in medium-sized rather than very large cities, whereas in the second, it is precisely the biggest cities which have absorbed the increases.

Postwar developments in the urban geography of Europe have therefore been very significant. It is fascinating, for example, to see how, in spite of the massive dislocation to urban infrastructure experienced between 1939 and 1945, remarkable continuity has obtained in the urban map of the postwar years. The strength of Europe's industrial heartland remains unimpaired and urban dominance in this area has been continued. The structural weaknesses of the older industrial areas have been pronounced, it is true, but by way of compensation there has been the conspicuous success of the urban zones of the Eastern Randstad, Cologne–Bonn and the Upper Rhine. Continuity in this century, indeed over the centuries, is remarkable. Metropolitan cities seem to do well in those corridors of trade and transportation where towns have thrived since the Middle Ages. Perhaps there is one strongly pronounced new feature, however. Tidewater locations, particularly on estuaries, no longer seem so important; the faster growing cities now tend to be inland.

Reconstruction sought to re-establish, though, not simply to conserve. As such it was seen as a physical exercise; it was place-specific as an activity, and people came second. In fact, over the years the insistent urban problems have been people-based, not place-based, and this has been the case across urban Europe. Patterns of social segregation have emerged, based on economic power and differential access to scarce resources, notably housing. Older city areas with low-income housing contrast markedly with outer city districts with higher-income dwelling stock. Lower-quality housing accommodates the ethnically disadvantaged Asians and Afro-Caribbeans in Britain, Algerians, Tunisians and Moroccans in France, and a variety of guest workers in Germany including Yugoslavs and Turks; European cities have become cosmopolitan. And in this period of social change they have become foci for social unrest, from whatever cause: the *provotariaat* ('provos') of Amsterdam, the students of Paris, urban terrorists, nationalists, race rioters and those demonstrating the pent-up anger of the inner city disadvantaged. These have been some of the features the planners for reconstruction could not have anticipated.

So the reconstruction years take their place in planning history. Embryo seeds for new urban forms had already been sown; the ravages of war provided the opportunity for new building; since then the fruits of achievement have been harvested. Urban processes have ben confirmed: out of urban problems arise policies, and those solutions beget new problems. Urban Europe may now be tackling the problems of affluence and growth, but the reconstruction phase continues to cast its shadow.

**Notes**
1. Paul M. Hohenberg and Lynn H. Lees, *The Making of Urban Europe* (Cambridge, Mass., and London, 1985).
2. Paul White, *The West European City: A Social Geography* (Harlow, 1984).
3. Martin Wynn (ed.), *Planning and Urban Growth in Southern Europe* (London, 1984).
4. R. A. French and F. E. Ian Hamilton (eds), *The Socialist City: Spatial Structure and Urban Policy* (Chichester, 1979).
5. Peter Hall, *The World Cities* (London, 1966).
6. Norma Evenson, *Paris: A Century of Change, 1878–1978* (New Haven, Conn. and London, 1979).
7. George Gordon (ed.), *Regional Cities in the U.K., 1890–1980* (London, 1986).
8. Edward Timms and David Kelley, *Unreal Life: Urban Experience*

in *Modern European Literature and Art* (Manchester, 1985).

9.   Lewis Mumford, *The Culture of Cities* (London, 1938).
10.  Royal Commission on the Distribution of the Industrial Population (Barlow Commission), *Report*, Cmd 6153 (London, 1940).
11.  Gordon E. Cherry, *Cities and Plans: The Shaping of Urban Britain in the 19th and 20th Centuries* (London, 1988).
12.  Gordon E. Cherry and Leith Penny, *Holford: A Study in Architecture, Planning and Civic Design* (London, 1986).
13.  H. Alker Tripp, *Town Planning and Road Traffic* (London, 1942).
14.  *Traffic in Towns*, Reports of the Steering Group and Working Group appointed by the Minister of Transport (London, 1963).
15.  Jonathan Barnett, *The Elusive City: Five Centuries of Design, Ambition and Miscalculation* (London, 1987).
16.  Peter Hall and Dennis Hay, *Growth Centres in the European Urban System* (London, 1980).

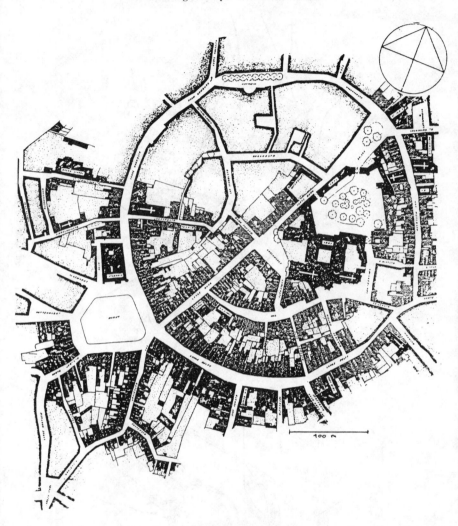

1.  Plan of Middelburg centre, 1939.

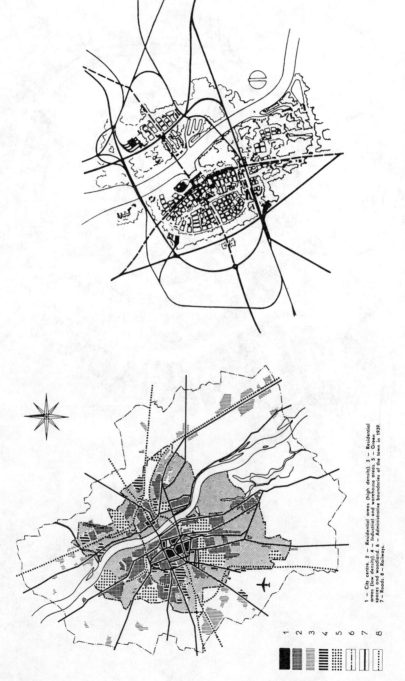

3. The Pabst Plan for Warsaw as a German city, 1939–40.

2. Warsaw, 1939.

1 — City centre. 2 — Residential areas (high density). 3 — Residential areas (low density). 4 — Industrial and warehouse areas. 5 — Green spaces and woodland. 6 — Administrative boundaries of the town in 1939. 7 — Roads. 8 — Railways.

**1** – Completely destroyed built-up areas. **2** – Partly destroyed and preserved built-up areas.

4.   Warsaw: destruction map, 1939–45.

5.   Warsaw: clandestine town-planning – project for the redevelopment of the High Bank
     in the city centre, 1943 (drawings by Kazimierz Marezewski).

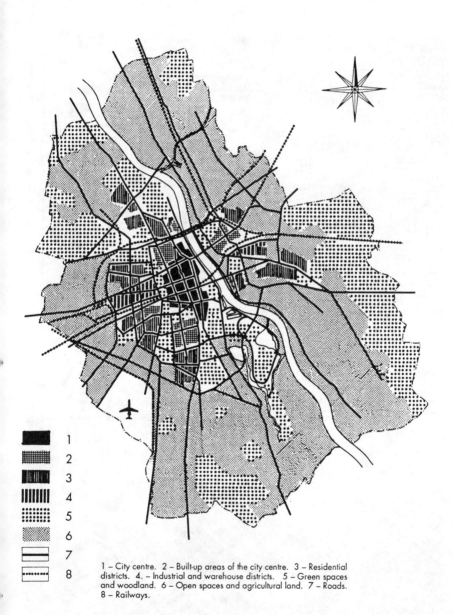

1 – City centre. 2 – Built-up areas of the city centre. 3 – Residential districts. 4. – Industrial and warehouse districts. 5 – Green spaces and woodland. 6 – Open spaces and agricultural land. 7 – Roads. 8 – Railways.

6. Warsaw: the First Reconstruction Plan of 1945.

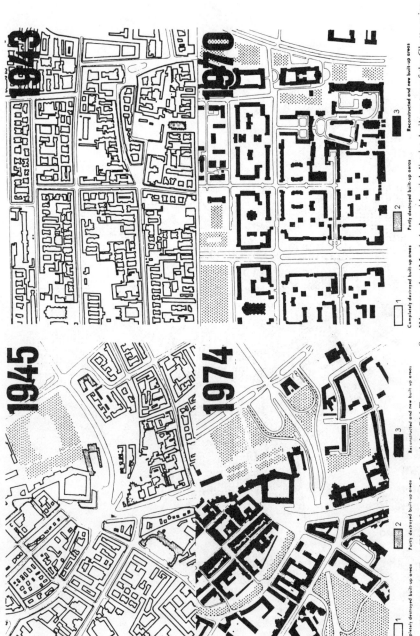

8. Warsaw: the 'Muranów' residential district, built on top of the Ghetto ruins.

7. Warsaw: the East–West thoroughfare and the Old Town.

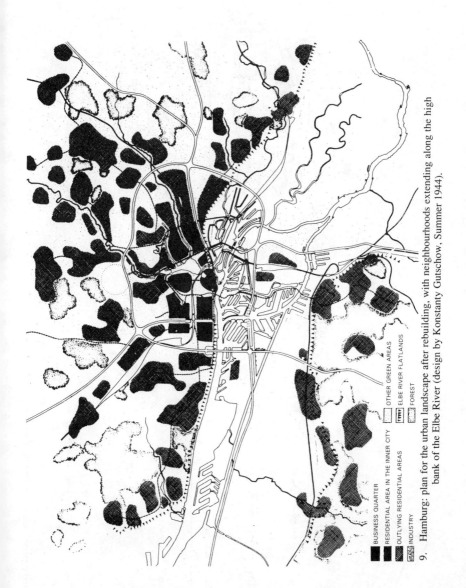

9. Hamburg: plan for the urban landscape after rebuilding, with neighbourhoods extending along the high bank of the Elbe River (design by Konstanty Gutschow, Summer 1944).

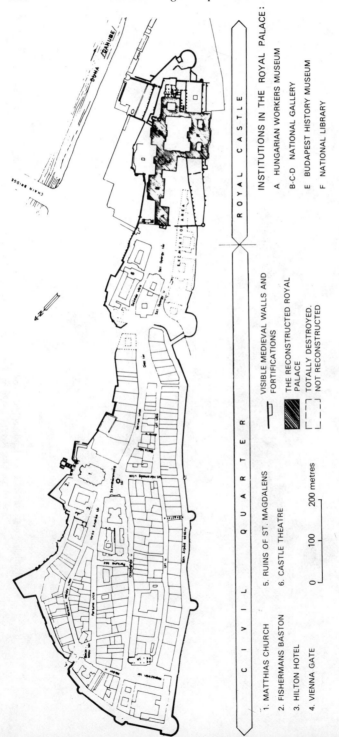

10. Budapest: ground plan of Buda Castle Hill (sketch map).

# Index

Abercrombie, Patrick, 8, 98, 126, 136, 213, 215
Acke, V., 52
anti-urbanism, 116, 119, 142, 211
Antwerp, 54
architecture
  historicist, 196
  Maréchalist aesthetics in, 33
  modern, 11, 32, 33, 38, 43, 45, 57, 61, 148, 158, 173, 184, 191, 193, 211
  monumental, 198
  postmodern, 186, 199
  regional / traditional, 32–4, 38, 40–1, 43, 57, 61–2, 64, 67, 68, 72, 74, 122, 157, 179, 184

Baburov, V. B., 83–4
Bakema, J., 148
Bardet, Gaston, 58
Barlow Report, 8, 103, 212–13
Bauhaus, 194
Belgium: see Chapter 4
  CGRP (Commissariat général de la restauration du pays), 48, 51–2, 54–7, 59–62
  collectivist ideals in, 55
  Commissariat à la reconstruction immobilière, 31
  Commissariat du royaume aux grandes agglomérations, 59
  Commissariat général au tourisme, 56
  Commission d'estimation des dommages de guerre, 56
  Commission royale des monuments et des sites, 50
  German occupation during World War I, 50
  German occupation during World War II, 51, 54
  Institut supérieur des arts décoratifs, 52
  Ministry of Reconstruction, 62
  Office des régions dévastées, 50
  OREC (Office du redressement economique), 51–3, 58, 61
  planologie, 59–60
  Service d'urbanisme, 58
  Service de l'urbanisme et de l'architecture, 61
  Service de la reconstruction (architecture et urbanisme), 52, 57
  Société nationale de la petite propriété terrienne, 51
  Société nationale des habitations bon marché, 51
  Touring Club, 56
  Vlaamse Toeristenbond, 56
Belgium Town Planning Committee, 49
Berlin, 10, 11, 196
  Alexanderplatz, 196
  Marx–Engels Square, 196
  Stalinallee, 194, 196
Bernoulli, Hans, 83–4
Berthelot, Jean, 40–1
Beyme, Klaus von, 3
Biegánski, Piotr, 88
Binder, Gottlieb, 138
Bloch-Lainé, François, 17, 26
Bolz, Lothar, 193
Bonatz, Paul, 194
Braem, Renaat, 57
Bremen, 197
Breuer, Marcel, 150
British Council Exhibition, 139
Brunfaut, Max and Gaston, 61
Budapest: see Chapter 11
  Castle Hill district, 155
  Castle Theatre, 156, 165
  Hilton Hotel, 163–5
  Institute for the Preservation of Historic Monuments, 157
  Matthias Church, 156
  Royal Palace, 155, 165–7
Burnham, Daniel, 134

Cassan, Urbain, 21
CGRP: see Belgium, CGRP
Chantier 1425, 21
Charter of Athens, 31, 45, 137, 174, 175, 193
Châteauneuf-sur-Loire, 35–6, 39, 42
Chernyshev, S. Y., 83
Chmielewski, Jan, 82
CIAM (Congrès Internationaux d'Architecture Moderne), 31, 34, 45, 140, 211
Ciborowski, Adolf, 89

Claudius-Petit, Eugéne, 25, 45
Collein, Edmund, 175
Cologne, 115
Coursimault, 36
Coventry: see Chapter 7
   City Re-Development Committee, 97
   Gibson plan, 100–1, 104–6, 111–12
   Labour Party politics, 95
   local opposition to Gibson plan, 99, 101
   opposition of central government to
      Gibson plan, 101, 102, 106
   prewar urban structure, 95
   social structure, 94
   town planning and local politics, 103–4
   town planning for, 96
CTRI: see France, CTRI
Custers, Joz. L., 55

DATAR: see France, DATAR
Dautry, Raoul, 19, 20, 23, 46
De Ligne, Jean, 62
de Man, Henri, 51
death memorials, 114
DeStalinisation, 183
DGEN: see France, DGEN
Dresden: see Chapter 12
   Altmarkt, 177, 179, 181, 182, 185–7
   Baroque architecture, 170, 181, 186
   Central Square, 178
   Department for Preservation of
      Historic Monuments, 178
   destruction of, 171
   Ernst-Thälmann-Strasse, 180, 182
   Frauenkirche, 170, 181–3, 186
   Frauenkirche as war memorial, 183
   Frauenkirche, demolition of, 173
   Gartenstadt Hellerau, 171
   historic centre, 181
   Hofkirche, 170
   House of Socialist Culture, 182, 184
   Kreuzkirche, 170
   Lasch architects' collective, 184
   'Magistrale', 177, 179–82
   planning competitions, 177–8, 180,
      184–5
   Prager Strasse, 185
   project for a skyscraper, 177–8,
      188–22, 184, 186
   in the romantic period, 171
   Royal Palace, 177, 181, 186
   shopping mall, 185
   Webergasse, 185
   Zwinger, 170, 177
Durth, Werner, 3
Dziewulski, Stanislaw, 79, 82, 84, 86

East Prussia, reconstruction programmes
   of 1917–18 in, 122
Eggerickx, Jean, 50
Eilenburg, 195
Eisenhower, Dwight D., 79
Elkart, Karl, 115
Ermisch, Hugo, 177
Exeter, 139
expropriation of private property, 65,
   104, 107, 158, 174, 191
fascist architecture and planning, 3, 7,
   114, 121, 133
Fehl, Gerhard, 3
Fischer, Karl Friedrich, 122
Fischer, Ludwig, 77
Flouquet, Pierre-Louis, 52, 58
Ford (City Engineer of Coventry), 97
Forshaw, J. H., 213
France: see Chapters 2 and 3
   La Charte de l'architecte-
      reconstructeur, 44
   CTRI (Commissariat technique à la
      reconstruction immobilière), 18,
      20–3, 41–2, 44
   DATAR (Délégation générale à
      l'aménagement du territoire et
      à l'action régionale), 22
   DGEN (Délégation générale à
      l'equipement national), 18, 20–2
   German Occupation of, 20, 32, 35
   Liberation, 17, 23, 45
   MRU (Ministère de la reconstruction
      et de l'urbanisme), 16–18, 20–1,
      31, 45
   OCM (Organisation civile et militaire),
      45
   reconstructors: and Vichy, 22; as a
      cohesive group, 19; education and
      training, 19
   survey on rural housing, 21
   the Resistance, 20, 21, 45
   town planning and politics, 23
   Town Planning Code, 22
   Town planning law, 18, 22
   UNITEC (Union nationale des
      ingénieurs et des techniciens),
      45
Vichy, 18, 21, 32, 33
wartime planning, 3
Frank, Hans, 77
Frank, Hartmut, 3
Frankfurt, as a possible capital of West
   Germany, 140–1
Freudenstadt, 195

Friedländer, Saul, 114
Functionalism: see architecture, modern

Gayk, Andreas, 124
Geddes, Patrick, 58
German Democratic Republic: see
    Chapters 12 and 13
    Academy of Architecture: see German
        Democratic Republic, Deutsche
        Bauakademie
    Advisory Council for Architecture, 175
    Decree for the Reorganisation of the
        Urban Centres, 183
    Deutsche Bauakademie, 175, 184
    German Academy of Architecture:
        see German Democratic Republic,
        Deutsche Bauakademie
    ideological 'Leitbild', 192, 193
    industrial building techniques, 183, 195
    Law Regulating the Reconstruction of
        Cities, 174
    'Magistrale' (monumental avenues),
        176
    Ministry for Reconstruction, 174
    National Programme of
        Reconstruction, 176
    nationalisation of the building industry,
        173
    new towns, 193
    Sixteen Principles [of town planning],
        174–7, 181, 183, 193, 194
    Socialist Realism in architecture, 184
    Soviet influences on, 175, 176, 191,
        195, 199
German Garden City Society, 171
Germany: see Chapters 8, 9, 12 and 13
    German Labour Front (Deutsche
        Arbeitsfront), 121
    United States Military Government
        in, 140
    wartime planning, 6, 7
    zero-hour myth, 116, 131
Gibson, Donald, 96–101, 103, 105
Gien, 35, 36, 40, 42
Graubner, Gerhard, 115
Great Britain: see Chapters 7 and 14
    King George VI, 100
    Ministry of Town and Country
        Planning, 8, 100, 106,
        213
    Modern Architectural Research Group
        (MARS), 212
    Town and Country Planning Act of
        November 1944, 102
    traffic planning, 215

Town and Country Planning Act of
    1947, 107
Gréber, Jacques, 45
Grebler, Leo, 2
green areas, 90
Gropius, Walter, 133–5, 139–41, 217
Gruen, Victor, 145
Gutschow, Konstanty, 121, 126, 135, 136
Gutschow, Niels, 3

Halberstadt, 197
Hamburg: see Chapter 8, 135, 136
    Association of Low German Hamburg
        (Vereinigung Niederdeutsches
        Hamburg), 122
    destruction of, 115
    emergency housing, 120, 125
    INTERPLAN (Internationale
        Studiengesellschaft für Planung),
        137
    Office for the new planning
        (Neugestaltung) of, 117, 119
    Office of important warfare operations
        (Amt für kriegswichtigen Einsatz),
        117, 121
    Reichsheimstättenamt, 115
    Neugestaltungsplanung, 114–5
    wartime destruction of, 117, 118
    wartime evacuation programmes for,
        120
    World Economic Archives, 136
Hannover, 115
Harlander, Tilman, 3
Helleputte, Joris, 49
Hempel, Oswin, 181–2
Henselmann, Hermann, 191, 194, 196,
    198
Henvaux, Emile, 62
Heuson, Robert, 119
Hillebrecht, Rudolf, 117, 136, 139, 140,
    185
Hintjens, I., 52
historic buildings, 40, 53, 73
    demolition of, 10, 71, 79, 173, 183
    new uses for, 70, 156, 161, 166
    restoration / reconstruction of, 9–11,
        64, 87, 157, 159, 182, 195–7
historic ensembles, 158, 178, 181, 186
historic preservation, 11, 122, 199
Hitler, Adolf, 114
Hoffmann, Herbert, 136
Holden, Charles, 214
Holford, William, 8, 214
Holvoet, Baron, 59
Hopp, Hans, 195

Hoste, Huib, 50
housing, 41, 58, 62, 68, 89, 120–1, 132,
    134, 139, 161, 171, 183–4, 190, 199,
    200, 212, 215
Houtart, Baron Albert, 51, 57
Hungary: see Chapter 11
    Historic Preservation Act, 158

IFHTP (International Congress of the
    Federation for Housing and Town
    Planning), 135, 138, 216
INTERPLAN: see Hamburg,
    INTERPLAN
Isaacs, Reginald, 141

Jankowski, Stanislaw, 78, 85, 86
Jasinski, Sta, 58, 61
Jensen, Herbert, 124

Kallmorgen, Werner, 124
Kampffmeyer, Hans, 136, 138
Kassel, 115
Kérisel, Jean, 36, 38, 39, 42
Kiel, 124
Knothe, J., 85

Laborie (French planner), 36, 39, 40
labour supply, 110
Lanchester, H. V., 58
landscape planning, 119, 124
Le Corbusier, 6, 26, 31, 33, 34, 38,
    45, 46, 98, 137, 211
Le Havre, 26
Leconte, André, 41, 43
Lehideux, François, 33
Leipzig, 196
Leucht, Kurt W., 181
Leurs, Stan, 52
Ley, Robert, 122
Liebknecht, Kurt, 176, 191
Liège, 139
Lier, Kazimierz, 82
Lijnbaan shopping centre: see
    Rotterdam, Lijnbaan
Lock, Max, 139
Loire Valley, 7, 33, 35, 42–4
Loire department: see Loire Valley
London, 126, 139
    City of London Plan, 214
    Conference of Foreign Ministers,
        140–1
    County of London Plan, 213
    urban planning for, 8
Lübeck, 115
Lurcat, André, 83–4

Maaskant, H. A., 145
Marczewski, Kazimierz, 79, 83, 86
Marrast, Jean, 41
Marshall Plan, 191
May, Ernst, 194
Meyer, Hannes, 194
Middelburg: see Chapter 5
    Stichting Herbouw Middelburg, 71–2
    Town Hall and Abbey, 68–71
    urban structure, 68
Morane, Jacques, 35, 36, 38, 41
Moscow, 115
Moutschen, Jean, 61
MRU: see France, MRU
Muffang, André, 41
Mumford, Lewis, 84, 96, 98, 146, 151–3,
    211

Nelson, Paul, 83
Netherlands, The: see Chapters 5 and 10
    German Occupation of, 64
Neufert, Ernst, 121, 140
Nordhausen, 197
Norway, reconstruction in, 7

oral history: see Chapter 2
Orléans, 35–9, 42
Ossowski, Stanislaw, 84
Ostrowski, Waclaw, 84
Otlet, Paul, 58

Pabst plan: see Warsaw, Pabst plan
Paulus, Heinz, 121
pedestrian zones, 149, 152, 185, 199
Pepler, George and Elizabeth, 139
Perret, Auguste, 26, 34, 41
Perry, Clarence, 211
Pétain, Maréchal, 34
Peyrouton, Marcel, 33
Pieper, Hans, 118
Piétri, François, 40
Piotrowski, Roman, 81–2
Plymouth, 126
Poëte, Marcel, 38
Poland, 9; see also Chapter 6
Potsdam, 197
prefabrication, 183
public works projects, 54–5

Rascher, Johannes, 177–9
Rauda, Wolfgang, 177–8
reconstruction financing, 105, 107,
    109–10
reconstruction planning
    and private property, 56

and tourism, 56, 68
central ideas in, 5, 36, 38, 39, 43, 53,
55, 57, 67, 72, 79, 81 ff., 98, 103,
115, 119, 123, 132, 146, 152, 174,
176, 194, 217
centralised, 65, 66
continuities in, 4, 17, 19, 31, 32, 34,
35, 44, 48, 49, 125, 132, 210
design competitions, 57
international influences on, 49, 131,
149, 150, 216
regional planning
in Belgium, 51, 58–9
in Germany, 139
Reichow, Bernhard, 114
Reith, John, 97, 101, 106
Remaury, Pierre, 41, 42
research methodology, 12; *see also*
Chapter 2
Ringers, J. A., 65
Rivière, George-Henri, 21
Romier, Lucien, 34
Rostock, 195, 197
Röthig, Kurt, 182
Rotterdam, 8, 139, 212; *see also* Chapter
10
Basisplan (the Basic Plan), 146, 152
collective buildings, 147
Groothandelsgebouw, 145
Lijnbaan Shopping Centre, 145, 185
pedestrian zone, 149, 152
Roux, Marcel, 45
Royan, 35
Royer, Jean, 36, 38, 39, 42
Rozanski, Stanislaw, 82
rubble removal, 156
ruins, images of, 38

Saint-Denis de, l'Hôtel, 36
sanitation systems, role in reconstruction
planning, 43–4
Schäfer, Paula, 138
Scharoun, Hans, 192
Schelkes, Willi, 135
Schmitthenner, Paul, 115
Schneider, Herbert, 177, 179, 181
Schwarz, Max Karl, 118, 119, 124
Schwarz, Rudolf, 7
Scott Report, 103
Scott, Giles, 106
Secrétain, Roger, 37, 39
Sharp, Thomas, 98
shopping mall, 185
Sigalin, Józek, 85–6
Sive, André, 45

Skibniewski, Zygmunt, 82–3
socialist architecture and planning, 9–10
socialist city, model of, 172, 192, 200
Soetewey, René, 59
Speer, Albert, 135, 196
Stalinist architecture and planning
theories, 175, 194
Stalmann, Gert, 124
Stephenson, Gordon, 139
Stepinski, Zygmunt, 85–6
Stiemer, Renate, 3
Stockholm, 216
Stoph, Willi, 192
Ströhlin, Karl, 115, 135
Suhl, 197
Sully-sur-Loire, 35–6, 39, 42
Surleau, Frédéric, 42
Syrkus, Helena, 82
Syrkus, Szymon, 82

Tamms, Friedrich, 114
Taut, Bruno and Max, 194
technocrats, 24
Belgian, 52, 60
French, 24, 33, 41
Terfve, Jean, 62
Tessenow, Heinrich, 122
Tolwinski, Tadeusz, 82, 84
Tournai, 62
town planning
Belgian, 58, 60
bureaucratic obstacles to, 23
centralised, 192
Dutch, 66
French, 25, 40, 45
town planning law, 6, 18, 36, 44, 57,
102, 107, 114, 174, 183
Belgian, 49–51, 55, 57
Dutch, 65
French, 32
Warsaw, 83
traffic planning, 38, 68, 69, 71, 90, 146
Tripp, Alker, 98, 215
Tyrwhitt, Jacqueline, 139

Ulbricht, Walter, 175, 176, 179, 191,
192, 194
Umbdenstock, Gustave, 38, 41
Uthwatt Report, 103

Vaerwyck, V., 52
Van de Velde, Henry, 52, 61–2
Van den Broek, J. H., 148–50
Van der Swaelmen, Louis, 49–50, 58
Van Esteren, C., 59, 83

Van Traa, C., 149
Verhagen, P., 68–74
Verwilghen, Charles, 52
Verwilghen, Raphaël, 49–50, 52, 57–60
Vichy, France: see Chapters 2 and 3
Vienna, 9
Viérin, Jos., 52
Vinck, Emile, 51

Wagner, Martin, 6, 133, 134
war damage, compensation for, 65
war memorials, 91
Wardill, H. R., 97, 99, 101
Warsaw, 126, 139; see Chapter 6
  BOS (Biuro Odbu
  owy Stolicy), 81–3,
    86, 88
  Civic Fund for Warsaw's
    Reconstruction, 88
  Commission of Town Planning
    Experts, 82
  Cooperative Building Enterprise, 82
  Department of Workers' Housing
    Estates, 89
  destruction of, 77, 79
  East–West thoroughfare, 85–7
  Faculty of Architecture, Warsaw
    Technical University, 82
  German Occupation of, 77
  Institute of Polish Architecture, 82

Ghetto, 78
  Muranów housing district, 79
  Nazi plans for, 78
  Pabst plan, 78
  Palace of Culture and Science, 90
  Planning Department, Warsaw
    Municipal Council, 81
  return of population to, 80
  secret wartime planning, 79, 81–3
  Studio for Architecture and Town
    Planning, 82
  Studio for Regional Planning, 82
  traffic planning, 85
  uprising, 78
Wartime damage
  in Belgium, 49, 53, 56
  in Budapest, 155–6, 165
  in Coventry, 97
  in Europe, 212
  in France, 35, 37
  in Middelburg, 68
Wilhelmshaven, 124
Winders, M., 52
Wolf, Paul, 173
Wolters, Rudolf, 7
Wright, Frank Lloyd, 211

Zachwatowicz, Jan, 82, 88